"Hi MOM, I'M O.K."
and Other Lies From Vietnam

By Howard Kalachman

Copyright ©2009

T0369258

Order this book online at www.trafford.com
or email orders@trafford.com

Most Trafford titles are also available at major online book retailers.

Printed in Victoria, BC, Canada.

ISBN: 978-1-4269-1894-0 (sc)
ISBN: 978-1-4269-1908-4 (dj)

Library of Congress Control Number: 2009938459

*Our mission is to efficiently provide the world's finest, most comprehensive book publishing
service, enabling every author to experience success. To find out how to publish your book, your
way, and have it available worldwide, visit us online at www.trafford.com*

Trafford rev. 2/05/2010

 www.trafford.com

North America & international
toll-free: 1 888 232 4444 (USA & Canada)
phone: 250 383 6864 ♦ fax: 812 355 4082

This book is dedicated to my fellow veterans of the Vietnam War and all wars past and present; both those who made it home and those did not, as well as to the families of veterans who had to deal with their own form of hell while their loved ones where overseas.

Also, a special dedication is given to my daughter, brother, & sisters, as well as to the loving memory of our parents, Abe & Sylvia.

I wrote *A Man Called Dad* at the time of my father's demise, some 20 years after my return from the Nam. It tells about him and why I am proud if anyone, even in anger, says, "You're just like your father!"

A MAN CALLED DAD!
THERE WAS ONE MAN EVEN A MAN CAN LOVE,
WE CALLED HIM "DAD!"
A SPECIAL FATHER, A DAD'S DAD; WE CALLED HIM LOVE.
WISE MEN SAY, "ANY MAN CAN BE A FATHER BUT IT TAKES
SOMEONE SPECIAL TO BE A DAD."
WE CALLED HIM "DAD!"
HE CALLED ME, "SUNSHINE", I CALLED HIM "DAD."
HE CALLED ME, "SONNY-BOY", I CALLED HIM, "POPPY",
THE MAN CALLED, "DAD."
A HAPPY GUY WHO BROUGHT JOY TO ALL.
MANY CALLED HIM, "FRIEND."
HE VALUED EDUCATION. THOU HE HAD LITTLE, AND WE HAVE
MUCH, WE CALLED HIM, "TEACHER."
A WISE MAN WHO COUNSELED US OFTEN, WE CALLED HIM "DAD."
BECAUSE OF HIM, WE KNOW WHAT'S RIGHT, WE KNOW WHAT'S
WRONG; WE CALLED HIM "DAD!"
A MAN AMONG MEN - HE COULD MAKE YOU FEEL VERY SPECIAL
BECAUSE HE WAS EXTRAORDINARILY SPECIAL,
THE MAN CALLED, "DAD!"
WHEN OUR DAYS WERE YOUNG, HE WORKED FROM DAWN TO DUSK,
THIS MAN CALLED, "DAD!"
SO WE COULD EAT. SO WE COULD DRESS. OUR SHOES WERE NEW,
BUT HIS HAD HOLES,
THAT MAN OF LOVE.
ALTHOUGH HE CAME HOME TORN AND TIRED, HE COULD SMILE FOR
US AND MAKE US LAUGH,
THIS MAN WAS, "DAD!"
WHEN WE NEEDED LOVE, HIS STRONG ARMS, AND BIG HEART
COULD COMFORT US WITH WARM, SECURE HUGS,
SUCH WAS OUR DAD!
WHENEVER SOMETHING BROKE, OR TORE, DAD COULD FIX IT. HIS
HANDS WERE GREAT!
THIS MAN CALLED, "DAD!"

2

HE WAS A BUILDER OF THINGS, AND PEOPLE, WE CALLED HIM
"DAD!"
THERE IS A LADY WHO LOVES HIM IN A SPECIAL WAY, WE CALL
HER, "MOM!"
SHE HELPED TO GUIDE US AND GIVE HIM STRENGTH.
TOGETHER THEY TAUGHT US ANOTHER MEANING OF, "LOVE", WITH
THE MAN CALLED, "DAD!"
WE LOVED TO SHARE OUR JOY AND DREAMS, WITH THE MAN
CALLED, "DAD!"
HE TAUGHT US LOVE AND FAMILY, WE WE'D HAVE EACH OTHER
WHEN HE WAS GONE,
WE CALLED HIM, "DAD!"
NOW THE SUN'S GONE DOWN, THE MIST IN OUR EYES, OUR HEARTS
ARE TORN,
BUT WE'LL NEVER FORGET THAT SPECIAL MAN - A MAN'S MAN - A
MAN'S DAD.
WE LOVE OUR DAD - I LOVE MY POPPY!!
WE'LL MISS THOSE HUGS - WE'LL MISS HIS VOICE -WE'LL MISS
THOSE SMILES -WE'LL MISS THE COUNSELING,
WE'LL MISS THE MAN CALLED, "DAD!"
HE LEFT US SOMETHING EXTRA-SPECIAL, HE LEFT US LOVE.
HE LEFT ME A PLAN TO BE, "DAD."
A GIRL HE PLAYED WITH, SHE CALLED HIM, "GRANDPA", SHE CALLS
ME, "DAD".
I PRAY I CAN FOLLOW HIS EXAMPLE, AND BE FOR HER, WHAT HE
WAS FOR US - A DAD! !
THE BEST COMPLIMENT YOU CAN GIVE ME IS TO SAY, I AM LIKE MY
DAD!
REST WELL POPPY, YOUR JOB IS DONE, I'LL CARRY ON FOR THE
MAN CALLED , "DAD!"
GOD GRANT PERFECT PEACE FOR THE MAN CALLED, "DAD!"

Chapters:

Preface:

It was early 1967. The Vietnam War was daily news in the papers, on the radio and television. We were also bombarded almost daily with news about the draft lottery. It seemed like there was no escaping it, and the draft was on the mind of every eligible guy. I was working full time for Flood & Purvin Esq., the house law office of Allstate Insurance Company, while attending Queens College at night and about to get an AA degree in Business Administration.

I wanted to go on for my Bachelor's, but wasn't sure what to major in. It would be nice to take some time off after receiving the AAS degree to decide what to do. A course or two in German had been taken to complete the language requirement. I wanted to visit Germany, but couldn't afford it, and certainly did not want to enlist in the Army for four years to get there. Completely oblivious to reality and very trusting, like a fool, I went down to visit my "friends and neighbors" at the local friendly draft board to try to ascertain my future. The agent I spoke to told me that if I pushed up my draft there was a very good chance I would go to Germany. I must have had "Idiot" stamped on my forehead because in a moment of total stupidity and naiveté I believed them and did it. You might say the lies started with those friends and neighbors. I was drafted in May of 1967. Big surprise, I did not go to Germany!

Many of my letters home from Vietnam had misinformation to protect my parents. Mom was a worrier (Isn't that the definition of a Jewish mother?) and dad had a heart condition, which claimed his life some twenty odd years later. When I found out I was going on an all expense paid vacation for one to beautiful, downtown Vietnam, I decided to adjust the truth, just a little. The first lie came in my first letter from boot camp. "Don't worry this is laughs!!"

My spelling and handwriting stunk, still does! Often my sentences had little or no punctuation whatsoever; they were sometimes one, unending run-on sentence. For the sake of clarity, most of my letters have been transcribed with many of my spelling & grammatical errors corrected for clarity. Others have been left in for authenticity or laughs. As an example, every time you see "you're", I most probably actually wrote "your". It is obvious to anyone who reads this that "received" was not part of the colloquial vocabulary I used in my letters, but "got" sure was!

5

Chapter 1 Basic Training

I was still oblivious…and ignorant. Not being in the best physical shape, to say the least, I was in for a big surprise. At this time, my letters were for the most part truthful. The first letter was the U.S. Army standardized form letter to parents reproduced below.

Letter:

DEPARTMENT OF THE ARMY
HEADQUARTERS, UNITED STATES ARMY RECEPTION STATION
FORT JACKSON, SOUTH CAROLINA 29207

Date

Dear Parent or Spouse:

Relatives of a person entering the United States Army for the first time may receive letters of solicitation from private business concerns. Some of these letters may imply that the Army indorses or recommends the products or services offered by such private concerns, and the letters may be signed by retired or reserve personnel no longer on active duty. Further, some concerns solicit by mail to avoid the requirements of state laws or Army Regulations.

We wish to emphasize that the Army does not divulge personal information about its Soldiers, their families, dependents or beneficiaries to any business concern for purpose of solicitation.

The purchase of any insurance, investments, or products by a serviceman, or by relatives, in response to such solicitation, should not be considered until the person solicited has sought competent service, either from the Unit Personal Affairs Officer in the case of the serviceman, or from family counsel in the case of relatives. Counsel in such matters, particularly insurance is always important, but especially so when solicitation is by mail.

William B Miller

WILLIAM B. MILLER
Lt Colonel, Inf
Commanding

AJJRS FL 112-R   (over)
1 Jul 66

7

Back of letter:

Dear ~~Mom & Dad~~, Mom, Marilyn

    I arrived safe and sound at the Reception Station at Fort Jackson, South Carolina, where I will undergo three or four days of processing. Upon completion of this processing, I will be sent to a basic training unit for basic training.

    Do not write to me at this address, since I will have left here before I could receive your letter. I have been advised to write to you as soon as I reach my training unit and receive a permanent address. Should any emergency arise at home, contact the local Red Cross, who will, in turn, notify me.

                Sincerely,

P.S. We'll be here 8 weeks + before I get home. I'll write as soon as I am able to. I'll be loosing the _rest_ of my golden locks! More info to follow. Sorry about handwriting, I've only 3 minutes to write.
Take care, don't worry, this is laughs!!

---

20 May 67

Dear Mom, Pop, Marv, & Marilyn
    Well you've got my letter of arrival by now. So far it hasn't been too bad but I haven't started my basic yet. I'm still in processing and will stay here till Thursday or Friday when I'll be shipped to my training unit. This will either be here at Ft Jackson or at Ft. Gordon, Georgia.
    So far we haven't done much because we arrived too late Friday for processing. I'll say one

8

thing about this place it is H-O-T!! Near 90° in the shade.

I pulled a latrine cleaning detail this morning it wasn't too bad. It's cooler in the barracks and the army provides long handled brushes.

I don't expect to be getting home for 20-21 weeks. A Sergeant told us they have done away with leave after basic, now you don't get any till after A.I.T. (Advanced Infantry Training) but I'll know more in a few weeks.

I haven't gotten much sleep so far. I couldn't sleep on the train because it rocked too much & last night I pulled fire patrol from 0200-0400. [Army time; translates to 2 to 4 AM] The guy who sleeps in the lower bunk can't stay in one spot for more than a minute. This weekend I should have some free time to catch up on my sleep.

We're in a barracks with a P.F.C. in charge who's a real S.O.B. He's worse than the D.I.'s, but so far hasn't gotten to me! Only five more days & I'll be out of his barracks. Maybe when I get to basic, I'll wish I were back.

I get along alright I just hide in the middle of a formation.

Well going to end for now, I'll write again, next week to let you know my training address.

Howard

---

27 May 67

Dear Mom, Pop, Marilyn, Marvin,
Hi! How's it going? You can disregard that postcard you received with my training co. address.

The army decided at the last minute to keep me and 100 other guys here at Fort Jackson for basic. We arrived yesterday on "the hill" as the basic area is called & it's no picnic. Haven't got much time to write so I'll just give you my correct Mailing address.

Pvt. Howard K....
CoD. 5th BN 1st TNG Bde;
Ft. JACKSON, SC 29207; 3RD PLT.

I'll try to call you soon again, maybe! If I can get permission. I'm enclosing a few pictures courtesy of the U.S. Army, they ruined and misspelled the last name. Please don't show these around. Will end for now.

Love
Howard

P.S. Tell Janet & Vic my address so they can write. Apologize for me for not being able myself. Time is precocious!

---

10 June 67

Dear Mom, Pop, Marv, Marilyn,

What happened? I tried to call today and find that you changed our phone number???? Is everything O.K.?

I've had a pretty tough week we had our first Physical Training test on Tuesday, which I failed but passed! Our company is tough and a passing mark of 300 is not enough for our company. We have to get 360 or better. So today I was retested I sure hope I passed this time because if I didn't I'll have to take it again every Saturday till I pass and it's tough!

I took a officers candidate test at the reception center and passed but I don't intend to sign up for 9 *or 10 more months even if it means I'll be an officer and earn more money by the end of the year.*

I did sign up for $5000 worth of gov't insurance at $1.00 a month premium with you dad, as my beneficiary. Also, I signed up for savings bonds with you as co-owner. This means you can cash them if you need the dough. You'll be getting one $25 bond every three months.

I'd like to save another $15-20 a month. I think the best way to do this if for you or mom to open a savings account in your own name and I'll mail you checks for whatever I want to deposit.

Most important, don't forget to send me our new phone number unless you don't want me to call you on the phone. At any rate write soon so I'll know all is O.K.

I have guard-duty tomorrow (Sunday) so I have to say good-bye now. Glad to hear everyone did O.K. in school.

> *Love*
> *Howard*

Yes, I admit I am a worrier - comes with being Jewish? Sounds like something the late Rodney Dangerfield would write, I joined the army and my parents moved, or in this case, just changed their phone number. Seems, I also got no respect!

The Army had taught us to hurry up and wait. You were rushed everywhere in the Army and then you were forced to wait on numerous endless lines. To this day many who went thru Army training hate lines, including yours truly. That was your life in basic. Add daily harassment, sleep deprivation, physical conditioning, some useful classes as well as many boring ones, and a few work details to round out your day.

I arrived as a 165 pound out of shape kid. My first mile took almost 12 minutes to run. By the time I left I could do a mile in less than half that and had redistributed my 165 pounds. I was a lean, not yet mean, not ready for fighting machine.

8, July 67

Dear Mom, Pop, etc

    Arrived O.K. at Fort. I went to guesthouse to check on rate they are ONE (1) dollar per person per night. You _must_ make reservations _well_ in advance.

    I tried to call you, but no one was home. So I made a reservation for you (for 3) for Thursday July 20th. These reservations must be picked-up before 6:30 PM on Thursday July 20th.

    Pop, You & mom decide what you want to do. Decide if you want to

1)   Come to Ft. Jackson at all

2)   Come on Thus July 20th or before

3)   Stay how long? (you must make reservations for the entire stay.

    If you do not want to come or, if you do want to come, but before Thursday July 20th, you MUST Let Me Know immediately. I have to cancel your reservation by Sunday or I can get into trouble and I may or may not be able to call you before that since I'll be on bivouac. The best bet is for you & mom to decide & then write two letters one to me and one to: Guest House
        Ft. Jackson, S.C. 29207

    The reservations are in the name of PVT Howard Kalachman D5-1 - Parent & brother.

    If you decide to come I'll be in touch to let you know how to get to guesthouse (which is just across the street form my co area.)

When you write let me know how you make out with the car and also if you decide you will come - how you will come (by plane, car etc).

If it will help you decide, I don't know where I'm going after basic but I'll most probably be shipping Friday afternoon July 20th. I'll try to find out if I have any leave but I doubt it.

Write - Soon

Love
Howard

P.S. - If you want you can call the Guesthouse but be sure to write me so I'll know you've taken care of things.

Chapter 2 – Advanced Infantry Training – AIT

At this point my family and I knew I had been assigned a M.O.S. or Military Occupational Specialty of 11B30, "Infantryman" and what was most likely in store for me. That MOS would be changed slightly in Vietnam to 11C30, "Motarman". I was assigned to Fork Polk, Louisiana, which we lovingly referred to as Fort Puke, Lousy-Anna

My concerns for my parents and myself are more obvious as I try to white wash the whole situation. You will see that I tried to give us some hope that my fate could be changed.

Had I only known then what I knew later. My mother's father had died quite suddenly. My parents could have pulled me out of training for my Grandfather's funeral. I was, after all, the grand child who most understood him and was closest to him. But, they decided to "protect me" from the sorrow of his funeral. Had I gone to the funeral, I would more than likely have been taken out of the loop, and might have avoided the Nam altogether!

Fort Polk, Louisiana

26 July 67

Dear Mom, Pop, Marilyn, Marv,

How are you all? Fine, I hope. Dad, you sounded a little out of sorts when I told you what the army has in store for me so I'm writing to tell you of my progress in getting my M.O.S. changed. I spoke to the chaplain and the only way to get my MOS changed is for medical reasons or if I go to O.C.S. I've been thinking about this and I've decided to try to get into Officer Candidate School for transportation in Ft. Eustes, Va. I've already passed the written exam as you know. All I have to do now is pass the review board of officers and have an opening in the school.

But, even if I don't make O.C.S., I can still go to my Advanced Training (Called AIT), and if I'm a good squad leader I can get recommended for drill corporal school. If I make it I'll be stabilized in the good old U.S.

If not, my drill sergeant at LPC has been talking to us. He is a veteran of the Nam and tells me M O S of motar-man is good because I'll be way back behind the riflemen. Also, I'll be an E-5 (Buck Sergeant) by attending this course and doing well in A.I.T. He said that the newspapers exaggerate a lot; the Nam is not that bad, and only sloppy soldiers don't make it. Further, I'm not defiantly headed for Nam as infantry also goes to Germany & Europe (if I'm lucky).

Right now I'm a lot relieved and I hope you are also, I know you would be if you spoke to SGT Bishop, my drill sergeant.

I'm hoping I can make O.C.S. transportation school. It will mean an extra 10 months of service but I'll be an officer, making more dough, be _Out of infantry_, and very possibly stateside. And my training will be in Virginia. It will be easy for me to get a good job when I'm discharged after having been an officer.

Well that's enough for now, I'll keep you posted about what's happening here. Probably by letter, phones are not as numerous as they were at Ft. Jackson, so I can only call sometimes - on Sundays or late Saturdays.

Sorry to hear about Grand-Pa. I hope Mom and Grand-Ma aren't taking it to hard.

By the way you did check to see that I had at least $40.00 in my account to cover my check?

You can pack up some of my magazines and get ready to send them as soon as I have a training company, which will be sometime next Friday. I'll call or write you the address.

I sent my Ft. Jackson Graduation book home, let me know when it arrives, it should arrive sometime in the next two weeks.

Not much time now, so I'll again say good-bye and don't worry, everything is pretty much under control.

Love
Howard

P.S. My address till Aug 4th is Pvt. Howard K.....
LPC Cl 30
Fort Polk Academy
Fort Polk, La 71459

My attempt to comfort my parents is obvious. I knew there was little chance of changing things.

Fort Polk, Louisiana

10 August '67

Dear Mom, Pop, & family,
I am just going to write a few lines as it is 0100 hours and I am very tired. I've tried every way I know to get my M.O.S. changed but its impossible so I'm forced to make one last ditch effort before I accept it. I've written a letter to my congressman, who I believe is still Ben Rosenthal. I don't wish to mail this letter from here as letters to congressman are taboos here. Please check and make sure he is still my congressman and then send him this letter do this as soon as possible and make sure you address the envelope "Honorable_____.

You can check with the League of Woman Voters for the correct congressman. Send this letter to him via Special Delivery (this will cost about 65 cents and Marv may have to go to the post office). Also make sure you put _my_ return address on the envelope.

Please write me to acknowledge receipt of this letter. Also let me know if you've received my money order and graduation book.

Take care of yourself and write soon. I'll probably be able to call you again a week from Saturday. Give everyone my regards.

Love
Howard

P.S. I hope this works!

Fort Polk, Louisiana

31 August 67

Dear Mom, Pop, Marilyn, & Marv,

Nothing yet on this end from Washington. I received the letter you sent and it sounds like my congressman is not going to do much. Well I only have a few more possibilities. I'm going to see the new C. O. and if that doesn't work try the I.G. I've heard of a few people who have gotten M.O.S. changes that way.

I tell you more when I call Friday or Saturday. Actually the main reason I'm, writing is to send you a few things

1) A sears I.D. card for Dad. They'll send them to me as long as I'm in the Army.

2) My L.P.C. (Leadership Preparation Course) graduation certificate, which turned out to be an expensive piece of toilet paper. Well, maybe I can use it when I get out of the Army and want a supervisory job.

3) The pull ring from an actual hand grenade. The second one I ever threw. Marv can have it to show off to his friends. It also makes a good key ring.

Well that's all for now. Be sure to let me know if your hear any news from Wash.
Stay well.

Love
Howard

In response my 31 August letter, my mother contacted Congressmen Rosenthal ...

September 11, 1967

Congressman Benjamin S. Rosenthal
Room 1530, House Office Building
Washington 25, D.C.

Dear Congressman Rosenthal,

On August 16, 1967 my son, who is in the Armed Forces sent a certified special delivery letter to your district office in Queens. On August 24, 1967, we received a reply to this letter stating you would try to help us through the Armed services in Washington, D.C.

If reference to this letter, Mr. Congressman, I am appealing to you in behalf of my son, my husband and myself to try to have my son's M.O.S. changed as soon as possible, since time is of great importance. On or about October 6, my son will finish has advanced Infantry training. His new assignment will then follow.

About two weeks ago, I came up to your district office in Queens regarding the above, and while there spoke to your associate over the telephone. I was told many times that you would call me, however, I never received such a call.

Mr. Congressman, I think it is very unfair that my son, who scored a 123 in clerical, and is very mechanically inclined, should be given an M.O.S. such as Infantry.

An important factor which should be considered, Mr. Congressman, is that my husband is a sick person, and worrying can be quite dangerous since he is now has both a heart condition and ulcers. My son, who is also a nervous person, is not only worrying about his M.O.S., but about his Father too.

I again appeal to you, as a supporter of the Democratic party and a former worker on the Registration Board, to do everything in your power to change my son's M.O.S. and in so doing alleviate the strain and pressure on my son, my husband, and myself.

Hoping to hear favorably from you, I remain,

Sincerely yours,

Sylvia Kalachman

Self-explanatory copies of the correspondence appear on the next few pages.

BENJAMIN S. ROSENTHAL
8th District, New York

COMMITTEES:
FOREIGN AFFAIRS
GOVERNMENT OPERATIONS

Congress of the United States
House of Representatives
Washington, D.C.

September 12, 1967

Private Howard Kalachman
TY-25 166th Street
Flushing, Long Island
New York 11366

Dear Private Kalachman:

Reference is made to your desire to effect a change in your MOS with the U. S. Army.

I am enclosing, herewith, a copy of the letter I have received from Lt. Col. Martin J. Cunningham, II, Assistant Executive Officer, Office of Personnel Operations, Department of the Army, Washington, D. C., which speaks for itself.

May I assure you that when I have any additional information on your case, I shall let you know.

With my kind regards, I am,

Sincerely yours,

On 29 August 1967 Lt. Colonel Cunningham just wrote that he had received the congressman's letter to General Beverley had been received an a further reply would be forthcoming in the near future.

Congress of the United States
House of Representatives
Washington, D.C.

September 20, 1967

Mrs. Sylvia Kalachman
77-25 166th Street
Flushing, Long Island
New York 11366

Dear Mrs. Kalachman:

This will acknowledge receipt of your letter of September
11th, relative to your concern over your son, Howard, who is in
the U. S. Army, assigned to Fort Polk, Louisiana.

As you know, when your son contacted me on August 10th I
immediately asked the Department of the Army here in Washington
to check into his case to determine whether or not there was any
possibility of effecting a change in his MOS.

I subsequently received a letter from Major General William
W. Beverley, Chief of Personnel Operations, Department of the Army,
indicating that favorable action could not be taken on the request.
I sent a copy of General Beverley's letter to your son, in care of
the home address, on September 14th. I am enclosing, herewith, a
copy of the General's letter, for your information. I believe it
is self-explanatory. I am sorry the report is not a favorable one.

With my kind regards, I am,

Sincerely yours,

21

DEPART... ...OR THE AR...
OFFICE OF T...
...C, 20310

EPPAS-A Kalachman, Howard
US 52 752 433

RECEIVED

SEP 11 1967

BENJAMIN S. ROSENTHAL, N.C.

Honorable Benjamin S. Rosenthal

House of Representatives

Dear Mr. Rosenthal:

This is in reply to your recent letter in behalf of Private Kalachman, who desires training in military occupational specialty 63A10 (Automotive Maintenance Apprentice).

As indicated in Private Kalachman's letter, each trainee is permitted to express a preference for training and station of assignment during his initial classification interview. No promises of future assignments, however, are made to individuals entering the Army for two years of active duty under the Universal Military Training and Service Act. They must be trained and subsequently assigned where the greatest needs of the service exist. While personal desires of service members are considered to the extent practicable, the military situation existing at a particular time places a limitation on the extent to which individual preferences may influence assignments.

Private Kalachman's desire to use in the Army the knowledge that he has obtained through civil schooling is certainly understandable. The Army's need, however, at the time he was selected dictated that he be assigned and utilized in MOS 11B (Light Weapons Infantryman). As a matter of information, Private Kalachman was considered for the Army's Scientific and Engineering Assistants Program. His attainment of an associate degree in mechanical engineering, however, does not meet the program prerequisites which are a baccalaureate degree in an engineering science and six months experience or a higher degree.

Your interest in Private Kalachman is appreciated and it is regretted that my reply cannot be favorable.

Sincerely yours,

William W. Beverley

WILLIAM W. BEVERLEY
Major General, USA
Chief of Personnel Operations

The body of this letter, which has not stood the test of time very well is reproduced below:.

"This is in reply to our recent letter in behalf of Private Kalachman, who desires training in military occupational 63A10 (Automotive Maintenance Apprentice).

As indicated in Private Kalachman's letter, each trainee is permitted to express a preference for training and station of assignment during his initial classification interview, No promises of future assignments, however, are made to individuals entering the Army for two years of active duty under the Universal Military Training and Service Act. They must be trained and subsequently assigned where the greatest needs of the service exist. While personal desires of service members are considered to the extent practicable, the military situation existing at a particular time places a limitation on the extent to which individual preferences may influence assignments.

Private Kalachman's desire to use in the Army the knowledge that he has obtained through civilian training is certainly understandable. The Army's need, however, at the time he was selected dictated that he be assigned and utilized in MOS 11B (Light Weapons Infantryman). As a matter of information, Private Kalachman was considered for the Army's Scientific and Engineering Assistants Program. His attainment of an associate degree in mechanical engineering however, does not meet the program prerequisites which are a baccalaureate degree in engineering science and six months experience or a higher degree. Your interest in Private Kalachman is appreciated and it is regretted that m y reply cannot be favorable."

It is obvious that this was getting me nowhere!

Fort Polk Louisiana

13, Sept '67

Dear Dad, Mom, Marilyn, Marv,

How's things on the home front? The reason I'm writing now instead of waiting for my call on Sunday is to convey some semi-good news.

It seems my name is on this instant N.C.O. school list. That means that if my name remains on the list I'd have my regular leave but then I'll go to Ft. Gordon for 14 more weeks of training which if I successfully complete will mean I'll be either a Corporal or buck Sergeant and my chances of going to the Nam is cut to 50%.

Also I get another leave after N.C.O. school.

I'm still working on getting in to see the C.O. I spoke to the sergeant today who said he would arrange an appointment. I hope I can get to see the "old man" without any help from the 1st Sgt. The acting sergeant said he can arrange this. I let you know what happens when I call Sunday. I just hope that if I see the C.O. & explain my problem & he doesn't help me, he doesn't do anything to remove my name from the instant N.C.O. list.

Marilyn, I received your letter and yes, I think that's a good idea to give Steve a surprise party. Of course you'll probably have to have a nice <u>blond</u> for me. The only problem is nothing is definite in the army, so it is probable something could happen to change my leave time. If you want to arrange the party and just invite a nice girl for me., that's fine, just warn her of the chances involved. Going to end now will call Sunday.

Love
Howard

PS:- Send Delta Airlines Sched. You can get it at travel agency on main street.

I was thinking about going home in a few weeks when AIT was over. An announcement was made that any Jewish personnel, who wanted to, could leave a few days early to get home in time for the Jewish high holy days (which by the way have nothing to do with drugs). I asked to see the unit's Commanding Officer (CO), a Lieutenant (Lt), and told him I'd like to get home in time for the Jewish High Holy days and his surprising reply was something to the effect of, "I can't be bothered with those fucking Jewish holidays." Not knowing I had options, I accepted that as final.

A while later I was asked by a Sergeant if I was going home for the Jewish holidays, so I told him what happened. Little did I suspect that he did know what the options were and he'd report that anti-Semitic statement to the Inspector General's (I.G.) office. I wish I could recall his name, as I owe him a debt of thanks.

Shortly thereafter, just before the Jewish Holidays, I was called in to the C.O.'s office where there was a lot of brass (senior officers) who asked me what had happened. The Lt tried to intimidate me with a "suggested" alternative to what had actually happened. Being basically honest, maybe a little stupid, or just plain pissed off, I told the I.G. what the Lt had said. He denied it and claimed I misunderstood. He had little choice so he told me there was a plane leaving the base in an hour and, if I could make it I could leave. I said I could, and he had orders cut for me. The same sergeant who had reported this incident drove me back to the barracks, helped me pack, and then rushed me to the airfield in his jeep. He, being black, no doubt had experienced prejudice first hand and was not going to allow it to be done to anyone else. I don't remember you're name but if you are reading this thank you!

As the small airfield on the base was behind some trees, we only saw the planes as they were taking off low over the trees. We saw the letters TTA on the fuselage and nicknamed the airline Tree Tops Airlines. Actually it was Trans-Texas Airlines.

Having never flown before, I anxiously and excitedly boarded the small, two engine plane and we took off. When we did, white condensation was flowing out of the vents. As it looked like smoke, I called the flight attendant over. Trying to be very calm and cool, I nonchalantly asked, "Do you know there is smoke coming out of the vents?" She advised it was just condensation and was normal. I then asked, "Where is the bathroom?!"

My arrival home was unexpected and it was quite early in the morning. It was chilly, the house was dark, and I did not want to wake everyone so I picked up a few small stones and tossed them gently at the bedroom window facing the front of the house. A few minutes later my younger sister appeared at the window. Surprised, she kept repeating, "Ou Howie, Ou Howie, Ou Howie.." I replied, "Marilyn, its cold can you please open the door?" which my Dad did, as her repeated exclamations had awakened the rest of the family.

My father had taught us the importance of family. My brother had a new job and a few dollars (very few). He knew I had no money but that then, as now, I was very dependant on a car for getting around. I had sold my car when I was drafted. My car was my freedom, independence, and one of the most important material things in my young life. You'll see that theme repeated. Marv decided **"we"** needed a car and helped me buy an old Ford Fairlane 500, which he gave me exclusive use of while I was on leave. That was very generous. It was very important to me then and obviously I never forgot it and never shall.

Chapter 3 – Arrival in The Nam!

After a month and a half of leave, thanks to that Sergeant, it was finally time to go to the Nam. The flight was a long one. We landed & stopped in several places along the way including Guam, Wake Island & Hawaii, not necessarily in that order. At Honolulu airport we were told not to leave the airport as our flight would be leaving shortly. Some of the guys did not listen and left to see a little of Hawaii. I should have also but was afraid of getting put on report as AWOL, or for desertion since we were on our way to a war zone. Stayed in the airport, mostly at the bar, for quite some time. A lot longer than the few minutes we were told we'd be there. What a schmuck I was! I could have seen at least a little of Hawaii.

We continued on, to Cam Rahn Bay in beautiful downtown Vietnam. Actually the base itself was tropical and beautiful from the air! Even on the ground it looked O.K., at first. It was in fact used as an in-country R& R (Rest & Relaxation) or vacation facility. But, this certainly would be no vacation!

Cam Rahn Bay:

8 November '67
1435

Dear Mom, Pop, Marilyn, & Marv:
    I arrived here this morning at Cam Rahn Bay.
The flight was very nice, we landed at Honolulu,
Wake Island, & Guam in route and spent an average
of thirty minutes apiece. We were allowed to get off
the plane at each of these stops. I only spent 35
minutes in Honolulu, Hawaii and didn't have time
to leave the terminal, but from what I could see at
the airport it sue is a beautiful place and I probably
will take my R & R there in July or so. Unless I find a
better idea. [We were actually at Honolulu for over an hour].

In case you're interested, Cam Rahn Bay is a secured area and considered safe. From what I can see of Vietnam from here, it looks like a beautiful place. There are many green rolling hills & mountains here. One thing though, it is H-O-T! The jungle fatigues the army issued me makes things a little easier since they are very light and loose.

I'm told that I'll probably ship out of here tomorrow, I don't know where. By the way don't write me yet as I can't receive any mail. The address I gave you is not good for here and neither is the return address on the envelope I'm mailing this in. I also can't do anything about getting my M.O.S. changed till I get to my next unit. I'll keep you posted on this! Did you have any luck with the Senator? Even tho I'm in the Nam, he may still be able to effectuate a change of M.O.S. for me. It might not be as bad to stay here for a year as a clerk. If you speak to the senator again you could mention that I also discovered that my DA-20 form (the one used to determine my m o s) is inaccurate and that's probably why I wasn't given a clerical M.O.S. The space for education had me down as an A.A.S. in Mechanical Engineering, my actual degree is in Business Admin. Also for civilian occupation the form has none! When I was a legal clerk for four years at Flood & Purvin. I'm going to bring this to the attention of my next unit commander if I can!

I'll write as soon as I have a mailing address. When I do, you can answer my questions, and also let me know how the constitution and transportation issues did in the election.

Its funny, but sitting here at 2:30PM Wednesday afternoon its had to contemplate that its only 2:30 AM Wednesday in NY.

Going to say good-bye for a while. Don't worry,
yet!

> Love
> Howard

P.S - It takes 2-4 days for my letters to reach you and
4-8 days for yours to reach me, so we may be getting
pretty mixed up.
I'm sending you my airmail stamps since I don't
need them here.

The 8 November '67 letter telling my family not to worry
"*yet*", was sent along with the official Red Cross post card about
notifying soldiers incase of family emergencies:

AMERICAN RED CROSS
EMERGENCY LEAVE
INFORMATION FOR FAMILIES

In case of the death, serious illness, injury or other emergency involving the immediate family of a U.S. Serviceman (or civilian member of the U.S. Forces overseas), the nearest Red Cross Chapter or Field Director should be notified at once.

The Red Cross will transmit the needed facts regarding emergency leave to the Red Cross Field Director on duty at the serviceman's military station. This field director will then notify the serviceman and also confirm the facts of the situation to the proper military commander who has authority to grant emergency leave. You will be notified of the military decision by Red Cross together with travel plans if leave is approved.

Financial aid to pay for transportation and expenses in the U.S. will also be provided the serviceman by Red Cross if needed. Depending on individual preference and financial circumstance this aid usually is provided as an outright gift, or by an interest-free loan that can be repaid in small monthly payments over an extended period.

The Red Cross services, like all Red Cross assistance to servicemen, are given free of charge through the contributions of the American people.

10 Nov 67
1830 Hours

Dear Mom, Pop. Marv, & Marilyn
　　Well my orders were held up a day because of a threatened typhoon. We were suppose to get the full force of the typhoon but only got some wind and lots of rain.
　　I got my orders a while ago, I'm going to a place called AN KHE with a bunch of my buddies. I don't know when I'll be shipping, but it'll be either tonight or tomorrow unless something comes up. I don't know my mailing address but you can be sure you'll know it almost as soon as I do.
　　AnKhe is in the Central Highlands so I should miss monsoon season. I'm told I'll be with the 1st Cavalry Division. One of the guys returning from his R & R says there is not too much doing there now.
　　You remember I was telling you about not writing return addresses because of a VC habit of picking up envelopes and sending home supposed gov't notifications. Well there's an official procedure, which is by an officer in person. I'm sending you this form also for you to read.
　　While here at Cam Rahn Bay I've been able to go to the Enlisted mans club and guess what. They have slot machines so I gave them a try. At a nickel a shot the darn one armed bandit stole fifty cents from me. Sorry about that.
　　Going to close now, keep well & don't sweat it!!
　　　　　　　　　Love
　　　　　　　　　Howard

PS - Give my love to Janet, Vic & family.

32

What I was trying to delicately tell my family in the forth paragraph is that, to demoralize us, the Viet Cong (VC) had a nasty little habit of picking up discarded letters and envelopes and sending home official looking letters that the soldier was Killed In Action (KIA). We'd been warned about it by the Army but never heard of it happening first hand.

Obviously this was before I was writing separately to my brother. As you'll see later on I was very wrong about missing monsoons and... but wait, I'm getting ahead of myself.

---

12 Nov '67
0730

Dear Mom, Pop, Marilyn & Marv

Not much time, I have to make a formation at 0745. Just writing to let you know my "permanent address"? I've been promoted to P.F.C. (Private First Class) and so I have one stripe.

My new mailing address is
P.F.C. Howard K...

1ˢᵗ Cav Div (A/M)
A.P.O. San Francisco 96490

I'll be at base camp eight days: Four days detail and four days jungle warfare training. Then I'll be going out to the field. This company stays in the field almost all year. I'll write more on this later.

I changed my bond so that beginning in January you'll be getting a bond a month instead of every three months. Dad, I purposely had them put you as co-owner so that you could cash them if the need arises. If you need a few extra dollars for Marilyn's wedding for instance. Its better to borrow from the bonds since I don't charge interest! [Added as an afterthought to distract from my real meaning of, if I were killed.]

I'm also going to try to get in on the 10% savings plan. I'll probably put $110-125 a month in this plan.

One favor Marilyn can do for me. In my closet in the back of the folder mark "Important papers & misc" are my checkbooks. Have Marilyn return the old books for credit to my account. Marilyn will know what I mean.

Will end now and try to write again this afternoon.

> Love
> Howard

---

12 Nov '67
1230

Dear Mom, Pop, Marilyn & Marv,

This is second letter to you today & so I'll keep it short.
Well it turns out we'll be going for jungle training today or tomorrow and we'll be going to the field

34

base camp Wensday or Thursday. I can't fill out my 1049 till I get out there but I'm told I should have no trouble filling one out but that I shouldn't expect it to be approved by the army.

I am going to keep this letter short because I'm enclosing a letter to Janet. I think she should know where I am. It'll sound worse if she finds out later that we kept it from her, she was angry about our trying to keep grandpa death a secret when she was pregnant with Annette. What do you think? (Probably by the time I get an answer the baby will be born. Mail takes 4-8 days each way, so I'm told).

Write soon & often.

Love
Howard

P.S. In case you didn't get my first letter my address is <u>PFC</u> Howard K....; 1st Cav Div (AM); A.P.O. S.F. 96490

PPS - The AM after 1st Cav stands for AirMobile. That means that we go by copter where we can. Otherwise we use our big feet!!

---

12 Nov '67
1245

Dear Janet, Vic & Annette

How are you all? Is junior kicking up a storm? I'll bet he/she is.

I'm sending this letter to mom & pop cause I have no more stamps and can't get to the PX till tomorrow.

Well I've been on a lot of work details doing everything from painting to moving. But it's not bad. The Army's quite different once you're out of *training. All the Sergeant's are friendly and they don't push or harass you.*

I've been promoted to Private First Class that means I can wear one stripe.

I'm putting my address at the end of this letter. Write as soon s you can but don't expect an answer right away as mail is very slow and it may take a week or more for me to get your letter.

Be sure to send me a picture of my newest niece or nephew as soon as you can and of-course make sure Vic or you write me as soon as the new baby arrives.

Well love to all. I'll write again as soon as I can.

Love
Howard

My new address:
P.F.C. Howard K.....

That line about not being able to get stamps or envelopes was a lie. I did not want my sister to see my return address. For U.S. troops in Vietnam mail was free – no stamps! I was not sure if my parents had told my older sister that I was in the Nam. As she was about 8 months pregnant, when I wrote her I was careful about what I wrote, and not to say anything that would reveal my location.

Commissioned as well as non-commissioned officers in the Nam for the most part treated their men well. That was often because they were regular guys too. However, fraging was always a danger for an over zealous officer. Fraging was when a live friendly (meaning one of ours) grenade just somehow happened to land & go off in the officer's quarters, if you get my drift.

When I arrived at Ah Khe I saw my future units motto painted next to the familiar yellow symbol. It read something like, "Yea though I walk through the valley of the shadow of death I fear no evil because I'm the meanest son of a bitch in the valley." Some guys had that motto on their helmets or on jackets, made by

Vietnamese tailors out of poncho liners, with the motto on the back. These jackets were great going home mementoes. Using Army issued ponchos for personal purposes is illegal but never heard of anyone who had one of those jackets who got into trouble. Fact is, you never know who supplied the tailors with those poncho liners. They looked cool and I had wanted to remember to get one of those somehow before I went home but never did.

```
FIRST   IN  MANILA

FIRST   IN  TOKYO

FIRST   IN  PYONGYANG

FIRST   AIRMOBILE  DIVISION

FIRST   DIVISION  TO  RECEIVE

PRESIDENTIAL  UNIT  CITATION

IN  VIETNAM

                    ALWAYS  FIRST
```

16 Nov 67
Time: 1730

Dear Mom, Pop, Marilyn & Marv,

Well I've gone thru three days of so called jungle training. It's the same training I already received from my A.I.T. at Ft Polk. The course takes four days. My group came in at the end of the day so were holding over till tomorrow (Friday) for our last day of training. We're going to learn how to repel from a chopper, that is how to get out fast using a rope & harness and we'll go through a booby-trap course.

I've spoken to some guys from my company and they've told me a lot, that I don't know if I should believe. They say it's better to spend my time in the field because time goes faster there. I've been told that mortarmen stay at the field base camp and get to sleep in houches (a type of Vietnamese shelter).

Unfortunately the PX's over here is not as well stocked as the one in Cam Rahn Bay was and there are several things I need. Some of them I'll get free once I get into the field, like a toothbrush and other personal hygiene needs. As soon as I've checked out the other PX or go out to the field I'll write you and let you know what I need.

The army issued me four sets of jungle fatigues, yet the guys tell me that I should only take one to the field for the year, since you have to carry everything you take on your back and even with choppers you still have to walk a little sometimes. It seems you wear the fatigues until they rip or start to rot, then you turn them in, you DX [Destroyed Exchange] them in Army language and supply issues you a new set via chopper.

About the only thing I'm told to take more of is socks since jungle rot is a bad problem if your feet stay wet too long.

Today has been pretty easy. I'm in between jungle school sessions. Right now I'm at "Club 54" an enlisted mans club enjoying a Tom Collins, well almost a Tom Collins its Wink & Gin (real gin). This will probably be my last drink for a while.

I've met my new first sergeant and it turns out he's Jewish, he made me feel a little better about being here. He said that since August they only lost four men and that was through their own stupid errors. He assured us he takes care of his men and that if the need ever arises he will and has personally assisted in getting a man out of a hot spot even tho he's not suppose to. It's true what they say about the Cav, it takes care of its men. As I was leaving his office he wish me that old Jewish greeting -Gazai Guzunth (excuse spelling). [Translates to something like, Be happy and healthy.]

I also discovered that I get three R&R periods, two in country, that is in Vietnam. There are certain spots here which haven't been touched by the war and are still considered resort and vacation areas. Plus one R&R out of country.

I'm still contemplating going to Hawaii. If I can save the money and can get the week I want (which is difficult). I can go to Hawaii and then fly as a civilian to N.Y. as long as I meet the flight going back to Vietnam five days later. This way I may be able to get to Marilyn & Steve's wedding but don't count on it. If I don't get that week I spend my five days in Hawaii.

I've also found out that if I extend my tour by three months I can get out of the Army from here, three months early. In other words when I come home I'm out and also when I extend I get to finish my tour on the main base where I am now. So far I don't intend to extend but I'll reserve my decision until next November. I also heard that if I go to college when I come home I can also save three months that way. I'll have to look into this further as this does sound very interesting. Well that's all for now folks, as the bunny might say.

Marv, did you sell that bomb yet? I certainly hope so, let me know how much you get for it!

Marilyn, how's school? What subjects are you taking this term? Of course I...

[water spots here]

40

Sorry paper is wet so I'll continue here - as I was saying - I haven't got any mail yet but as I said already that's par for the course. I may not hear from you for a few weeks yet even if you've already written. No more room to write so-long for now

Love Howard

At this point I was trying to hide as much of my fear as I could by writing what I though would be comforting thoughts. However, I'm sure they were not that comforting to those at home. Jungle training was something the army came up with to allow new guys to accommodate to the tropical Vietnamese weather, and retrain after our month (or longer) leave. I had not yet learned that whenever the army says something is permanent, it means "today" or "at this moment" not forever.

Another lie was that every "grunt" gets three R& R's. Infantrymen in the field, as I was about to be, were called, "grunts".

Yes, we often rode to a new area by chopper but mostly we walked and not just "a little sometimes" as I'd written. The army measured how far we walked in Kilometers or, as we called them, "Klicks". We often walked 10 or more klicks a day, cutting a path through unknown jungle in full combat gear. That's about 6 miles!

---

19 Nov 67
Time" 1000

Dear Mom, Pop, Marilyn & Marv-
Just been looking over some of my price lists on new cars. I have about eight months before I'll be ready to order but I want to be sure I get what I want so I'm checking now. Marv, can you do me a favor, I'd like the new car brochures for the Chevy Chevelle Malibu convertible and Pontiac Firebird convertible. Also if they came out with it this years

Rambler "X-Ray". You can get it anytime you have a chance there's no big rush.

By the way Marv, have you sold your car yet? I hope you've taken my advice to sell. If you feel you must have another car look at the Army Times ads for "Kardon". Some of the used cars seem O.K. make sure it says "ec" (east coast) next to the price then let me know and I'll get car for you. You can put money in my checking account. Now if that doesn't convince you that I want you to sell I don't know what will.

I'm on K.P. again. I think I go see the C.O. this afternoon and try to get out of further K.P. I don't mind it once in a while but this is getting ridiculous. I wish reassignment orders would come down already.

<u>1730</u>

I've just been informed that starting tomorrow I'm to have permanent green-line detail. That means I'll be living in a tower by the perimeter (inside the perimeter) and pulling several hours of guard a day. I'm told it's a pretty good detail. I'm confused though as to whether this change is temporary until my reassignment orders come in, or if this is my reassignment. I'll have to check on that & let you know. Actually this is good because it's an easy detail, as we don't see much action here and no more K.P. If I find it is a permanent reassignment, I'll keep it till I complete my USAFI course and then apply for a change of MOS to Wheel Vehicle Repairman.

Have you heard anything as yet? You should get a reply from the Army as to what action they've decided to take.

42

In answer to letter of Dec 12th, "Yes", you should receive the bonds; probably this month. Also send my mail and magazines and stuff here, cause even if I should get a new address they'll be forwarded to me and I need something to read.

I'm glad Marv is finally getting rid of the bomb I got him, it makes the first part of this letter unnecessary. How much did he get for it?

Will try to write tomorrow about green-line detail.

> *Love*
> *Howard*

PS - I just asked my company clerk and he said green-line detail is just that a detail until I get reassignment order, if I ever do - anyway I'm still at AnKhe base camp.

I believe USAFI stood for United States Armed Forced Instruction. The course I refer to was a correspondence course. I left the date error in; obviously I was referring to Nov 12th.

Chapter 4 - The Boonies

As you may have figured out, much of my writing is in the stream of consciousness style with misspellings and run on sentences. Most of the time there was some thought of what not to write, as I knew those at home were worried and I did not want to add to that worry. You'll see more of that, now that I had arrived in the place of death.

One-way of dealing with being in the Nam was to spend time thinking about going home. I became preoccupied with the idea of being able to buy my first ever new car when I returned home. It was the same for many guys. As noted earlier the car represented freedom and independence for me. It also was a way of thinking positively, that you were in fact going to make it through the year and go home.

On the way to the boonies I saw my first dead VC. Actually it was the first dead body I'd ever seen. His hands and feet were tied to a pole and two Vietnamese soldiers were carrying him like another piece of dead meat. That image has stuck with me to this day.

At every village we passed there were papasons (fathers), mamasons (mothers), and babysons (their kids) as we sometimes referred to the locals. The Vietnamese language had been bastardized before by the French, and now by us.

The Vietnamese culture is more lay backed then I, as a New Yorker, was used to. Actually that can be said of almost anywhere compared to New York City, Can't it? We often saw the Vietnamese resting in what came be to known as the "gook squat". It was the position the VC took when they were captured. We found it hard to be comfortable in that position. They squatted without touching the ground by sitting on their haunches, bending at the knees and stayed in that position. It looked they were taking a shit. For Americans that position could be painful after a while, or at least fatiguing. It was easier for us to just sit down on the ground.

Mamason in doorway

Locals try to sell us stuff when we stopped

Vietnamese towns

Town outside AnKhe

Cobra (Gun Ship) on base

Huey's in assault formation

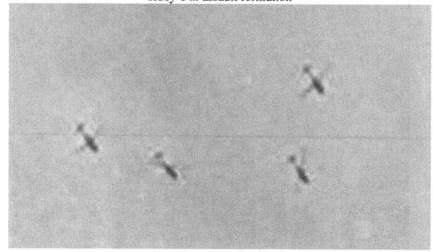

Huey's return to base

"Birth Control" Chinook Gunship:

20 Nov 67
Time: 0820

Dear Mom, Dad, Marilyn, & Marv,

 Well here I am out in the "boonies" at the field camp. Arrived here yesterday. I took a plane from AnKhe to an LZ (Landing Zone) near here. The plane developed radio trouble and we put down at Phu Cat air base in route. Let me tell you those airman know how to live; their camp looks just like a base camp at home. They had paved streets, plumbing, barracks with inside plumbing and good chow. I was there only a few hours but it was nice. From there we went to LZ Baldy where I got a chopper here. I'm at LZ Ross below Chu Lai. Three of the four companies in the battalion are out in the field a few miles from here walking back to base camp here, clearing as they move. I'll probably be joining them this afternoon. I hear all they've been meeting the last few days has been light sniper fire.

 I've met a few guys from my company, they're a real nice bunch.

 I told you I'd let you know if there was anything I needed. Well I got most of what I need so far. But I've been unable to get small batteries for my pocket flashlight. Can you send me about four Penlite Size (AA I think) batteries. There the same size as the ones in my radio if you want to check it. Make sure you wrap them in plastic or some other waterproof material.

 Although I still have 351 days to go and I'm not exactly a short timer I'm sending you a copy of a letter printed up for short-timers to send home. I

52

think you'll enjoy the humor! I did. Keep this letter for me I may want to use it when I get home.

Let me know how things are at home. I sure miss you all and can't wait till I get some mail. The boys say it'll probably be another week or two before my mail catches up to me.

Well that's about it for now. Take care & happy Thanksgiving.

Love

Howard

P.S. - Letter for Janet enclosed. This time you'll have to make the excuse for my sending it through you!

No lies here. I did downplay the snipers but that was more due to the fact that I hadn't yet encountered them and thus wasn't aware of how deadly they were. Dead is dead weather from a sniper, booby trap, or firefight. I was feeling quite lonely as I was with strangers and had not received mail from home in a while. Regardless, I was still thinking about protecting my folks. That's why I sent them the humorous preprinted letter. You will see that letter one more time. Can you guess when?

The put-down at Chu Bai was interesting and after I got to the field I thought about how much nicer it was to be in the Air Force.

South Vietnam

Dear Civilians, Friends, Draft Dodgers, Etc.,

In the very near future the undersigned will once more be in your midst, dehydrated and demoralized, to take his place again as a human being with the well known forms of freedom and justice for all; engage in Life, Liberty, and the somewhat delayed pursuit of Happiness. In making your joyous preparations to welcome him back into organized society you might take certain steps to make allowances for the crude environment that has been his miserable lot for the past twelve months. In other words he might be a little Asiatic from Vietnamesitis and

53

overseasites and should be handled with care. Do not be alarmed if he is infested with all forms of rare tropical diseases. A little time in the "Land of the Big PX" will cure this malady.

Therefore, show no alarm if he insists on carrying a weapon to the dinner table, looks around for his steel pot when offered a chair, or wakes you up in the middle of the night for guard duty. Keep cool when he pours gravy on his dessert at dinner or mixes peaches with his Seagrams VO. Pretend not to notice if he eats with his fingers instead of silverware and prefers C-rations to steak. Take it with a smile when he insists on digging up the garden to fill sandbags for the bunker he is building. Be tolerant when he takes his blanket and sheet off the bed and puts them on the floor to sleep on.

Abstain from saying anything about powered eggs, dehydrated potatoes, fried rice, fresh milk, or ice cream. Do not be alarmed if he should jump up from the dinner table and rush to the garbage can to wash his dish with a toilet brush. After all that has been his standard. Also, if it should start raining, pay no attention to him if he pulls off his clothes, grabs a bar of soap and a towel and runs outdoors for a shower.

When in his daily conversation he utters such things as: "Sin Loi" and "Choi Oi" just be patient, and simply leave quickly and calmly if by some chance he utters "Di Di" with an irritated look on his face because it means no less then "Get the h___ out of here." Do not let it shake you if hew picks up the phone and yells, "Skylark Forward sir" or says, "roger Out" for good-bye or simply shouts, "Working!"

Never ask why the Jones son held a higher rang then he did, and by no means mention the term "Extend." Pretend not to notice if at a restaurant he calls the waitress "Numbah one girl" and uses his hat for an ashtray. He will probably keep listening for "Comin' Home Soldier" to sound off over the Armed Forces Radio Station. If he does, comfort him, for he is still reminiscing. Be especially watchful when he is in the presence of women – especially a beautiful woman.

Above all keep in mind that beneath that tanned and rugged exterior there is a heart of gold (the only thing of value he has left). Treat him with kindness, tolerance, and an occasion fifth of liquor and you shall be able to rehabilitate that which was once (and is a hollow shell of) the Happy-go-lucky guy you once knew and loved.

Last, and by no means least, send no more mail to APO, fill the ice box with beer, get the civvies out of the mothballs, fill the car with gas, and get the women and children off the streets---

BECASE THE KID IS COMING HOME!!!!!!!!!!!!!!!!!!!

23 Nov 67
Time: 0830

Dear Mom, Pop, Marilyn & Marv, -

Well I'm out in the field at last and, except for the load I have to hump, it's not as bad as I imagined. My load now is close to 80 or 90 lbs. It'll be less as soon as I get on the gun crew. Then, I'll be carrying part of the gun instead of three rounds.

Our company has been on a very dangerous & important mission. Ha Ha! We've been a bunch of cow-hands and pig herders. The company has been moving some captured water buffalo, pigs, & chickens to give to some refugees. This is the Army; you never know what you'll be doing next. Today a mortarman, yesterday a pig handler, tomorrow - who knows?

By the way dad, I forgot to pay the parking ticket. I believe its on Marv's desk.

I wish you a happy thanksgiving. We'll be going in for Thanksgiving dinner.

Not much left to say right now. I'm sending you a copy of an Xmas card my unit puts out. They gave me about 15 and I mailed them all. Save this one for me.

By the way the yellow and black insignia is my division patch I'll be wearing it when I come home in 347 days!

Love
Howard

When I arrived in the field, I was told to dig a hole. I took off my shirt and my back was facing the other grunts when I felt something hit me hard in the middle of my back. Assuming it was a stone thrown by one of the guys as some sort of initiation or harassment, I ignored it. Actually it was a piece of friendly shrapnel from one of the artillery rounds that were being laid down to protect our perimeter. It hit me flat side first, if it had hit point first, as it hit directly behind my heart, it would have killed me. The guys came over in amazement at my having this piece of shrapnel bounce off me like Superman. I carried that piece of shrapnel around as a kind of good luck charm.

I omitted that incident from this letter to avoid worry; the next time I might not be so lucky and I knew Dad could figure that out.

Also omitted from these letters is any mention what so ever of the various field missions and air assaults I was part of or the fact that we often had sniper fire. I now knew how deadly they could be! We were, after all, out in the jungle on "Search and Destroy" missions. Which meant find and capture or kill the enemy.

One of my first nights in the field I was trying to sleep but couldn't because of a sickeningly sweet smell. I told the lieutenant about it. Turned out I was bedding down on a shallow, freshly dug grave. Ycch!

One of our Sergeants, a Native American was a mortarman. There is a correct way to drop a mortar round into the mortar. You hold the round on the sides and slide it in quickly moving your hands down the out side of the mortar tube and out of the way. You hold your thumbs out and out of the way. Although he was an experienced pro and knew better, he didn't load one round correctly or move quickly enough and had his thumb taken off by the round. Anyone else would be yelling in pain. It's been said that Native Americans have high pain thresholds. Chief just looked at his hand and kept saying, "Son of a bitch, Son of a Bitch." He had what was known as "the million dollar wound", one you could walk away from but got you sent home. He was medivaced back to the base hospital and we never saw him again.

When we went in for Thanksgiving dinner we had to pitch our tents. Drinking alcohol was a court martial offense in the field. For some reason, there was no such rule for marijuana use, maybe because it was a more recent occurrence. I had never used any recreational drugs other than alcohol. The guys had marijuana and asked if I wanted to join them. As I was not comfortable using any drug and did not want to lose control, I declined. I just wanted to get some sleep. I lay down in the tent. They smoked right outside and the smoke wafted into the tent. I had no experience so did not know about contact highs or understand while I was feeling kind of dizzy, strange, and very hungry!

The Vietnamese barber on base was piss poor and often cut us when we got a haircut. Having just come out of the boonies some of the grunts were a little rough around the edges. One of our guys took out his bayonet, stuck it to the barbers throat, he said, "You cut me, I cut you." Amazingly, he got a haircut without getting cut.

---

25 Nov '67
Time 0805

Dear Mom, Pop, Marilyn, & Marv-

Well, I had another chopper ride yesterday, and if mom could see me she'd probably have conniptions. We put seven men in a "Huey" and since I was one of the last ones to get on (purposely), I had to ride sitting on the floor of the chopper with my feet dangling over the side of the chopper. These chopper rides are really great, you can see for miles & miles with no distortions as you have with windowed craft. Its really great, and even tho I look like I'm only hanging on by my seat and will fall if the chopper banks hard, its really quite safe, the armies been doing it for years & never had a soldier go "airborne"! Also, it's quite a thrill.

I got a few extra copies of my orders, promoting me to P.F.C., which I'm sending home. My name is next to the last on the back.

I purchased a camera already but no film yet. One of the guys is going on R&R said he'll pick me up a few rolls of film. The camera I got is the "Minolta-16" a miniature spy camera that I can carry in my pocket. As soon as I get some film I'll send you some pictures. You'll probably have to have them developed for me, make sure you can get these

57

size (16mm) single frames developed. There is quite a bit to take pictures of here, the land, the people.

These people have some of the cutest children. When we returned to base for Thanksgiving dinner we came through a small town outside the field base and were flocked by children trying to sell beer & soda. Some of these kids couldn't be more than five or six years old. The beer & soda they sell is American and costs 60 cents!

So far, I finally got one piece of mail from Marv. Thanks Marv, you were almost right I'm only the most popular in the battalion! We are all separated by battalions. By the way what's the name of the office you work in, one of the guys here worked in the Chase buildings also & is interested!

Well, in the what you can send me department-

I need a plastic case for my wallet, the one I have is ripped & allows water to get in.

Also religious type medals are pretty popular here. So far I don't want one. I still have my star in my watch box at home, but if I should change my mind I'll let you know, meanwhile just check on the price of a gold colored mezuzah. The one I'm interested in is a square type one not rounded in front. The only reason I don't ask for one now is because I have to see how the language is here, you're not suppose to be cursing with that on your neck.

Will close for now, Happy, Happy Anniversary, Mom & Pop!!!

I hope my mail will catch up to me soon so I'll know what's happening. Till then I'll still write as often as I can.

Love
Howard

After saying I'd send copies of my orders I forgot, but sent them out later that day. I did not keep letters sent to me for reasons previously explained.

Being in a war zone I was more religious that I'd ever been before, or would be. During AIT, two of my friends, a Catholic, a Protestant, and I decided to go to each other's services. What we discovered is that apparently one person wrote all three prayer books, as they were exactly the same except for a few words that referred to whom we prayed to. Don't know if visiting each other's services had anything to do with it but all three of us came home!

On my first combat air assault, we loaded onto one of the Huey assault choppers. We had on full gear, which included a backpack with supplies and ammo as well as two mortar rounds. The chopper would get to the landing area, with some gun ships providing cover fire. The Huey hovered about 10-20 feet off the ground. We'd quickly jump out and roll to secure the landing zone. The first time I did this I jumped out of the chopper, on the edge of a bomb crater, lost my footing and rolled all the way into that crater. If it had been a hot LZ my ass would have been grass and that crater could have been my grave.

Another little incident I "forgot" to mention to my family was when I ran into what I thought was a "trip wire" as I was running to catch up with my unit that first day. Turned out it was not an explosive, but the moment I hit it, my body clenched up so tight I only had one ass cheek, I thought I'd be dead or missing a limb. My heart was pounding out of my chest for many minutes after that. It's an experience one can't forget.

After we had crossed a creek we were often full of leeches, which we had to remove from ourselves, and for those that they could not reach, from our buddies. This happened frequently in the field. We had to strip down quickly to get them off, usually with our bayonets, before they got too well attached. Not something this soldier would write home about.

Many of the Vietnamese were poor farmers. The water buffalo was their tractor. These huge creatures were very intimidating to us, although they often could be, and were handled by the farmer's young children. There was a standing rule that we could not kill them unless we received permission first as they could be the key to survival for a farmer. However, when you see one of these monsters charging at you it's hard to remember that rule. In reality what happened was *after* a water buffalo had been shot & killed, they radioed in for permission. Since the animal was already dead, and to avoid a lot of nastiness & paperwork, the permission for the kill was given. I found that upsetting even though I later discovered that the army recompensed farmers for that kind loss. Of course if that was with the usually army speed and efficiency, that farmer could be dead of starvation, or more likely anti-American, and even a V.C. before that payment was received.

Yes, the children were the cutest and often another source of sorrow for me. There were so many orphans. We saw them at every town and sometimes even in the jungle. They were also beggars and thieves. I didn't hold that against them. What else could they do under such heinous conditions?

If you really thought I had met someone who coincidently happened to work in the same Chase building and that's why I wanted my brother's address you'd be wrong. It was difficult to write the truth home knowing my father's medical condition and my parents' propensity for worry. Someone should know the truth and that someone should be my brother! I believed he could handle it.

Orphanage we passed on one of our convoys

Water Buffalo

Rice paddies:

Vietnamese Monsoon Wear:

27 Nov 67
Time: 0930

Dear Mom, Pop, Marilyn & Marv,

Good News - some of my mail is finally catching up to me. I only received one letter from home, one from Janet, one from Marilyn, Steve & some friends.

I haven't yet received the other letters you sent without return addresses.   It's O.K. to put return addresses on your letter since you now know that the Armies method of informing next of kin is personal, & if you should ever receive communication by mail or telegram that anything has happened to me be sure to notify the Army. Although you should never have this problem as I burn all my mail as soon as I answer it.

As far as my other mail goes, you can send it all, except my magazines. I have a few books to read now & I don't want to carry more that I have to. I let you know when to send them.

A few other things I need here are a toothbrush (the travel type), my lighter (it should be in my closet in the box on the shelf), we do get to cook our "C"s here but matches get wet easily. Also ask Marilyn to get me a calendar card for 1968 from our bank (cause it has the jewish holidays on the back) as soon as they come out.

I'm glad of the way the elections turned out, even tho I didn't vote.

My diploma probably isn't ready yet, but Marilyn can check in the registrar's office if she wants to.

As far as monsoon season goes - well it's raining right now and rains every night and almost

64

every day but we do get some sunshine. As a matter of fact I got myself a little sunburn on Friday!

I'm glad you told Janet about my being here. It'll make it easier to write her! That's just what I'm going to do now.

Marilyn - don't believe everything you hear - your co-worker is very wrong. AnKhe is a secured position and hasn't even been mortared since August. But, I'm not in AnKhe; I'm in the field near "LZ Ross" (that's not on the map) it is near Chu Lai.

Marilyn & Marv, thanks for writing. I hope you don't mind me not sending you separate letters, but it's easier this way! Instead of repeating the same thing in three or four letters.

Well, now that I've started getting mail, keep those letters coming!

Love from Nam
Howard

Now that mail started arriving my tone is defiantly happier. Rain was something I associated with Vietnam. As luck would have it I would go through more than one monsoon.

At the time this was written An Khe was considered a "safe" location in Vietnam.

There was never any mention in any of my letters about the many patrols I was part of or of the minefields we crossed with the expected casualties.

When we came upon a village, we had no way of knowing if it there were friendlies there or not, or if it was booby-trapped. Many a good man had lost limbs or life to bobby traps.

There were also the unmentioned tunnels we uncovered. One in particular I remember appeared to be just a piece of junk wood lying on the ground behind a hooch. When we lifted it we found a tunnel. As I recall we shouted, fired a few rounds, tossed in grenade before a few of us went down to check it out. It was dark and tight but bigger than it appeared from above. Tunnels were all over the Nam and in my short time in the field I had seen a few. One did not want to be the smaller guys in a unit, as they were the ones who often went down to check out those tunnels. Being lean at the time was not an advantage for me. Of course that info never went home.

Chopper Views:

Notice authors foot bottom in picture (intentionally photographed):

Chapter 5 – The Eyes have it

After all my emails trying to get my MOS (Military Occupational Specialty) changed from 11B (Infantryman) or 11C (Motarman) to mechanic or clerk, I get called out of the field because of my eyes. The eye examination did not change my life, but while waiting for the results something else did. I did not wish for it to happen that way but it did.

---

30 Nov '67
Time: 0830

Dear Mom, Pop, Marilyn, & Marv,

Don't get your hopes up, but an inquiry came down from Washington about my eyes. Yesterday I was pulled out of the field and I'm now on my way to AnKhe, where I'll probably be sent to Quan An, where the ophthalmologist is. They're mainly interested in my night vision. I suppose Senator Javits started the inquiry. The reason I say, "don't get your hopes up" is that the eye doctor in NY found nothing wrong and even if they do find something there's no guarantee I'll stay out of the field. I'll let you know more about this when I get through with the tests.

No action yet, my company has been on the same LZ for about a week. I think they'll move today but I don't know where.

Right now I'm at " [LZ] Baldy" waiting for a plane out to AnKhe. Just now I had a small type problem. They have this pet monkey across the road, which I and another fellow went to look at. Well he jumped up on me & went looking in my pockets. He took my camera and I had to get him -this is easy since he's tied up by a long piece of rope. As if that wasn't enough, he pretended to be looking in my top pocket and then dashed up my arm & grabbed my glasses. He reminded me of the deer at Catskills Game Farm. He wasn't satisfied; he tried & succeeded in getting my glasses at least another 3 times! Boy, he sure is a clever little animal. You should excuse the expression; he made a monkey out of me! Well I guess that's the trails & tribulations of war in Vietnam!

Nothing else right now - except food is improving & we're getting more fresh milk & even fresh eggnog! Also I get free candy & personal items in the field.

So long for now & wish me luck in failing this eye test!

Love
Howard

The letter from the senator was not the only reason I was sent back. In fact, I had severe night blindness as a result of my nearsightedness. While on night maneuvers I stepped and fell into a very deep hole in the ground. I do not know how deep the hole was as I never reached the bottom. I put my hand out when I was in the hole to break and halt my fall. Although I was fully in the hole, a few of the guys were able to pull me out. Perhaps this was an entrance to one of the well-known V C tunnels. Whatever it was, this was not something I could write home about. Those in charge now also knew of my night blindness.

Relating the monkey tale makes this letter somewhat humorous. Again, this was intentional. Knowing that my parents were worried I augmented and wrote home about every funny event. If someone had taken pictures of that monkey incident it would no doubt have been on TV.

Dear Mom, Pop, Marilyn & Marv,

    The examination part of the inquiry is over & now I have to wait for the decision on whether or not I'm to return to the field. My vision is 20/300 in each eye uncorrected, and 20/20 with glasses. I saw two doctors, the first one wrote that I complained of nytalopia (night blindness), I was severely myopia (near sighted), and suggested I be held out of the field, but it turns out I had to have an ophthalmologist examine my eyes so I went to Qui Nhon. The ophthalmologist did the same test (looking into my eyes) that the doctor did back here & wrote that my eyes were good with glasses. I asked that he recommend that I be kept out of the field but the S.O.B. was not as friendly as the doc here & all he wrote was that "if it be the policy" to keep myopias out of the field I should be kept out but otherwise my vision is normal.

    Checking Army regulation 40-501 Chapter 3 I find that it could go either way now depending on the interpretation given to that chapter. I'm hoping the doctors' report from here suggesting I be kept out of the field is the balancing factor that may get me a desk job. I'll let you know as soon as I hear something.

    Please don't worry about me. I haven't even seen a sniper yet. The only enemy I've seen is captured NVA regulars & suspected cong. I'll tell you when I'm seeing action, if I do. Right now I'm back at the base camp, for a few days anyway. The mortar platoon of my company hasn't lost a man in quite a long while; we don't go out on patrol like the line platoons. We stay back at the LZ.

Hope you & mom enjoyed "Fiddler". I hear it's a great comedy & it's a change of pace for you. You two should get our more often & enjoy yourselves.

Marilyn, thanks for those pics. I'll keep them in my wallet. I'm glad to see you're writing pretty often. Don't worry about giving my address to any of my friends, I've already written to all of them (including Nancy). No, I haven't received mail from Gail, just Steve.

Sorry Marilyn, but don't expect me at your wedding unless you believe in miracles or know an important General. Be sure to take lots & lots of movies so I can see them when I come home & save me a dinner. I also wish I could make it. I have eight more months to think of some way so I haven't completely given up hope yet.

Thanks for the luck piece also. I'll keep it in my wallet. At this point I'll try anything.

Marv, I want you to do me a favor find out if Chloroquine & Primaquine Phosphates, and Dapsone Tablets prevent Malaria or just prevent it's symptoms. Check it in the library or maybe ask Vic's brother. I've been trying to find out and we're in some disagreement here.

Well nothing else except that twice I tried to call home via MARS (Military Auxiliary Radio Service) which radios stateside & has the stateside connections "patch" a call. It's a collect call from wherever in the U.S. the radioman can reach. Ours usually gets Ft Lewis in Washington (state) but the contacts don't last too long. I waited over three hours each day but they couldn't get good contact. If I stay here at AnKhe, I'll probably try again so don't be surprised if you should hear something like,

72

"Hello Pop & Mom -crackle, buzz, buzz crackle- this is- crackle crackle - Howard over.......
Good Bye - "out"

Love from Nam
Howard

Yes, mortar men stay at the forward LZ or in the bush. We saw the same action as the other grunts getting to that forward area. What I wrote about not seeing a sniper was for my parents' sake. I did not say we were not shot at by a sniper, just that I had never seen one. I hadn't at this point, but I had seen their muzzle flashes.

The medications I asked my brother about were those we took to prevent malaria, which is very prevalent in the tropics.

More time on my hand so I'm writing longer letters. Continues to be lots of spelling and grammatical errors. I have corrected many of them to make my meanings known.

Mortar crew

4 Dec 67
Time: 1530

Dear Dad

This morning I went to the education office & signed up for my first USAFI (United States Armed Forces Institute) correspondence course. The first course cost $5.00 but all the rest are free. They want to ensure sincerity of their pupils. I signed up for the first of three Auto Mechanics courses. After I take these I'll take some physics courses that I can use to advance in college. The mechanics courses are for my own pleasure & also may help me to better understand my Auto Engineering Courses. Also, they'll make me eligible for the adjustor's job with Allstate after my discharge.

The car price I've enclosed is just for you to look at. In order to buy you put down a minimum of $250.00 and pay the rest on delivery so you can get it financed. Your suppose to order about 60 days before DEROS (date you return to states). That'll be in August or September for me. I'm not sure what car I'll get but I'll know better this summer when my auto magazines have the previews of the '69's which is what I'll probably buy. There are places in the states that sell cars to serviceman overseas at prices even less than PX. These are advertised in the Army Times. If you're interested in getting a new car next year & I can get two just let me know. You can check out some prices by buying the Army Times at any base (probably you can get one at the reserve center on 118 st. It's a quarter per issue) if not, you'll have to let me know & I'll send you the auto ad pages from a copy.

Dad, as I said before, don't worry too much about me. My last letter should have given you a pretty good idea of what I do in the field. While I'm back here what I do is hide during work call. So far in the five or six days I've been here I've been found twice but the work details aren't bad. I got dumb jobs like putting brackets on beds for mosquito nets.

The summons should be on the corner of the desk pad. If it's not there check the area it might have fallen or be under the pad. If you still can't find it check the bookend up on the top of my closet. If you still can't find it - forget it till you get a warning of a citation. Tell them I must have got it & never told you & now I'm overseas. Actually you don't have to tell them anything, just mail the money if they send you a citation warning. You can get a copy of the ticket by writing the M.V. Bureau in Albany explaining the truth that I got it & lost it & you'd like to pay it.

Tell Marv he's stupid to try to fix that car. The bearings are going bad and the car will soon need a new engine. (The bearing will either seize & melt part of the engine or cause a piston to pop). Tell him to sell even at a loss, I'll make up the difference. It's better than getting stuck with an immoveable piece of junk! We only paid $75 for it. I'm sure he can get $100 or $125, but it's better to sell now at $50 then to a junkie for $10!

Which 3 month deal do you want to hear about, the college one or shorter E.T.S (Estimated Time Service - discharge date) after an extension in Nam?

I don't' think I can come home even for a few day except if I get to go to Hawaii for R&R.

75

That Caddy [wedding limo] *sounds very nice. If you could find out where to rent it, it doesn't cost more that $50.00, & Marilyn would like it, rent it. It'll be my wedding gift to Marilyn & Steve.*

I miss you too, pop & I don't want you worrying. I can see in your letters that you're thinking too much & that means worry. I know no matter how much I say, "don't worry", it's natural for you & mom to worry about me. Well there's someone above looking over me & I think that can alleviate most worry. So far He's done O.K. for me. I don't want you getting your pressure up about this damned mess, cause that will worry me!

Love
Howard

Although, that last paragraph says a lot about why my letters did not tell everything or the truth about what was occurring, the line about someone above looking over me was true.

My preoccupation with cars is very obvious and continued through my tour for the reasons previously stated. It was something "normal" to write to my dad about. Before I was in Nam we often talked about cars.

---

5 Dec 67

Dear Mom, Pop, Marilyn & Marv –
WOW, WHOPPEE, hooray etc. I've just been told confidentially that I've been reassigned and all I do now is await order. That means I stay here at base camp.
Great news isn't' it.
Pop, I sent already for some car info on the ad I checked. I write more when I calm down. Right now I'm going to get inebriated or something. I'll let

76

you know my new address as son as I have it. Meanwhile you can continue writing me here, (It'll only be a change in the second line of the address). Tell Janet about this. I'm too excited to write any more.

Love & Stuff
Howard

P.S. Thanks Mom & Dad

PPS - Sending pictures of my former means of transportation the UH1D chopper

My confidant's information was not exactly correct and my excitement was a bit premature. While waiting for new orders I was assigned various details each day. One of them would be nearly fatal. But again I am getting ahead of myself.

---

10 Dec 67
Time: 9:30

Dear Dad, Mom, Marilyn, & Marv -
Dad, today I received your letter of Dec 2nd, which I'm now attempting to answer but I see a communications problem. It takes almost a week for your letters to reach me & vice versa. While I'm now answering your letter of Dec. 2nd (and you'll probably get this on Dec 15 or so), things are happening all the time & your answer to my letter of Dec 4th will probably be getting there about the same time you get this letter. (Are you confused yet?) Well what I suggest is that you hold my letters a week (4-8 days) before answering them. That way we'll be closer in time & less prone to misunderstanding each other. (I think now I'm confused, can you figure this out?)

Well I've been in almost two weeks now. I'm still trying to dodge the work details but it ain't easy. The night activity here on post is O.K. Most nights I go over to the E.M. [Enlisted Man's] club for a beer or something stronger then I go to "the theater under the stars" an open-air movie (free of course). I've seen some good movies this week including "Hawaii", "The Happening" & " The Greatest Story Ever told". Also, last Thursday we had a group of entertainers at the EM club including singer Vicky Carr, in a miniskirt no less! The next few Thursdays are also scheduled for some live entertainment. Also, Martha Ray & Co. will be here December 12th. I hope I can get to see her.

No news yet on my new assignment. I asked the C.O. (Commanding Officer) about it & he said he'd called Brigade (Headquarters) & they had nothing as yet.

You're right Pop, all overseas soldiers make P.F.C.; & I thought I could fool you. Oh well, they say you can fool some of the people.......

Just to give you an example of what I was talking about before, I know your attitude toward this thing has improved but also I believe that you've already sent me a letter reassuring me.

Don't worry about foods, I don't get enough to eat (at least not enough for me) but I have a very well stocked PX (Post Exchange) where I'm able to buy canned goods to supplement my diet. Also I have fuel for cooking so there is no problem there.

One thing you can do for me now is to send me my mail & magazines...

Marv, thanks for the Chanukah card. As soon as I get some change I'll be sending you some "Pia" or "Dong" that's Vietnamese money you can save as souvenirs.

Marv, how's things in school? What courses are you taking?

Marilyn, how are you & Steve getting on? Are you nervous yet? You know I've been getting mail from both you & him. He's O.K.! (I thought you might want my blessings.)

You should really consider Hawaii as your honeymoon spot. It's very beautiful but unfortunately also very expensive. Do you have any plans yet for your honeymoon?

Well this is page 3 & I think that's enough for one day.

Love to all

Howard
P.S. - Any problems reading my handwriting?

Not all is true here. I had not been dodging duty as I had written several time. Had details just about every day! The movie under the stars was mortared more than once.

Yes, that really was page 3. The paper we used was 5" x 7" and I wrote on both sides of each page. Transposing my letters to this form uses a lot less paper.

As I write my letter of 17 Dec., I was unaware of the letter below from General Steger. Events were about to unfold that would make it moot.

DEPARTMENT OF THE ARMY
HEADQUARTERS UNITED STATES ARMY, PACIFIC
APO SAN FRANCISCO 96558
Office of the Chief Surgeon

IN REPLY REFER TO
GPMC-AD

13 December 1967

Mrs. S. Kalachman
77-25 166th Street
Flushing, New York   11366

Dear Mrs. Kalachman:

This is in further reply to your letter of 8 November 1967 concerning the medical condition of your son, Private First Class Howard Kalachman, and his qualifications for continued service in Vietnam.

Upon receipt of your letter, I directed medical authorities in Vietnam to conduct a thorough review of Howard's condition. Subsequently, I have been informed that Howard's eyesight was examined by a physician on 2 December 1967. That physician has reported that Howard's eyesight is deficient but there is no evidence of any disease of the eyes. Due to the large number of persons in our society who wear spectacles, it has been made official policy that if a man's vision is sufficiently corrected he will be considered qualified for almost all of the same duties as a man who does not require glasses. As Howard's vision is fully correctable with the use of properly prescribed spectacles, he is considered fully qualified for duty in Vietnam.

As a parent myself, I know full well the worry you are experiencing. I sincerely hope this information will help to allay your fears and concern for your son's welfare.

Sincerely,

BYRON L. STEGER
Major General, MC, USA
Chief Surgeon

80

17 Dec 67
Time: 1420

Dear Mom, Dad, Marilyn, & Marv -

Glad to hear the good-news of Douglas Henrys birth. I knew it would be a boy,

Sorry for not writing sooner but there's nothing new yet. I spoke to the C.O. again and asked him if I should put in a 1049 (Personnel Change) form to get into the motor pool since I'm qualified as a motor maintenance apprentice. (All you have to know is safety items & how to service batteries & change tires) He said he doesn't know! I have to ask the clerk what he thinks, he knows more than the Captain...I think.

I got the batteries yesterday with the good news but broke the bulb putting in the batteries - Oh well, I guess I can't win. I'll go to the PX & get a few bulbs.

Unfortunately I got picked for K.P. again today. I was going to go down & pick up my pay & send Janet & Vic a money order but that'll have to wait till tomorrow. Anyway, I'll make some woman a good wife!?

Thanks Marilyn for your letter also, that makes 5 so far telling me of the birth, but from each one I got a little different info so I did O.K. I wonder what this afternoon's mail will bring?

Marilyn, as for your wedding, as I said, I don't think I can make it but I'll speak to the C.O. Maybe he has some ideas, though, I doubt it.

That coin you sent me may be good luck now, but if I'm found with it I could be arrested. You're not allowed to have any United States Currency over a penny here even if it's a good luck charm, only MPCs (Military Payment Certificates) which are paper money & Pia (Vietnamese money).

Nothing else to report here. Will write again soon or when orders arrive.

Congratulations Grandma & Grandpa, Uncle & Aunt.

81

Love
Howard

These were the days before symbols like :) . I assumed my family understood my sense of humor, which was often in my letters. However, sometime I did not want them to misconstrue what I wrote so I'd write "Ha Ha" to note humor.

The military did not want any of our currency to fall into the hands of the VC, NVA, black marketers or those who could counterfeit it.

The last line was in reference to the birth of my nephew.

I was about to get a life changing duty. It would be almost a week before I'd be able to write again!

Convoy :

Chopper views of return to base:

Chapter 6 – Ouch!

I was on a routine detail helping shore up a Chinook (double rotor helicopter) hanger bay. That hanger consisted of sandbags sandwiched between 100 plus pound pressed steel plates (PSP). We were adding more sandbags, a never-ending chore with the rain. As we were working, a nearby Chinook was taking off carrying a heavy load, requiring more uplift. I never saw what hit me but found out later. Apparently the prop wash from the Chinook picked up a few of the 100 plus pound steel plates and flung them thru the air like paper. One hit me in the back and opened up my neck. Luckily it hit me strait on, flat in the back and the point only opened up my neck. If it had hit me sideways it could have decapitated me. I was knocked unconscious and later told my heart had stopped from the impact. If that was true and I was dead, I saw no light just blackness.

I gained consciousness in an ambulance not knowing where I was or what had happened. I felt my wet clothes (blood soaked) and a tag on my foot. My first thought was that I was dead (as I believed those tags were only used for the dead) and I was concerned about how the Army would break the news to my family. I can laugh at that thought now, but it was no laughing matter at the time. Soon, as I became more fully awake, one of the medics asked me what happened. Half in shock and half trying to be funny, I answered, with that old line from the joke (about the crowd that formed when a guy falls out of a window. Some one in the crowd asks him what happened, and he says,) "I don't know I just got here."

I was taken to the hospital where I discovered I'd lost movement in the left side of my face as my facial nerve & artery had been cut. The Chaplin, Captain Black, came to see me and asked me how I was. Still upset, groggy, and in shock, I answered, "Not so good they ruined my whole fucken social life." Then I was taken in for emergency surgery and came out with 19 stitches. When I awoke and realized what I had said to that man of the cloth, I was very upset.

After I got out of the hospital I looked up Captain Black. I reminded him of whom I was and told him how very sorry I was for the language I had used. My mother had taught me to show more respect for all holy men. He lived up to his chosen career and let me off the hook gently saying, "Don't worry son, I've said worse myself" We became friends and had many philosophical discussions in the ensuing weeks.

Getting back to my letter of 22 December, it was one of the most difficult letters I had to write. I had to let my parents know what had happened without getting them too worried. I refer to the incident as "a slight accident", the cut as a "small cut", and did not say anything about the number of stitches I'd received. I even joked a little to make everyone believe I was better than I was.

Pictures at the hospital were ruined by time & dust. Note scar on neck!

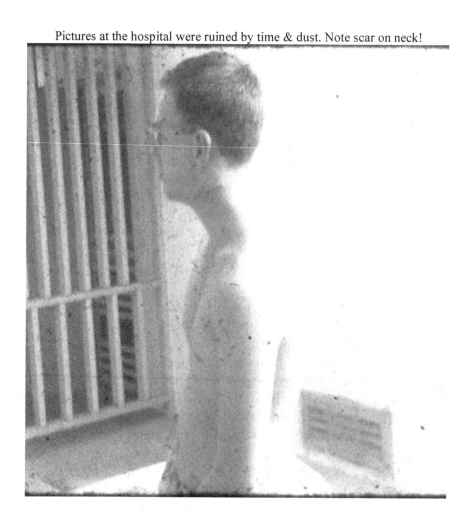

87

22 Dec 67
Time: 0945

Dear Mom, Pop, Marilyn & Marv
    No, I'm not on the green line detail. It seems
they put it off a day so I could be on the
sandbagging detail at the chopper field and I had a
slight accident there. I had worked about an hour
when the chopper on my pad started to take off. We
all stopped working and secured the equipment since
quite a wind is created by the chopper blades. Well
anyway I sat on some empty sandbags and turned
my back to the Chinook (chopper), so I wouldn't be
beaten by the sand. Well something must have hit
me cause the next thing I remember was waking up

in an ambulance with a sore back and small cut in my neck. They took me here to the 616th Medical and I was X-Rayed and then the doctor performed some minor surgery on my neck to see if he could find any foreign body in my neck cause the X-ray showed none. He found nothing so he closed the cut and I'm now at the 616th medical for a few days, (that's the field hospital here at AnKhe). I'm O.K. though, no pain and I'm not confined to bed. As a matter of fact I'm even helping the medics with some of the other patients.

I don't intend to tell Janet what happened, at least not yet. The only reason I'm writing you now is to prevent you from worrying in case the Army sent you any word of my being hurt.

Well anyway I'm allowed to stay in bed as much as I want to so I'm catching up on some lost sleep. Also they have American Woman as nurses here, only their all officers and therefore off-limits to me. I knew I should have gone to O.C.S. (Officer Candidate School) Oh well, there's still the Red Cross girls who are civilians!

That's all for now. Just wanted to let you know I'm O.K. I've got to think of a good war story to tell when I get home to explain the scar. It's sure to be, "The Greatest Story every Told".

Let me know if the Army did notify you I was hurt because they're not suppose to unless I'm hurt bad.

Love from Nam
Howard

24 Dec 67
Time: 1230

Dear Dad, Mom, Marilyn & Marv -

Arrived yesterday at Qui Nhon, at the very same hospital I took my eye exam at several weeks ago. The Doctor at AnKhe, Captain Lucero (a surgeon) sent me here and said that I may be sent from here to Japan but they tell me here that they'll be removing the stitches tomorrow and I'll probably be returned to AnKhe a few days after with a profile (light or no duty order), of course that's the nurses opinion so it doesn't mean it's final yet. So far all I've done is play cards and read and go out to the PX a few times. They have some conveniences here like showers (indoor with heat), and you should excuse - toilets with a flushing handle and water. Also there's a TV in the ward and a movie at night a few wards over.

The ward has two Vietnamese civilians also, one is a 10 year old boy whom we believe is an orphan, thanks to Charles. He's very sad and most of us try to keep him amused but that's difficult with the language differences. Maybe we can show him a good time tonight for Christmas Eve.

You should still write me at my same address as all my mail is forwarded from there. Of-course you can expect it to take a little longer for your letters to reach me.

Nothing else to report. Hope you al have a Happy Chanukah.

Love
Howard

P.S. Map of Vietnam on envelope Qui Nhon & AnKhe Marked off.

Even today, the thought of that poor orphan makes me sad. Children get the worst of war.

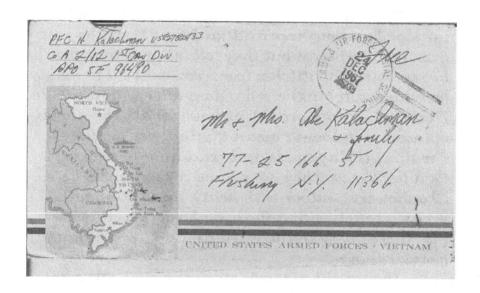

27 Dec 67
Time: 1220

Dear Mom, Pop, Marilyn, & Marv

Today the Doc removed my stitches, so I should be returning to AnKhe soon. While here I was visited by General Tolson, the commander of the First Cav. It was very nice of him to visit me and the other first Cav people here at Qui Nhon but I would have preferred Bob Hope & Rachel Welch.

I'm sending home two letters for you to hold for me. One is from General Tolson and one is from the Chairman of the Board of Allstate Ins.

I already wrote to Janet about what happened, only for her I played it down. Since I feel fine, I see no reason for anyone to worry.

Today I received my USAFI course in mechanics so I'm going to be short since I want to get my first lesson finished today.

Love
Howard

P.S. _ I'll try to find out if & when I'm going back to Ankhe or if by some slim chance I'm going to Japan.

When I said I played it down for my sister, I meant, but did not say, played it down *more*!

All my life I was blessed with fast healing. This time it worked against me. Had I not healed so quickly, I'd have gone to Japan and then home, but then my story would end here.

We were supposed to see Bob Hope & Raquel Welch. At the last minute, due to enemy activity in the area, they changed the area to a yellow zone. Civilians were only allowed in green zones.

Major General Tolson visited us a day after we found out we weren't going to see those stars. He came over to my bed and asked how I was. Don't know what got into me but I said, "Not so good sir, we were suppose to see Bob Hope and Raquel Welch and all we got is you." He laughed (thank goodness) and said I brought you some Red Cross girls. I'd have felt a little better if he gave them to me but he just let them visit.

Shortly before the General's visit, I was asked about the incident for my Purple Heart. Since I was not in actual combat with the enemy at the time of the incident, I did not feel right accepting that medal so I refused it. You only had to be in a combat zone supporting troops to earn that medal, which I was. So I was entitled to the award. It was a decision I later regretted.

At the time I was drafted into the service, I was working for the local legal office for Allstate Insurance. That is why I received their chairman's holiday letter. It was a nice holiday wishes, hope you're O.K., and hope I'd return to them when I came home, letter.

---

29 Dec 67
Time: 1100

Dear Mom, Pop, Marilyn & Marv -

First let me thank you for your cards. Second - some good news I'm going back to AnKhe tomorrow. Today I received your letter of Dec 14th. Of course my mail has been slowed somewhat by rerouting to the hospital and probably several letters will be roaming around for another week or so before I catch-up since they'll be coming here & then be returned to AnKhe.

I also received a letter from Janet dated Dec 19th in which she describes the birth. She seemed a little concerned over the fact that he was losing a piece, but that's the breaks if you're born a Jew.

Annette is welcome to use my bed or my "big shoe's" anytime she wants to, if she can take the squeaks. By the way, what do you mean with that crack about "big" shoes? Are you saying I have big feet?...Ha.

Janet's letter indicates that Annette 's not doing too good a job of toilet training her brother. As a matter of fact she gets squirted.

I doubt whether the recruiting officer was more than a sergeant. If he had stripes on his arm that's all he is. Army maps can be very useful and cover every part of the U.S. but you have to know how to use them. You should have told him you were the I.G. or the I.G's wife, that's Inspector General and it creates fear for all soldiers. He's the man or woman who inspects you & your facilities and completion of duty.

I'm sure if you'd have told him that he'd have given you a ride over to the restaurant in an official vehicle. Although maybe it's better you walked. Any 50 year old soldier, officer or not, is dangerous to women.....enough said.

I still haven't received the mezuzah you said you mailed. It may be due to rerouting of my mail. I'll let you know if I don't get it in another week or two.

I'll probably be sending home a few rolls of film soon. One of them has a few pictures one of the guys took of me a few days ago before the stitches were out. They should look pretty scary I meant them that way. I can invent a good story to go with it and counter my office manager's stories of winning WWII without firing a shot.

Love to all for now. Auto lessons coming along fine.

Howard

Going back to An Khe was anything but "good News" going to Japan would have been good news!

Again I down play the pictures with that ruse about wanting them to look that way & telling stories. I had no such intention but knew the pictures might scare my parents.

My niece, Annette was about 5 years old. She went into my bedroom and had come out wearing a pair of my "big" shoes. Hence the humor.

GPMC-AD

2 January 1968

Mrs. S. Kalachman
77-25 166th Street
Flushing, New York   11366

Dear Mrs. Kalachman:

    This is in further reply to your letter of 24 December 1967 regarding the qualifications of your son, Private First Class Howard Kalachman, for continued service in the Republic of Vietnam.

    Upon receipt of that letter, I reviewed the correspondence and medical reports I had received as a result of my previous inquiry. Unfortunately, I do not feel it would be appropriate for me to take action regarding an MOS change for your son. The proper and most expeditious way of accomplishing this would be for Howard to initiate through his commanding officer a request that his MOS be changed. At that time his Commander would review Howard's past record, his physical fitness and his proven ability to perform in his present MOS. The decision regarding a reassignment would then be made and any appropriate action initiated.

    Your continued concern into the welfare of your son is understood and appreciated.

Sincerely,

BYRON L. STEGER
Major General, MC, USA
Chief Surgeon

Seems like my last resort to not return to the field has been lost. Most of what I have been writing & saying had been to allay my parents fear. I really was in the field even on an LZ. Unless you were at AnKhe, you were in the field, more at risk then at base camp.

---

1 Jan 68
Time: 1100

Dear Dad, Mom, Marilyn, & Marv -
   Received your letter of Dec 24ᵗʰ yesterday. Dad I Already have received brochures from American Motors, Walker Bros, Karden, and one other firm, so when you get your brochures you keep them so we can compare notes. Don't undersell the Rambler dad, it's not a bad car. I'll be able to judge better when I've completed my USAFI correspondence course in mechanics. I've already done the first two lessons and I didn't realize there was so much basic information I didn't know.
   Dad, I know what the surgeon general must have said, just what that S.O.B. at Qui Nhon wrote on my medical report. But there's still several things I can do. Also my C.O. told me that before I got hurt he was speaking to the C.O. of the 1/5 who was looking for a man with some college to do some bookkeeping work, he asked me if I'm interested and of course I said "Yes" and told him I took some Accounting in college. He said he would check and see if they're still looking and if so he would recommend me. I sure hope something comes of it, though if I don't see the C.O. today I'll have to wait a few weeks for an answer since he's going on R&R today.
   If nothing else works I can always go to the Chaplin or I.G., I'm told they will help in my case.

96

Also I have a first Sergeant of another co. who has offered to help me, several weeks ago, when I told him of my problem as we were shooting the bull. I'm saving him for last.

As for New Years eve, I went to the EM club for some _free_ booze, but there was no show last night, so I left early & went to see the movie. Then I came back and had a drink and barbecued steak outside the supply office. I didn't want to stay up to twelve though. I was tired so I turned in at 10 P.M.

I guess you spent your New Years babysitting at Janet's? At least Janet said Mom & Pop - I guess she meant you. Sure am looking forward to 10 very fast months.

While in the hospital I got another humorous but true composition from the Red Cross. I'm sending it to you to read & then put with my other papers.

Sure am glad Marv smartened up and sold the car. Though I hear you may have another transit strike. That's good old New York. Let me know how you make out if there's a strike. I remember last time it was pretty bad. The average speed was 05 MPH Both engines & drivers were overheated. Good -Luck - if it gets too rough call in & say your car broke down - don't fight it.

Love from Nam
Howard

P.S. - Dad & Mom - I also have another problem with getting sent to the field. When the metal hit me it also scraped my back and now I get backaches and probably will get them all year - (understand what I mean?)

97

Once again I talk about a lot of mundane things and say things believing they will alleviate my parents worry & concern for my well being. My back was actually badly injured in the incident at the chopper field and I had backaches for many years thereafter but I wouldn't say that to my parents so tried to lead them to believe it was not real.

This is all about to change in one way. I will now start writing more of the truth to my brother.

Below is that cute (author unknown) composition I received form the Red Cross. It is somewhat similar to the one I sent home a month prior.

WHAT IS A SOLDIER? ? ? ? ? ?

AFTER THE SECURITY OF CHILDHOODAND BEFORE THE INSECURITY OF SECOND CHILDHOOD WE FIND A SOLDIER. SOLDIERS ARE FOUND EVERYWHERE, IN JEEPS, IN BARS, INTROUBLE, ON LEAVE, IN LOVE AND IN DEBT. SOLDIERS COME IN ASSORTED SIZES, WEIGHTS, STATES OF SOBRIATY, MISERY AND CONFUSION. GILRS LOVE THEM, MOTHERS TOLERATE THEM THE U.S. SUPPORTS THEM AND SOMEHOW THEY MANAGE TO GET ALONG WITH EACH OTHER. A SOLDIER IS LAZINESSWITH A DECK OF CARDS, A MILLIONAIRENWIHTOUT A CENT, BRAVERY WITH A GRIN, AND THE PROTECTOR OF AMERICA WITH A COPY OF PLAYBOY IN HIS POSSESSION. A SOLDIER IS AS SLY AS A FOX, HAS THE ENERGYOF TURTLE, THE BRAINS OF AN IDION, THE STORIES OF A SEA CAPTAIN, THE SINCERITY OF A LIAR, THE APPETITE OF AN ELEPHAN, THE ASPIRATIONS OF A CASANOVA, AND WHEN HE WANTS SOMETHING IT'S LIKE A WEEKEND PASS OR A STAND-BY. HE LIKES GIRLS, WOMEN, FEMALES, AND MEMEBERS OF THE OPPOSITE SEX. HE DISLIKES ANSWEREING LETTERS, WEARING HIS UNIFORM, HIS SUPERIOR OFFICERS, AND GETTING UP AT REVILLE, NOT TOMENTION ARMY CHOW, ARMY REGULATIONS, THE WEEK AGTER PAYDAY, AND HIS GIRLS'S FATHER'S CURFUE. NO ONE CAN WRITE SO SELDOM YET THINK OF YOU SO OFTEN. NO ONE ELSE CAN GET SO MUCH FUN FROM YOUR LETER, CIVILIAN CLOTGHERS, AND SEX MAGAZINE. NOBODY ELSE CAN CRAM INTO ONE SMALL POCKET A LITTLE BLACK BOOK, A LETTER FROM HOMW AND A PIN UP FROM ESQUIRE OR PLAYBOY, A PAIR OF DICEOR A DECK OF CARDS, AND THE REMAINS OF LAST PAYDAY.

98

A SOLDIER IS A MAGICAL CREDATURE, YOU CAN LOCK HIM OUT OF
YOUR HOUSE BUT NOT OUT OF YOUR MIND AND HEART. YOUJ CAN
TAKE HIM OFF YOUR MAILING LIST BUT NOT OUT OF YOUR HEART.
YOU CAN TAKER HIM FOR WHAT HE IS BUT NOT OFF YOUR MIND.
YOU MIGHT AS WELL GIVE IN, HE'S YOUR LONG-DISTANCE LOVER,
YOUR BRIGHT-EYED GOOD FOR NOTHING BUNDLE OF WORRY. EVEN
SO, ALL YOUR SHATTERED DREAMS SEEM INSIGNIFICANT WHEN HE
COMES HOME TO YOU AND GREETS YOU WITH THOSE INNOCENTLY
SPOKEN WORKS:

"HI HONEY"

Chapter 7 – Letters to Marv

The truth at last! (More or less) I decided to title this book the way I did being very aware of my father's heart condition and how my being in the Nam was affecting him. I figured if I talked about cars, and other bullshit it would normalize things somewhat for him, my mom, and the rest of the family. I often wrote little lies or tried to make them think I was out of harms way. I dared not tell them what was really happening or how afraid I was that I'd never see them again, but felt someone should know the truth just in case I did not make it home.

You will notice some differences between what I wrote my parents and sisters and what I wrote my brother. Yes, I still watered it down, even for him, but he got most of the truth.

My first letter to my brother explains it as I saw it at the time.

---

5 Jan 67 [of course it was 68 not 67]
Time: 10:45

Dear Marv,

No one really asked for your address, it was the only way I could get you to send your address without arousing suspicions.

Marv, You know I can't write home everything that happens because I don't want Dad to worry with his heart and Mom will only worry Dad if she knows what is really going on, same with Marilyn. You, Marv, I've always trusted with secrets and so I'll be writing to you from time to time at the office, if it's O.K., letting you know what's really happening.

I'm going to write Mom & Pop about my cut, and tell them the truth. Of course I won't tell them that another ¼ inch and I could have hung it up. I guess someone up there really is watching over me.

Marv, my Company out in the field got hit bad Jan 2 & 3 at LZ Ross, the forward base. There were

100

quite a few K.I.A.s & M.I.As (Killed & Wounded in action).

The last few nights we've been having red alerts about 0300 every morning. Cong has been mortaring the chopper and airfields. There's no danger to me cause I'm nowhere near either the choppers or the airfield, but it's annoying getting up at 0300 to go into a ditch.

That's it for what's happening here. Now how's things in the world, does Dad seem very worried about me? Congratulations for selling "it" for $190! Boy, you sure are some salesman!

Don't bother sending me Playboy I can see it at the Red Cross.

Marv, how's your social life? Are you dating regularly, a little, a lot? Marv, don't make the same mistakes as me; don't let your school work ruin your social life. You know I really regret the way I've ruined my social life, I really wish I'd found the right girl before I came here, but that's another story.

Marv, if you have any problems please write me no matter what, money, school, social, or sex. I can help you cause you'll probably have the same problems as me and I can also keep a secret. I already have $400 I can get my hands on if you or dad needs it for emergency or part of it for non-emergency.

I'm gong to end now Marv. I suggest that you don't even take this letter home just read it and destroy it that way there's no chance of someone accidentally seeing it.

Write soon,

Brotherly love (Ha Ha)
Howard

Dear Mom, Pop, Marilyn, Marv—

Received your letter of Dec 29ᵗʰ yesterday. Glad to hear all is well at home. All is good here also.

Dad, you ask me for the details about my accident, O.K. I'll tell you all but remember I'm O.K. except for a scar on my neck and the back aches. I went to sick call this morning about my back. The doctor gave me 5 days light duty profile and pain pills. He said my muscle is bruised and it should go away soon.

Now for all the gory details -are you ready? O.K. here goes….what the chopper picked up was PSP (Pressed Steel Plate), a large slate of steel used to make runways out here, its' about 5 ft by 10 ft and weighs over 100 lbs. When it hit me it knocked me out instantly. I never knew what hit me or even that I'd been hit until I woke up and realized I was in an ambulance. As far as the real dope on my injury, the PSP hit me in the neck and back. My back was bruised pretty bad and my neck was cut. Also my facial artery and the nerve controlling part of my face were cut. When I woke up, I was only able to move half my face. I could only move the right side of my face, to smile for instance. I was taken to surgery where Dr. Lucerno (or Capt. Lucerno, if you like) sewed up my nerve, artery and neck. My neck took 19 stitches. I've regained full control of my face but there's still a small spot where my neck is numb. The doctor says it'll take awhile for me to get complete feeling back. Well that's the whole story….

Oh - I was almost given a Purple Heart until they found out that I was in AnKhe, which is considered non-hostile, when I was hurt. - That's it on the accident.

I expect I'll receive your package in a day or two, maybe more if it's more than 5 lbs. Whenever you send anything, make sure it's in packages of less than 5 lbs. they go a different way and get here faster than the heavier packages.

Oh - I guess you know I told Janet about the accident although the version I gave her was even more watered down than what I told you. I figure it's better to tell her now so when she sees my scar, she won't be hurt that I didn't tell her.

Love from Nam
Howard

Mostly true but did you catch where I slipped and wrote "…even more watered down". Obviously I told the truth, mostly. It was I who refused the purple star as previously noted, because I didn't feel right taking it. AnKhe was in the war zone and a combat area. I wrote that "they" to further allay any fears my parents might have that this was a battlefield injury. However, as you will see that did not convince them.

---

9 January 68
Time: 1815

Dear Mom, Pop, Marilyn, Marv—
I don't know if the newspapers there have been carrying the story but my whole battalion has been making contact for the last week, since New Years. My battalion has two LZs out forward. LZ Leslie and LZ Ross, where I was when I was in the field. Both have been hit hard. Leslie was overrun on the 3rd but was recaptured. At LZ Ross, where my company is, there

103

was 24 hours of mortar fire coming in on Jan 3-4. Then on Jan 7th the Colonel's chopper was shot down and my company and C Company went out to see if there were survivors. They were ambushed and quite a few were killed including a few friends that I know of so far. Radio contact has been poor so I don't know yet how many more of the guys are hit. We get most of the news from the guys coming in to AnKhe for R&R or to go home. *Because of this I've been helping out in the orderly room (that's the office) typing up sympathy letters.* One of the guys who came in today said that as of noon today there were no more contacts. We suspect 3 regiments of North Vietnamese Regulars are in Que Son Valley. I don't know what the Army intends to do about it but I certainly hope they do it quick. Don't tell Janet about this cause she'll worry even though I am back here at AnKhe, and in case the papers mention my unit (2/12) being hit, remind Janet that I'm at AnKhe and not in the action.

Tomorrow if I have time I'm going to ask the C.O. for the mail clerk's job, he goes home next month. The sergeant here suggested it to me so I should be able to get it.

Haven't received your package yet but I did get a package from the Jewish War Veterans which included some goodies like a can of sardines and a can of gefilite fish and a lot more.

Dad,….[More BS about price lists for cars]

Don't do anything with my tax as yet. First of all you need my army W-2 and secondly I don't have to fill it out till I get home at the end of this year and then I have 180 days. Of course if I do get a big refund I might be a good idea to fill it our over here, *send me the forms when you get my W-2 from Allstate and I'll check with the legal office and finance here.*

As far as what you said about my accident being to help me, could be - I was here at AnKhe while my company is getting battered and I'll probably be staying here if not for my eyes, there's always my back.

Well time for theater under the stars and it's getting too dark to write anymore as you can see from my handwriting, so bye for now.

Love

Howard

This was the beginning of some very bad times for my unit. Most was covered in the daily news reports.

The orderly room (S-1) is really a tent. My mother always said things happened for the best. This is an important letter for me, especially the line bolded in italics. Because I volunteered to help with the typing as indicated in this letter, my mother's philosophy would have some merit.

---

16 Jan 68

Dear Marv -

Received your letter yesterday and first of all let me set one thing strait. I got hurt just the way I said I got hurt. It seems no one believes that; everyone from Janet, to Uncle Jack, & Aunt Judy is writing asking me the same question.

You know Marv; I think you may have misunderstood my meaning in my last letter. I didn't mean to imply that your social life is more important than your schooling. Definitely don't allow your social life to adversely affect your

105

schooling. What I meant in my last letter was that you should find a medium between study & enjoyment with school being the most important. Also I'm surprised to find you're still going with the same girl, you should be playing the field more now, while you're still young so that you'll meet a lot of different women and then when you're older you will be able to decide what characteristics you like in a girl and be able to find a more compatible mate. Also that girl was older than you wasn't she? You know it's always better to date a younger girl, I've found. Women mature faster than men and you have to find a younger woman if you want her to enjoy most of the things you enjoy. Maybe I'm being a nosy-body Marv, but if I were you I'd try to date other girls. Of course break off with your current girl very friendly so you can always get a date with her if you want it. Well, that's all I'll say on that, if you think I'm being nosy just tell me to mind my own damned business.

Don't worry about an account for me. I save over here. I have $125.00 taken from my pay each month and when I go home I get <u>10%</u> interest. By the way you can get me some car brochures if you get a chance. If Rambler has that X-Ray book this year get that ad send it, it covers all the cars. Otherwise get brochures for Olds F85, Pontiac Firebird, Chevelle Malibu, and Corvair.

By the way Marv, I haven't heard from home in almost two weeks. Is everything O.K.? I've heard about the cold spell and flu epidemic and was worried about everyone especially Dad.

What do you mean about having broads write to me? What broads? It sounds interesting.

106

As far as over here, nothing much happening,
I'm still working on awards. The sergeant told me
this morning that intelligence expects us to be
attacked between now and Feb 2ⁿᵈ but they probably
mean another mortar attack so I'm not worried.
I probably won't be able to write home today,
these awards really take up alot of my time and I'm
only getting out a letter or two a day, sometimes.
Write again soon, tell me if it's cold enough for
you. Also, what you think of the cars I've chosen.
Take Care.

> *Your favorite Brother*
> *Howard*

Nobody did believe that the accident happened the way I had written. My repeated efforts to get that straight were in vain.

My statement, "I'm not worried" was a lie on the theory that if I'm not worried you shouldn't be either.

Note my every changing brotherly advice about dating. The reason for my advice? I wanted to protect him. Just before I went to the Nam we had met a few women. The one my brother met was older than him by a few years. I believed that she was more experienced, if you know what I mean, and didn't want to see my brother get hurt.

---

17 Jan 68
Time: 0730

Dear Dad, Mom, Marilyn, & Marv —
Received your letter yesterday, was happy to
hear from you. How are you all getting along in all
that cold and flu?
As far as my back goes, I've only been to sick
call once about it & they said there was nothing they
could do for it, it was bruised & would heal by itself.

Right now, I'm working on making a favorable impression in the orderly room typing up those award recommendations.

I'm sending home a package that contains some Army clothes I won't need over here. You can put it with the other two boxes when it arrives in three weeks or so. I still didn't receive your package. Packages over 5 lbs are extremely slow in getting here cause they're usually shipped by boat.

I'm sorry that I can't write as often cause I'm very busy on this typing thing.
Tell Marilyn I receive all those letters from Steve's class and I've already answered them.

Dad, I'm thinking about the following cars: Olds F-85, Chevelle Malibu, Pontiac Firebird, Rambler Marlin or Rebel SST, Corvair. I haven't made any decision as yet. I'll watch the reports in my car mags. I expect I'll be getting a 69. How's your car holding up?

By the way you can start looking at some color T.V. sets. I have $400 in my accruals, as soon as I get $500, I want to buy you a color T.V. for $400 or less.

Going to end now, write soon - you too Marilyn.

Love
Howard

As mentioned previously, I was very preoccupied with cars. Not only was the thought of being able to buy a new car thrilling for me, it was also a way to focus on something positive. It has some "normalcy" in it. It was easier to write about than the situation in the nam.

A theme that repeats is my wanting to buy things for my family. I had no real concept of how little money I really was making and saving. Since I could spend little of it in the Nam it accumulated. Having grown up somewhat poor, I had not had much money before this and the accumulated funds looked to me like more than it was.

I wish I had kept the letters Steve had his third grade class send me. Some of them were quite charming and very funny like the youngster who sent me a recipe for chocolate chip cookies, or the one who wanted to know if the war ended at 5:00 so we could go home for the day!

---

18 Jan 68
Time: 0900

Dear Dad, Mom, Marilyn, Marv –

Just returned from Sick Call where they finally wrote "Back Ache" on my records. The doc leveled with me, first he gave me an injection in my back of "Xylocaine" or something like that. He said one of my muscles is still spastic and it'll take 5 or 6 weeks for it to heal. He said it may heal.

I'm returning the Jan 1st letter from the General. Dad, thanks for leveling with me, if I don't know what's happening I can't react properly.

Don't be bothered by my accident. I'm not, and wasn't when it happened. I'm also not interested in getting disability on my back when I get out of the service. My company clerk tells me they won't send me back to the field and I have the first doctor's report on my eyes advising I be kept out of the field.

As far as disability, I may be able to collect that anyway because the doctor said I may or may not get feeling back in that 2-inch area below my left ear.

The doc here knows I'm not a faker cause there a scar on my back that show's I've been injured. Don't worry about weekend passes; I can't get any here until I'm ready for R&R.

Glad you renewed the lease. I hope the landlady didn't increase the rent. Did she?

By the way, I was surprised to receive a $25 check as a belated Christmas gift from my office in New York. I already sent them a thank-you letter.

Love,
Howard

What actually occurred at sick call is that the doctors tried to dissuade many from claiming they had a backache by telling us the treatment was a very large and painful shot in the back. They did this, as there were many who faked backaches to get out of work. As my pain was real, and pretty bad, I elected to try the treatment. It was a big and painful needle! As I recall it required several shots. Each only helped for a short while.

COMPANY A
2nd BATTALION, 12th CAVALRY
1st CAV. DIV. (AIRMOBILE)
APO SAN FRANCISCO 96490

21 Jan 68
Time: 0810

Dear Mom, Pop, Marilyn & Marv-

How's everything at home, fine, I hope. The last time I wrote you I told you to expect a package from me with some of my army duds that I wasn't using. Well, I also sent a second smaller package. This smaller package was sent Air Mail parcel Post so you should be receiving it soon if you haven't already. It contains a souvenir of Vietnam for you.

By the way my package finally arrived yesterday. Thanks for everything. That Mezuzah is just what I wanted.

This Stationary was given to the people of Company "C" as their Christmas gift. I borrowed a few sheets & envelopes from a buddy in Charlie Company. That's my unit crest on the left of the page and my favorite type of chopper on the right (a Huey).

I'm also sending you two rolls of film to be developed into _slides._ It was Kodochrome II _16mm_ slides. I'm sending them in the envelope from Minolta but I don't want them mailed cause if mailed you pay for shots whether or not they come out and these may not. Most companies send credit slips if they don't come out. Since I've sold this camera, I won't have any use for credit slips. (I'll be buying a Polaroid or Konica Auto S). Also I took shots before & after the numbered film so there may be extra shots. I guess Marv can take this down town to be developed at any of the camera stores in his area.

Make sure you let me know when you get this letter & film & how it comes out.

Also - don't let that picture of me in my PJs & stitches scare you. I had it taken when I looked my worse.

Going to end for now.

Love
Howard

P.S. - If you can't find someone who develops slides form a "Minolta 16" (that's the camera) then I guess you'll have to use the mailer.

The souvenir I sent home was a mounted doll of a Vietnamese woman in typical garb and hat. I also sent one to my older sister.

Only a few pictures were usable from those roles of film I sent home.

(N.Y.: 23 Jan 68
Time 2400)

24 Jan 68
Time: 1200

Dear Marv---

To answer your first question about the mail; the reason it takes 6 days for a letter to reach me & only 3 days to get to you is because of the time difference. It's 12:00 noon the 24th of Jan here and 12:00 Midnight the 23rd in New York. So you see if you convert both times to N.Y. time it takes a letter 4 days each way.

Thanks for letting me know how you're doing at home. I've had a lot of trouble trying to find some spare time to write. Each of the awards I do are lengthy. I type up a narrative of what a witness (usually an officer) says happened that deserves a medal. Then I type it two more times, once using standard Army form for each type of medal & another time as a statement.

Glad to hear all is well at school. Remember you can always write me.

As for the Coast Guard Reserves, the physical isn't tough.

As far as not going back to the field, what I wrote Janet is what the clerk told me & I think it's true.

Now for some more news - confidential - very soon now the 1ˢᵗ Cav will be moving out of AnKhe, except for a few offices. We'll be setting up a new base camp, clerks & all, at Hue which is only 20 miles from the D.M.Z. It's suppose to be the 2ⁿᵈ largest city in Nam. The battalion has already moved up to secure the area. We may move up there anytime from now to three months from now. Since my address won't change I'm not going to say anything to Dad & Mom till I know exactly what's happening & how secure the area is.

I'll make a little mark on the map on the envelope where Hue is so you can look it up on the regular map if you want to.

Do you get to read the letters I send home? I'm going to end now & get back to work. I'll try to write home this afternoon.

Love from your favorite brother

Howard

There was a lot of work in writing up an award as this was before the computer age and each had to be typed up individually. Computers with cut and paste would have made life easier

Does the name "Hue' mean anything to you? Read on!

---

28 Jan 68

Time: 1230

Dear Mom, Pop, Marilyn, & Marv

Time has been moving along pretty well since I've been in the orderly room. I didn't even realize that it's been a week since I last wrote.

Yesterday I got back one of my letters of Jan 9ᵗʰ saying that it was undeliverable. No such number, addressee unknown. That annoyed me, so I just took

another envelope & typed out the address. I expect you've received it by now. If I have another letter returned I'm going to complain to the Red Cross.

The Jewish Chaplin is suppose to be in this evening, If I can get to see him I'm going to ask him if he knows any way I could get to Marilyn's wedding.

The snack you sent me really went fast. Since I've been in the orderly room I've been mooching off the other guys when they got packages so of course when I got a package I had to retaliate. Pretty soon I'm going to send you a grocery lit of what I want to be sent. Right not I'm too busy, I don't even have time for my USAFI course.

The last few nights we've been having alerts almost every night. I and my buddies have been losing all types of sleep, that's another reason I haven't been writing.

There's a chance that the 1st Cav Div may move its base camp North in the very near future. I'll tell you more about that in a few days.

For now I say goodbye, and write soon & often.

Love
Howard

---

30 Jan 68
Time: 0730

Dear Mom, Pop, Marilyn & Marv

I hope by now you've got the doll and the film I sent you. I don't expect you've got the box of clothes I sent home yet since it was over 5 lbs.

I've been reading and hearing a lot about the Korean problem. Most of us here are watching very carefully everything that's happening. Some of the guys are worried because if we declare war on Korea, the President will have the power to extend us in Vietnam till the end of the war. I'm not worried cause that's never been done to Army enlisted men, only to aviators and officers.

I haven't been getting much mail lately. I hope all is well at home.

I sure hope you are getting my letters. Since that letter was returned to me from flushing, I don't know if you're getting any of my letters.

Will end now so I can get this in today's mail.

Love

Howard

The S-1 tent inside

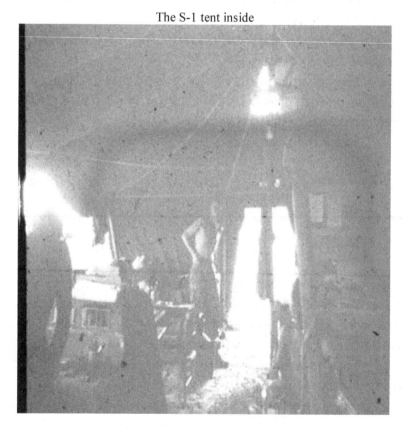

S-1 from outside

The rest of the S-1 crew:

Chapter 8 – Some Good News & Some Bad News

February 1968 was hell for my unit. For me personally, as you'll see in my first letter that month, things were looking better. However, the First Cav was reputed to be General Westmorland's (or Westy's, as we called him) favorite unit and he sent our unit in whenever he had a difficult situation with the expected results. This was difficult for me, as I knew many of the guys personally from my time in the field. Many of them had helped me and taught me the strings. We were brothers under the skin.

Too often, one of the early M-16's jammed under the damp jungle conditions and the mud. When I left the field I had one of the newer M-16's which was less prone to jamming. I gave it up so one of my buddies in the bush could have a more dependable weapon. In it's place, I received a 45-caliber side arm. Since I got to know the supply sergeant pretty well, he taught me how to not only clean it, but strip it all the way down to it's basic parts. That was way more than the average soldier knew. Unfortunately, or maybe fortunately, it's a skill I have since lost.

Since officers were sniper targets, they often did not wear their ranks on their collars, neither did I. Because I wore a sidearm, and a clean uniform, like an officer, I was often saluted as I moved about the bases.

1 Feb 68
Time: 1700

Dear Mom, Pop, Marilyn, & Marv;

Yesterday I recieved two leters from you. Sure was glad to hear from you. Unfortunately due to the fact that most of the battalion has moved up north to the new base camp, the APO has been shifted up there. That means that until I move up there my mail will be slower in getting here since a courier will be bringing it down here once a day if the weather and enemy conditions permit. Before it was the other way around; the courier brought the unit mail from here to the unit and sometimes the week was here several days before conditions permitted him to get up north.

First thing I want to do is tell you the good news. The sergeant here informed me that The captain has decided to keep me here at S-1 (Orderly Room) as personnel and assistant awards clerk. All my hard work was not for nothing. My hours are 1200 to 2400 with time off for meals and we are not pushed too hard. I'll be typing up the awards as I have been doing, and also making out a daily personnel strenght award. I will also be getting the use of a jeep since I have to take the report to headquarters every night.

After that news you probably won't be able to finish reading this letter! So far I haven't recieved the package from the "Top Spot" store but I'm watching for it. If you get any more of my auto magazines please send them to me. Also send me that letter from the Retired Major, its from one of the car places I wrote to.

Dad, as far as the bonds go starting with January you should start recieving them xxxxx once a month. I'm glad you had the front end of your car repaired , I sought of thought it might be ball jointe thats why I suggested you have it checked out when I was home.

Dad, you mentioned an article in the News about the commies sending Prostitutes with VD well I don't know who sends them but the town right outside the gates known as "Sin City" and the VD rate there is over 90%. Many of the guys go down there and come back with a case, as a matter of fact VD is so common here that a standard greeting among the guys is "Hows it dripping?" Several of my buddies including the medic have had it. Sam warned us about that back in Fort Polk, and again when you arrive in country.

I recieved the pictures of Douglas last week and was happy to finally be able to see what my nephew looks like. He cute as a baby (thats a pun).

As far as my health goes I'm in all this sunshine so I don't worry too much about it. Right now I'm fine the recent good news did wonders for my back although its not completely healed yet. You never know whats going to happen in the army.

By the way the reason I'm typing this letter is so the sergeant will think I'm working.

The weather here has turned quite warm again its been in the 80s and 90s here. I may even get a sunburn this winter. I'll try to send a little bit of hot sunshine in this letter to warm up New York City.

I'm all typed out as far as this letter goes so I'll end for now. Take care and write soon.

Love

P.S.- Have you recieved film or packages yet?

PPS- Marilyn send me a recent picture of you and steve, I have a picture of Janet and everyone wants to see if my other sister is as pretty.

After all my attempts to get my MOS changed by writing this politician and that, it was my good deeds that would finally effect that change.

6 Feb 68
Time: 1930

Dear Mom, Pop, Marilyn, Marv----

Well it's been over a week since I've gotten any mail. The way things are going it'll be at least a few more days before I get any. I explained in my last letter why I'm not getting any mail and went into it in even greater detail in my letter to Janet yesterday. I don't want to go into the whole story again cause I'll be writing all night.

My company clerk said he's going to put me in for promotion to Spec 4 and change of M.O.S. at the end of the month so that should make it final.

You know my company gave out a lighter and a combination penknife nail file etc. for the holidays, but I was at the hospital at that time. When I tried to get mine, cause they have the battalion crest, my 1st sergeant just said, "You don't need it, you don't smoke." He's a real S.O.B. I think he just wanted to keep the extras himself.

The 1st Cav Div has moved its base camp north as I mentioned in my last letter. The rear detachment (that's me) is presently scheduled to move up there 21 Feb. I've been told that date will probably be pushed forward again since the area isn't secure yet and rear detachment will only move after the area is secure since we have all the records etc. which are confidential.

Going to end now, probably won't write for few days till I get some mail unless I have new news but don't you stop writing. I answer all letters at once when I get my mail.

Love
Howard

One of the guys I knew had a portable typewriter that typed in script. I borrowed it to write my next letter. I liked it so much that when he went home I bought it from him. Since the handwriting is not an issue that letter is presented below without corrections.

Note the reference to my Dad's health checkup in the second paragraph. I knew he was more worried than ever since the incident at the chopper field and I was in turn worried about his health.

COMPANY C
2nd BATTALION, 12th CAVALRY
1st CAV. DIV. (AIRMOBILE)
APO SAN FRANCISCO 96490

10 Feb 68
Time 2200

Dear Dad, Mom, Marilyn, & Mary

I finally recieved some mail today, I recieved letters you wrote on Jan 28th and 31st. I hope tomorrow or the next day I'll be able to get the rest of my mail. I also got the letter from Marilyn about my diploma. Marilyn make sure you tell me when I get it, and thanks.

In answer to your question about my back and neck, yes they are alot better. My back only acts up when its damp and even then its not really painfull just annoying. Glad to hear that your check-up showed everything to be OK, Dad, now make sure you continue to take it easy. Don't worry about my neck, its too early to tell if I'll get any feeling back in the damaged area but it doesn't matter cause if I don't I can collect on it and it only bothers me when I shave because it gives me a weird tingling feeling when I run my blade over it.

I haven't recieved the package from Tom Foot yet but that may be due to the foul up in the mail.

As far as my films go just let me know how they came out if you haven't already in a letter that I may not have recieved as yet. I'm afraid they'll be damaged or lost if you send them to me.

As far as my misunderstanding what you said about the lense, just remember one thing although I'd like to come home to the same home I left from but I prefer to have you move rather than break your back to pay any extra rent Doris may wish to charge.

I'm not going to start this sentence with "as far as" as I just noticed I've done for the last three sentences.

There's not much action here, we get incoming mortar at the airfield but thats on the other side of the base (about 4 miles from here) and town is off limits now but except for a few nights of lost sleep due to false alerts, I have been unaffected.

I've spoke to several people about getting home for Marilyn and Steve's wedding and it looks like the only way I can legally get home for it is to extend for six months here in Vietnam. By doing that I can get a 30 day leave and choose where and in what capacity I will work on return from my leave (as long as its somewhere in the Nam). This would mean I would be in the Army an extra month. This doesn't sound too exciting to me what do you say?

I hope I'll recieve my tax forms soon so I can take care of it before we move forward (which is now pushed to March).

I got my military drivers licence a few days ago and everything was alright for my first day driving stick with my sergeant in the jeep. He was very calm and coached me as I drove him to division headquarters. I told him that a few more trips with me and he would be eligible for a medal for bravery. Then yesterday I made my first trip alone in the C.O.'s jeep to pick up one of the guys at division. Everything was going fine till I got within 100 meters of my objective than I did it instead of shifting into 3rd gear I went over too far and shifted into reverse locking the gears. I almost had a heart attack right there on the spot. Fortunally another vehicle from my battalion was at division at the time and I knew the driver. The driver got a friend who tried to free the gears but was unsuccessful. He told me the transmission and clutch was ruined and I could see myself back in the field or paying 1800 dollars for a new jeep. Well the friend went and got the mechanic from our battalion who fixed it in about an hour. Boy was I relieved. Of course it'll be awhile before the guys stop kidding me about it. The CO has also teased me about it. In case you forgotten the gear pattern on a jeep it looks like this:

Well that all for now. Be well and write main soon. How do you like my new handwriting? Actually its a typewriter (as if you didn't know). Love

Dear Mom, Pop, Marilyn, Marv..

Well how did you like our first phone patch? Yesterday one of my friends told me they were getting through between 9-10 AM Vietnamese time (approx 8-9 PM the day before NY time) so I decided that, since most of the Cav has already moved north, there would only be members of the 173rd Airborne, who are taking over this base. Sure enough I went up there & there were only 3 people waiting before me. The reason I sounded so tongue-tied was that I didn't really expect to get through.

It's too bad I didn't get to speak to Dad, but if I stay here another two weeks maybe I can try again.

Let me try to explain the phone patch jazz. Actually what is done is the MARS station here calls a MARS station in the states & that station calls you & connects you to his radio. That's the reason you have to say, "over" after each transmission. Since you're on a radio, which is a one-way transmission. You pay for the call from the MARS station in the state, which is usually Ft. Lewis, Washington.

I had hoped there was a 24-hour difference instead of 25 so that you would only have to pay the $1.00 after 9:00 rate. It is 9:00 for the reduced rate now or has it been changed to 8:00?

Another thing is I can't say where I am or mention troop movement over the phone patch since it's not a secure means of communications.

The radio operator on my side monitors the call to assist (such as advising you to say over) & to make sure no information is given over the phone patch which shouldn't be.

We got a call from forward that they need a casualty clerk at the new base _now!_ That means either myself or one of the two other clerks will be going forward in the next few days. I'm hoping I can stay here till the whole rear detachment ships out, because they'll be going convoy & I'd get a chance to drive and also a few days off for traveling. If I do get to stay, I'll try to call home again in a few weeks, before I leave.

Dad & Marilyn, I sure am sorry I couldn't speak to you but don't worry I'll call again either in the next few weeks or when I go on R&R.

Marv said I sounded different, well that's because of the radio. You also sounded different but I sure was happy to speak to you, Marv & Mom.

Mom, a little more training and I can bring you over here as a R.T.O. (Radio Telephone Operator) to carry the ANPRC-25 radio for the command post. Another thing to know in radio language is, "Out" which means end of transmission & unlike television shows is never used with "Over" which means continue. There's no such thing as, "over & out." You can say, "Roger, out" which means, "I understand your last transmission, end of transmission. Enough said for radio talk.

How did you like the phone patch? I'll bet I really surprised you. I actually didn't think I would get through & when we did I was also so surprise that I didn't remember anything I wanted to say.

I guess that's all for now on radio.

Be well, and write soon.

Love from Nam
Howard

OUT!

126

As you can see from the last few letters much has been going on. I had finally received my military license and could drive again. That was a big morale booster for me, even if learning to drive a standard shift army jeep was a little awkward. The transmission on a Vietnam era jeep was strange in that there was no gate between 3rd gear and reverse so it was easy, until you got used to that, to accidentally shift from 2nd to reverse putting the jeep in a spin and meshing the gears. I did it a few times. Before I got that down pat I learned how to remove the transmission cover and undo the mess myself.

My call to my family was another morale booster for both them as well as me. My mom had some difficulty at first with remembering to say, "over" but then got it down. That's why I kidded her about being an R.T.O.

You may have noticed my tendency to repeat things. Sometimes I was unsure what I had written, other times I just got too into what I was writing at the moment to think about whether I was repeating myself. You will see that repeatedly. Pun intended.

There was much going on in Khe Sahn & Hue that I did not write home to my parents about. I don't believe I was even aware of the full extent of what was happening to my field units at this time.

Jeep Pictures:

20 Feb 68

Dear Family-(that's shorter than Mom, pop...)
    Glad to hear you got all my clothes. You did
get my first packages (2) of clothes from November,
didn't you? You can pack most of it in my blue
suitcase to keep it together (except for the boots of
course). I know what you mean about getting that
Army smell out.
    You say my pictures are small didn't you get
slides? If you did ask Vic to bring his slide projector
next time he comes & you can view them on the
screen. That should improve them a little. How many
of the 40 or so pics came out? Did the picture of me
with my moustache come out? As for the scar, I sent
Janet a Polaroid shot of myself taken yesterday by
one of my buddies. It's a picture of my left profile &
as you'll see my scar isn't even visible on the picture.
    My back doesn't bother me much (except for
very damp weather).
    I got my tax form but it'll be a few days before I
can get my W-2 from "Sam".
    My office is pretty safe now and although the
new base is north of here, it's still considered safe.
There are no front lines here and you can
have action anywhere. Right now the hottest spots
are Saigon & Khe Sahn. My new base is about 30
miles from Khe Sahn, but my unit is in Hue, which is
about 10 miles from the base.
    Charlie is expected to <u>try</u> to make one last big
effort soon up at Khe Sahn but I'll still be safe. The
experts say that if he gets past Khe Sahn we can hang
it up (we being the US) cause we have quite a few
thousand troop up there. If they do get through I'm
one person who will lose all respect for my country's

129

Armed Forces. I don't think all of North Vietnam and half of Red China together could get through Khe Sahn now, & I think Charlie knows it.

My area in the new base is the farthest area from the airfield & that's good because if he shells, that's his target. No, I'm not worried about the move.

Yesterday the mechanic here said that I'm a good driver & he's gong to assign the adjutants jeep to me cause he knows I'll treat it right. He says that my sticking it in reverse was a mistake that even he could make & that the tranny was shot anyway. So, in a few days I'll have myself a jeep!

I should be SP/4 (Read Spec Four) Kalachman in a week or two. The request for orders has already been submitted.

As far as what I want, I could use another "care" package, keep it under 5 lbs & include some canned Italian foods. I hear there's no mess hall yet up north only good old "Cs" which are sometime better than the mess they serve us in the mess hall.

Love & stuff, keep well

Your son
Soon to be SP/4
Howard

Yes, they did instill lots of esprit de corps in us, but once again I down play the danger. Charlie did briefly overrun the Marine base at Khe Sahn but the Cav helped them reclaim it. I wrote home about my move north, as I believed it would be on the news and I didn't want my parents to catch me in that lie. I was surprised that I wrote them about there being no front line, even though it was true.

Whenever there were injured or killed I had to go over to the medical unit to get the reports. I could either drive over in the jeep or walk the quarter mile. When my unit got hit I drove over in the jeep as usual. I took the report. There were a lot of KIAs and wounded, many of whom I knew and had served with in the bush.

Must have been in shock, as I forgot I had driven over and walked back. Next time I went to use the jeep it wasn't outside the S-1 where I always left it. I reported it missing to the MPs who quickly found it by the medical facility. Got kidded about that incident and I tried to laugh it off but knew the reason it happened was not a laughing matter.

---

20 Feb 68
Time: 0810

Dear Marv (My favorite brother)

Yesterday I received your letter of 29 Jan. As you can see the mail situation hasn't improved much.

As far as the DMZ goes it is kind of hot up there near Khe Sahn but the Cav's new base is not in that area. Khe Sahn is about 30 miles from the new Cav base. Marv, I told you when I first started writing you that I was going to tell you the truth about what's going on even if I sought of color it for Dad & Mom's sake in my letters home.

One of the guys who's been up to the new base says that it's getting motared every night. He also said that the mortar was on the landing field & that just like this base the airfield is at the other end of the base so I don't have to worry too much. We're scheduled to move up there the 28th or 29th of this month & that date may or may not be postponed.

My unit has been fighting in Hue, which is about 10 miles from the new Cav base temporarily called "Camp Evans."

Thanks for the offer of stationary, I have plenty for now. I'll let you know if I start running short.

Don't worry about your letters I don't keep any mail. I destroy my letters as soon as I answer them.

Waiting to hear how you made out on your physical.

Received letter from home telling me how pictures came out but not mentioning if they all came out or not.

Marv There's something I meant to do last time but forgot & that was to send you a list of my friends in case anything should ever happen to me you could inform them. No, I don't expect anything to happen to me but I also didn't expect to get hit by a PSP & have half of my neck tore open. Keep this list someplace safe.

Marv, you weren't lying to me about doing well in school were you? Don't say I told you but Dad's letter indicates you're having some trouble - why & what is your trouble? Can I help? What are you doing for transportation? Using Dad's car?

Well Marv, I'm going to end for now, take care & be sure to write soon.

Your Handsomest Brother
Howard

Also your
Bravest
Smartest
Strongest
Richest?
Biggest Brother

P.S. - probably by the next time you write I'll be SP/4 Howard K...

That list of friends and family was included.

I was not yet aware of the full extent of the additional heavy casualties my unit had sustained.

Dear Mom, Pop, Marilyn, Marv---

The last letter I received from you was dated 8 February. I believe the letter before that one was 14 or 15 Feb, I'm not sure. Well in two days I'm going north. Most of S-1 went north today, only myself, Sgt Dissel, Capt Mack (the adjutant) and one other clerk remained behind. I'll be glad when this move is over and we're settled in Evans. All my records have been shipped north so I'm really stuck for something to do to get the info I need.

I was given the jeep a few days ago but haven't been driving it much. First the transmission went, then the starter, and now who knows, it still doesn't run well but at least I'm driving again. The Captain teases me about my not so smooth shifting but he's really O.K. Yesterday when the starter gave out <u>he pushed me</u> to get started. There aren't many officers who would do that.

I'm glad to hear that Dad likes to play with my doll, if he likes it that much, I'll send the real thing next time. How about it Dad would you like that?

Mom, what kind of work are you doing at the Nurses Ed office of Mary Immaculate? I guess I'm really in good with the man in charge of us all with sisters & Jews both praying for me. I know a little about Catholic & Protestant services because when I was in basic & A.I.T. my friends & I went to each other's services.

Annette is not the only one who likes pizza, I intend to get a few when I go for R&R. Mom, and I really miss your delicious meals!! The slop the army calls food even my dog refuses to eat. I don't know if I told you about "Jack", he is a 4-legged type. He

133

follows me around & likes to play with old clothes and my arm. He likes to chew on my arm, all in good fun of course. He actually belongs to one of my buddies here but he said I could have him if I want. Since it's quite expensive (over $150) & quite a bit of red tape involved in taking him home, I won't be taking him stateside when I return.

Mom, I would like some of your peanut-butter cookies but you have to wrap them in cellophane & package them so they won't break up.

Don't worry about my back, it hasn't bothered me for six or seven weeks now.

Yes, I have received and answered letters from Grandma & Uncle Irv

I had intended.... Sorry for the interruption. I had to pick up Captain Mack at Brigade Headquarters. What I was going to say is I intended to call you tomorrow since I'll be going north in a few days. I don't know if I'll be able to call or not but since it takes only a few minutes to call you'll know before you get this letter. I wanted to talk to Dad. If I don't get to call I'll try to tape my messages & send them to you.

How's things at home, you know if I don't get shot at too much this is not too bad a tour. I get to miss that coooold in New York City. No, I'm not serious, I'd rather be cold then in this damned army.

Well I really have to end now so I can write a few other letters to Janet & others. So, until my next letter.

Probably after I get to Camp Evans I'll find about 30 letters from you & Janet.

Love & Sunshine
Howard

Ah, Jack. I didn't adopt him, he adopted me. I was his human! He was a mutt who roamed the base doing what dogs do, fighting and making puppies. He was never leashed; he just hung with me for a time.

---

28 Feb 68

Time: 1900

Dear Mom Pop, Marilyn, Marv-

Well here I am at beautiful Camp Evans - boy what a dump! This place is just mud for as far as you can see or as deep as you can step.ecch!

Mail is only slightly better. I received a letter from you dated 18 Feb & that's about 8 days mailing time, which isn't too bad but I also received some mail from 30 Jan that was waiting for me.

This place is semi-secure. In other words the base is secure from ground attack but every once in a while they have an incoming round but again 2/12 lucked out & we are stationed atop the highest hill in the area with no equipment or airfield nearby for the cong to use as a target. So far they've had no incoming round in this sector & it's secure for us since we have the battalion personnel records here. Just to be safe though, we sleep in bunkers.

My battalion has been hit pretty hard these past two months, so finally today they came into base camp for a rest. It's about time!! It's easy to see Sam doesn't worry enough about our boys here. It sure is good to see some of the guys I was in the field with.

I'm glad you were home when I called, though I too was disappointed that dad wasn't home. Unfortunately I didn't get a chance to call you again before I got here. Mom, your & Marv's voices also sounded different - radio isn't quite as clear as telephone.

I remember the story Dad told me about his jeep almost going off a cliff.

Dad, as soon as I can get a Polaroid or the Konica I want (possibly when a buddy I can trust goes on R&R to Japan) I'll send you boo-koo (many) pictures of me & this lousy country.

I received the tax forms & yesterday my magazines. Keep the mgs coming. Next time you send them to me also include that days L.I. Press. I miss the news here. You at home probably know what's happening here better than I do. We get a paper here usually, but lately it's been hard to get it.

As for foods, I'll leave the choices up to you since I've been away from the world so long I can't remember what they have

Sorry Dad, the scar on my neck is permanent but you <u>can't</u> see it on the picture I sent. Janet you don't have to worry because it's not as bad as it looked in the hospital.

I don't remember my exact salary but I get $49 a month more as a SP4. I save about $130 a month in soldiers saving, $18.75 a month for bonds. I get $30 per month for spending & the rest of my money stays in an accrual account in finance.

What was done on the transmission of your Rambler Dad?

Well I'm going to end for now.

Love
Howard

We arrived at Camp Evans right after monsoons. The ground was so wet that even tracked vehicles got stuck.

Much of what I write is in response to questions asked. I don't knew who wrote me about salary but the answer is interesting in terms of what a soldier was worth then.

What I never said is that as I was sitting in the passenger seat in a duce and a half (Army mid sized truck) moving thru a very beautiful pass we were sniped at. Once of the snipers bullets came thru the truck window. I heard it and felt it wiz by my head. Had we been going just one mile per hour faster I might not be writing this. I refused to take that sitting down (literally and figuratively). We were told to speed up. I climbed out of the window and up to the top of the moving truck to return fire. At the time all I had was my 45 side arm. I fired it at the muzzle flashes on the mountain. Shortly thereafter there were some terrific explosions. No, I did not have a new Army secret weapon. The Army had called in air support, which had just arrived firing rockets and napalm at the coordinates my unit had provided them.

It was said that the things the V.C. were most afraid of were:
1) Dogs from our canine units. Even we were afraid of them. They were trained to respond only to their handlers and they were deadly vicious.
2) Korean soldiers who, it was rumored, like nothing better then to put down their weapons and kill the enemy with their bare hands. Worked with one for a while who was liaison to our unit and fortunately was a language teacher who knew English. He was a regular, down to earth guy.
3) Mutilation. In one of the main Vietnamese religion's it was believed one could not get into heaven with a mutilated body. Although it was forbidden to mutilate a body, even that of the enemy, it was rumored that at least one of our sergeants had a collection of V.C. ears. I did witness some evidence of mutilation in my time in the bush. Maybe that's why the V.C. did not like to engage our unit.
4) Napalm, which burned everything it dropped on including humans. Burning to death is a horrible and sometimes slow death.

On just about every convoy I was in, we saw bombed out vehicles which had been rocketed, booby trapped, or had hit land mines. I loved driving so this was not a deterrent. Not that one could say they wouldn't drive if they were so ordered, but in my case I preferred it.

---

29 Feb 68
Time: 1330

Dear Marv---

Received your letter of 15 Feb a few days ago but this is the first chance I have to write you.

I'm anxious to know what the eye doctor said about your eyes, can they be corrected? Marv, you know my vision is 20/200 in both eyes or worse & you always said yours was 20/200 in your bad eye when actually it's 5/200 so I guess you were right about that eye being worse than mine. The physical you took sounds more like an induction physical than a reserve physical. I'm glad at least one service gives you a decent physical even if the doc grabs your balls.

I'd like to call more often but now that I'm at the new base, I can't unless they build a MARS station here. Probably the next time you hear from me will be when I go for R&R, probably in July. Thanks anyway for the offer to pay, money is no problem here since there's not much we can buy.

I keep hearing Nancy is asking about me but she hasn't answered any of my letters but don't you say anything.

I guess you know I'm at Camp Evans, the new army base camp of the 1st Cav Div. I arrived here at what I hope was the end of monsoon season & the place is all muddy. It's pretty secure, though I'm told they get an occasional mortar or rocket coming in.

138

I came part of the way by convoy. Boy was that exciting & scary. There were trucks off the road & blown up all over the place. We drove right through the center of Quang Tri. Boy, that city was almost completely leveled,

We got here so, so far, so good.

How did you do in school this term? I hope you got some B's & A's, did you?

Well I'll say good-bye for now & I'll write you again when I'm over 24 (about 1 or 2 days over).

> *Your favorite, handsomest,*
> *smartest, bravest,*
> *Most intelligent &*
> *richest brother.*
> *Howard*
> *(Sp/4 Type)*

You might have picked up my concern that my brother might also get drafted and sent to Vietnam. He was virtually blind in one eye but I did not trust the Army doctors so I later sent him official pages of the requirements for passing the exam in one of my letters to him. It turned out he got deferral without any help from me. He actually saw a military doctor who found his issues! Amazing!

The part of the way I came by convoy was though booby-trapped and mined areas. The trucks we saw off the road was proof of their effectiveness.

The remark about 24 was a reference to my 24th birthday, which was less than a week away.

Working with Jack behind me:

"Dufus" & "Asshole" were not Jacks pups.

Travel by convoy thru Vietnamese village

Vietnamese Market:

Poor Market

Richer women often wore white and long pinky nail to show wealth

Vietnamese Church

Mined vehicle in forefront:

DaNang Pass:

Called in smoke on Sniper's ass:

Mud claims mule:

Mud claims truck

Mud claims tracked vehicle

Chapter 9 –Birthday –Schmirthday

My March birthday passed without fanfare. It was a sad time in the Nam; my unit was involved in constant fighting with heavy losses. One of my jobs was to compose letters home to next of kin. It was standard operating procedure in my unit to give a medal to each of those KIA's. There was a format for the sympathy letters but we individualized them with as much personal information as we could get about each of the guys.

One young man I had worked with before I came to the Nam was a kid named Ari. He was more a competitor than a friend. We competed at our job for promotion and for the attention of a girl. He was not nice to me. When I heard he was coming to the Nam I was without emotion. Unfortunately he was KIA almost as soon as he arrived. He may not have been one of my favorite people, but his tragic death was disturbing and undeserved.

My new job as company clerk was similar to that of "Radar" on the popular M.A.S.H. TV show, only we were a forward combat company, not a medical unit.

Not only was I exposed to confidential information, but was told that since I typed sensitive information and was privy to even more sensitive information I had been given clearance equivalent to "Top Secret". I also had responsibility for the secure safe in our S-1 building, which once again was not a brick & mortar building but a tent. S-1 was the name used for administration. Whenever the safe was to be opened I had to stand there with my .45 cocked, poised, and ready to shoot.

Working all morning meant from at least midnight to noon! Twelve to sixteen hours in S-1 was still better than all day and night in the bush.

We did have our fun and jokes to break the tension. One of the lubricants used in servicing weapons had a thick consistency and white color. One of the S-1 Sergeant's was a very proper kind of guy, a bit of a ball buster, and a little naïve. We loved to tease him. One time we had a tube of that lubricant. As we saw the Sergeant approaching the S-1 tent I turned my back to him and just as he entered I made some grunting sounds and quickly squeezed a few squirts of the lubricant out of the tent, timed perfectly to my grunts.

Thinking I was doing something improper, he began shouting, "What are you doing? What are you doing?" We all had a good laugh, except the sarge.

---

4 March '68
Time: 1645

Dear Mom, Pop, Marilyn & Marv-

Well I'm now officially an SP4 with a 71B20 MOS which means I'm a clerk. I've been working in the S-1 putting in 15 hours a day & working in the same place as the Captain, Major, & Colonel! This is bad because the Sergeant who's in charge of S-! is pushing us more. Yesterday after working all morning I was reading my auto magazine over lunch & was told there's no time for reading. I almost told off that Sergeant on the spot but decided it would be wiser to hold my temper. Of-course I won't be able to write you as often as you can already see. Speaking of writing, now that I've come north I see the mail slowed down at this point, it slowed down before it even got to my unit probably in getting to this base since the Airfield isn't built yet so only choppers are operating.

Well they finally called in my battalion for a short recuperation after a month that produced more causalities than were produced in the last five months.

Dad mentioned last time that I may be exposed to confidential information. Well I wasn't until I moved here (except of course for casualty figures & battalion strength figures). Since I've moved here I've been exposed to quite a bit more since the colonel uses this office. He holds his "State of the Battalion" meetings here almost every night &

I'm finding out what's really happening here. I understand a lot more about what we are doing here now.

One thing I wanted to say is that the base may, (it hasn't so far) come under Rocket or mortar attack so don't worry if you should hear on T.V. that we've been attacked, as I told you before, I'm in a good location on the base.

Haven't had any mail in almost a week, hope to get some tomorrow. It sure is lonely not hearing from you in such a long time. I wish this dammed mail situation would get better but with this new communist offensive it'll probably get worse.

Probably I'll be transferred to Headquarters Company which doesn't involve anything except a change in my address since I'm already working for Headquarters Company but don't worry about that change of address till I send it.

Sorry for the lousy handwriting but I'm writing fast so I can finish & get back to work. Tell Janet that I can't write so often because of this crash program to clean up our backlog of _500_ awards.

Well so long for now hope to hear from you soon.

Love
From 24 yr old   SP/4 Type
Known as
Super Jew - Expert Typist
Alias
Howard
Oy-oy-6 ½ (Israel Bond)

Did that sign-off indicate that I hadn't lost my sense of humor or was it that I was trying to make my family believe that? What do you think?

Some of my depression may be showing thru. It was the day before my birthday, already my birthday in NY and no mail. If you have friends & relatives in the armed forced do write or call them often. Even 24 hours seems like an eternity when you're "alone", in a strange land, away from your loved ones. If you picked up nothing from this book else pick up the loneliness a soldier can experience, even surrounded by & interacting with hundreds of people.

---

8 March 1968
Time: 0230

Dear Mom, Dad, Marilyn, Marv -

Thanks for the birthday card. It arrived on 5 March & was the only piece of mail I got that day.

Before I answer your letter or give you any further news, effective immediately my new address is: SP/4 Howard Kalachman ; HHC 2/12 Cav; Cav Div (AM); APO SF96490

The only change is that you now address the letters to HHC instead of A Co since I found out that one reason my mail was slowed down was that the mail clerk was sending it out to the field instead of pulling it so I spoke to the adjutant (that's Capt Mack, my boss) & he told me I should have my mail sent to Headquarters & Headquarters Company instead of A Co. & that he would give me an official change as soon as he could.

Please notify the relatives of my new address including Janet since I won't be able to write her till tomorrow.

I'm working a night shift now but at least I'm back to twelve hours & no one bothers me. As you can see by the time (above) I'm not working all night.

Dad, if you're thinking of changing insurance companies, I would suggest you check with my Agent, Dave B... of Liberty Mutual Ins Co. They have a pretty decent & cheap package deal. His office is in New York but he'll come to you & I got pretty decent service on the one claim I made for the burn on my car seat.

Make sure you speak to him if you call & not another salesman if he's not in. Tell him you're my Dad, he knows me. As far as Allstate, their prices are cheap but they may give you some trouble since they have some crap on their records about you not being a good risk. I think you had Allstate Insurance through Sears in B'klyn several years ago (remember)? You cancelled with a short fee Allstate said was due, which you refused to pay & that gave you a risk rating. But if you do get good rates try my Allstate agent whose name is on my life insurance policy, he was my supervisor & friend's brother.

Don't worry this job is permanent! I have no sweat about losing it especially now that I have the MOS for the job, which is how the Army classifies you, not by wounds received. Those who are so badly wounded are either sent home or transferred out of the unit to a "strap unit". [A strap unit was an easy unit on the main base.]

I'm glad you finally got to see my pictures through Vic's projector. Those pictures of me in my PJs were taken at the hospital in Qui Nhon. Too bad about the pictures not coming out with my moustache I guess I'll just have to grow another one.

Well I'm now in the 2nd, 3rd of my tour with _only_ 243 to go. It won't be long (only 7 months & days) till I get to see Douglas Henry for the first time & see my favorite family again.

Not much happening here except finally having some warm weather & the mud is drying up. This place may even be livable.

Well, will end for now remember my new
address (HHC) & give it to the relatives.
                    Love
                         as always

                    Howard
                    The Old one (24)

Dear Marv -
     So far no action here, had a few alerts but
nothing came of them. Thank goodness no incoming
rounds have troubled us here & that's surprising with
the new Phase III offensive Charlie's putting into
operation. You've read about it haven't you? The new
policy of the commies is supposed to be constant
attacks. It sounds like a last ditch effort to me, what
do you think?
     I'm glad in a way that you got that bad eye
especially since it'll probably keep you out of the
service. Did you try the Navy reserve at Whitestone?
That's where I was accepted, only it was 3 yrs - 1
inactive followed by 2 active. That's why I didn't sign
up even though I passed all that. I can kick myself in
the ass for not signing. If you get called for a
physical by the Army (which you probably will within
the year) remember to play up the eye thing.
     Glad to hear you're doing better in school keep
it up & you'll be a genius like me -ugh!
     Remember that since I've been promoted to
Specialist 4 (called Spec 4) & had my MOS changed
my address is slightly changed to HHC.

Your Bravest, Smartest, Richest,
Handsomest, Biggest Brother
(Got to keep you brain washed)
Howard SP/4 Type

Since a lot of what I write home at this point is truer so there was less "truth" to write my brother. My main concern was still that he never be drafted and/or put in the same situation I was in.

---

10 March 68
Time: 2145

Dear Mom, Dad, Marilyn, Marv –
It seems that every time I write you I forget to ask you one thing so I'll start this letter by asking you to check with the board of elections about getting me an absentee ballot for the November election.
My deros is 5 Nov, which is Election Day, & even though you usually get home 3-4 days early I don't want to take any chances of missing my voting rights. They'll probably tell you that it is too early, but even if they do, find out when you can get me a ballot. Also, keep me informed of what each of the candidates is doing. A good way of doing this is to clip various articles & send them with your letters & also call the Woman's League of Voters and give them my address & they'll send me an unbiased account of the candidates and their platforms.
Received today, birthday card from Marilyn. Thanks Marilyn I did have a blast? But I didn't get blasted. By the way Marilyn, I'm sending you one of the covers of a pad I got while in the hospital. It has

154

the address where you can write for a booklet about trousseaus.

If you're interested in reading about my battalion, there's an account of the Jan 2-3 action in Que San Valley (LZ Ross & LZ Leslie) in the 29 Jan edition of Newsweek.

No new news except I'm back to working days but down to 12 hours.

Write soon
Love
Howard

We had a troubled officer who constantly corrected my letters to next of kin. As I felt I was a pretty good writer, I took this personally until I found him correcting newspaper & magazine articles and then posting them on the bulletin board. He, no doubt, had some issues.

At one point our troops were surrounded and vastly outnumbered by NVA regulars. It was a moonlit night. He formed up his unit and marched them four abreast right through the middle of the NVA's waving at the NVAs. The NVA believing it was just another NVA unit, allowed our boys through without a single shot being fired. They even waved back! It was an extremely risky strategy, but it worked and made him a hero. Shortly thereafter he was taken out of the field, with a promotion and movement away from our unit and field duty. The scuttlebutt was they knew he was nuts and the next time he might not be so lucky. He was, as they say, kicked upstairs.

If you read the article I referred to, or almost any article about my unit in the war in Vietnam you always see that the gooks had something like a thousand dead and we lost like two men. While a grunt, I participated in a few body counts. They were interesting. A dozen men went out to count enemy casualties, more often than not, counting the same bodies; they reported back the numbers, which were added together. That is one reason why the number of enemy dead was often so far off. Yes, thank goodness we did, in fact, usually have many more of the enemy dead than our boys but the numbers reported tended to be spurious.

---

15 March 68

Dear Dad, Mom, Marilyn, Marv-

Well today I got your letters of 5 March. Thanks for the good wishes. Yes, I got the Hershey's kisses from the Sister. I guess I'm covered all around with Sisters praying for me also.

I'm looking forward to all that food & especially the Italian food & Mom's peanut butter cookies.

Unfortunately when I moved I couldn't take "Jack" so I left him with his original owner who's suppose to bring him up in the convoy if he can, which I doubt. I guess I won't be seeing Jack anymore but Jack is a friendly dog & I'm sure his owner will have no trouble finding someone to take care of him.

Sorry Mom about offering to send Dad a real doll. I only figured that it would be a nice toy for Dad to play with (Ha Ha). Don't worry you have nothing to fear from a gook. I haven't seen one yet half as pretty as any of the woman in my family.

I also read about Cam Rahn Bay being mortared but it was not the first time & it was only a few rounds. There's an editorial cartoon in the Army Times, its caption is, "Ho's other Army" & it's a picture of American Newspapermen. It's very appropriate to Cam Rahn & other incidents here. True, there is no safe place here, this is a war zone. That's why I get $65 a month combat pay. There are only relatively secure places and some are safer than others.

I'm not worried I have a nice deep bunker to jump into if & when we get incoming rounds. Today is the anniversary of Dien Bien Phu and supposedly Phase III of the communist offensive, mainly at Khe Sahn is expected to begin.

I already received and devoured the Salami Uncle Jack sent & have already thanked him for it.

As for my driving, I drove a "mule" today, which is a ¼ ton vehicle, used to tote supplies. It's a flatbed vehicle with no body, just one seat and a flat surface. It looks like a miniature Railroad flatcar.

As for the jeep I did like driving it but I don't think I'll be doing much driving. My jeep is suppose to come up with the "phantom convoy" & there's a fellow here with a driver MOS. That's his only job. I'll let you know when I'm driving again.

Dad, you were concerned about my opening the cans before I eat them - you forgot about Uncle Sam's "Cs", which I've been eating, are all canned.

Dad, don't forget if you need money for Marilyn's wedding let me know by that time I'll be able to send you $500.00 if you need it but you must let me know at least a month in advance because it's hard to get more than $200 per month unless you're going home or on R&R. It's a new policy to make sure we don't spend too many American dollars here & don't engage in black market selling.

Well now that I've answered your letters I think I'll end here & rest. Hope all continues to go well here & at home. <u>Don't Sweat it</u> somebody up there likes me!

Love
Howard

---

19 March 68
Time: 0300

Dear Dad, Mom, Marilyn, Marv -

I guess my division has been in the papers quite
a bit lately. We sure have been jumping in Charlie's
S__t as they say here. The reason my division was
moved north is because it's the only unit in the Nam
which has been consistently successful in its
operations. My unit is especially good & keeps getting
moved around & getting committed to every firefight in the area. We've been changed back to 2nd
Brigade again (from 3rd Brigade) last week so the
unit will probably be a reaction force if Khe Sahn
pops. Unfortunately because my unit is so good it
hasn't had a rest at base camp of more that a few
days since I believe July.

I've changed my mind I think I'll take Steve's
camera & about 6 packs of film.

Dad, did you have "Cs" in WWII? You say you
sent me a can opener - O.K. I'll return the favor, I'm
sending you one of my can openers for C rations -
can you figure out how to use it? You'll find it's good
for beer & soda cans but most steel cans are difficult
to open. By the way in case you didn't know, Cs are
canned vacuum-packed foods in 12 assortments
each containing a food unit, a bread unit (usually
crackers), a spoon & an accessory pack (sugar, salt,
coffee).

I'm not sure which college I want to attend but
it'll probably be City since with them I'll get credit for

158

all my courses & it's a very highly rated college for Mechanical (auto) Engineering.

Dad, I'm still confused about college. I like the idea of Automotive Safety Engineering but I don't know if I could make it, it's very tough. Well, I still have over a year to think about it & Vic said he'll introduce me to some people he know who worked on the Safety Car Project at Republic Aviation.

Dad, I sure am sorry about that bit on the car. That place as I now remember does that all of the time. They did the same exact thing to me twice, once with my Power Steering & once with my valves. Although they usually do good work & charge a rate right from the manual, they are also jip artist. I certainly hope I didn't recommend them to you (I'm speaking of Bellerose Transmission alias Tabs Motors).   Dad, it's very hard to find a good mechanic who won't sucker you. Did they replace your whole transmission? Ben Razenson is honest but he's a long way from home.

Everyone keeps saying something about a penknife file combination which I lost sometime ago. Since that time I've obtained two of them so I no longer need it.

Marv, did you get my letter of 8 March? I got yours of 9 March today. Marv when you write Army time you leave out the ":" , it's 1800 not 18:00 (which is 18 o'clock - no such animal). It's eighteen hundred, or as now -0330 - zero three thirty hours.

Marv, did Marilyn tell you Jack got here the day after I wrote you that I might not see him again? I'll be sure to give him his cookie when they arrive.

By the way if you haven't guessed by now (see time), I'm back on night shift - oh well it's a hard ship tour - Ha Ha

Until my next words of wisdom & truth in my next action packed letter - same time - same station - I'm--------? Who am I again..well whoever I am, I am signing off.

Signed off..

Love from Name

Howard

Once again my attempts at humor in closing are obvious. Firefight = battle.

Night shift was nice in that I was alone and not bothered by the sergeant or brass unless there was some emergency in the field or on our base. I was glad to have Jack back as a companion to help fight the loneliness.

Because I was getting food from home I became friends with one of the cooks. We shared most of what we got from home including that green – salami. It was after all food from home so I just cut away the green mold and ate the rest. Because of the hot, humid weather and the time it took for packages to reach us it was not unusual for food to be on the route to ruin by the time we received it.

Beer rations when we got them from the Army were served warm. We developed a taste for warm beer.

---

23 March 68

Time: 0330

Dear Dad, Mom, Marilyn, Marv -

How's it going? Dad did you figure out how to use the can opener I sent you? I'm sending you another with the instructions.

I got the bill from Allstate today & sent it to finance with a note to send Allstate a check from my

160

accrual. I don't know how long it takes for them to react but I believe it should get there before the due date.

By the way I sent Marv, a sample of the prices I can get for the two cars I'm interested in & the accessories I want. These aren't the cheapest prices since I have two other places which I'm still waiting for replys from. I'll let you know if they are any cheaper.

I've been told that I may be able to get my best price from a dealer in New York so I asked Marv to check one. It may be true since they usually give you a good price if you have no trade-in.

Well, my friend jack is sitting right here watching me write & he says he can't wait to get his cookie.

On that insurance, that was a partial payment for last year. The only thing you might check is whether the amount is right. I believe Dad has my policy if not check my closet.

What's new at home? What do you think of Kennedy joining the race at this point? What have you heard about Nixon's pledge to end the war if elected?

Going to sign off now & get back to typing.

Love
Howard

Chapter 10 – Mood Swings

Mood swings were an occupational hazard in the nam. I tried to keep my letters and myself cheery, but that was not always possible. We were, after all, in a war zone, miles from home, surrounded by death and danger. You'll note I'm sending fewer and fewer letters to my brother so I did not have that outlet. With depression, tended to write more honestly what was on my mind.

Notice how much a religious article had a lot to do with my feelings. As I've already mentioned, it seems like everyone in a war zone gets religion. The Mezuzah took on almost magical, charm like powers for me. It was like the lord would not protect one without it. Sounds crazy now but I'll bet all of you who are or were soldiers in a war zone understand. When I lost mine I hoped my family would send me another. My hints were not subtle.

Of course. there was that looming religious R&R that might elate my morale a little.

---

27 March 68
Time 0005

Dear Dad, Mom, Marilyn, Marv –
I'm feeling pretty blue, because I lost my mezuzah. I lost it once before at An Khe but found it again the same day. This time I think it's gone for good. I've retraced all my steps & can't find it. Last night while I was working something, I thought, fell off my desk & into the garbage pail. I thought it was a paper clip so I didn't even check it out. I think that was my Mezuzah. Unfortunately, the trash is burned every morning.

That's too bad, it was just the type I wanted. When I asked you to get it I said I needed a strong chain, well the chain was strong enough but the little ring connecting the mezuzah to the chain wasn't. It broke in Ah Khe & when I found I bent the large piece to make a new ring but I guess it broke again. I should have had it soldered.

I'm sending home the chain. Maybe I'll be able to use it when I get home for something.

I'll bet it was an expensive mezuzah also. I really feel bad about it. I must have looked like a nut crawling around on my hands & knees sifting though the sand & mud this afternoon. I looked everywhere in the hope that I'd find it but to no avail, & I still got seven months over here. Oh well enough of my troubles.

I spoke to the battalion doctor today (he works right next door) & told him that I've been getting some pain in my neck & face. He says that's because I'm getting feeling back in my face & that's good to hear.

Well now you know the latest about your dumb son who loses mezuzahs.

How's it going at home, it should be getting warmer already!

I'm going to close now so I can write Janet & Vic & send Annette & Doug M&Ms.

Love from Nam
Howard

Literally spent hours looking for that lost mezuzah checking, rechecking and then rechecking again in the hope it would magically reappear or that I had somehow missed something. Losing things has always been an issue for me and this was seen as the loss of my life protecting charm! It was also a gift from my family, and that made the loss all the more painful.

31 March 68
Time: 0145

Dear Mom, Pop, Marilyn, & Marv-

Haven't had any mails from home in a few days due to mail slow down (again). But, I have received a few packages. I got your Peanut butter cookies two days ago, all that's left are some crumbs & the can. You haven't lost your touch Mom, now if I could only figure a way to wrap up an Apple Pie I'd be set.

Guess what? Yesterday I got your package of car prices mailed 29 January. Only 2 months - that's pretty bad. Most of them I had already except for EP Kovory. His prices were about $25 less but they are for Detroit delivery. Even though I intend to go to Detroit when I get home (to check out some schools) I don't want to buy a car too far from home because of service & warranty problems. (Although I think this year they came out with a warranty that's good at any dealer).

Tomorrow I have to give my name in for my Passover holiday in Da Nang at China Beach. It's from 12-20 April but don't know how much of that I'll get maybe the whole week. I'll let you know more when I do.

Marv, have you got some time to check out some colleges for me?
First the colleges: Stony Brook campus of State U of NY
Ohio State U   GM Institute (Flint Mich)
U of Detroit   Detroit Institute of Technology
U of Mich   City College (N.Y. City U)
Conn U   Bridgeport U
The info I want: Do these colleges offer an Undergraduate course in Automotive Engineering, if not what about Mechanical Eng. Find the deadline

164

for applications to spring Semester as a transfer student & send me the title of the person & address to write for an application & bulletin (such as the Director of Admissions Dead of Admissions, Admissions Office, etc.).

Marv, Lou's brother in law took his physical & is now eligible for the draft. I wrote that he should get in touch with you about the reserves since you know (from experience) which ones are open. I don't know if he will call or not.

If anyone wants to send me a nice gift, how about a bottle (even a pint) of Seagram's 7 Crown or some other good whiskey. Hiccup Hiccup.

I hear there some new action at Khe Sahn & guess who's the ready reaction force - you're right 2nd of the 12th, my unit. They'll b e moving up there in a few days. Some of them have already moved up there.

Marilyn, I finally got the letter that was lost. I already answered it. So how's my little sister doing? I'll bet things are really hectic.

Marilyn unless I get sick enough to be medivacd to the world I will not be able to be home for your wedding. My Hawaii idea is also no good because I found out it's a violation of general order to leave Hawaii without permission & it's also expensive, about $300 one way.

I'm thinking of taking my R&R in Australia instead. I'll save Hawaii for my honeymoon (that should be in about 10 years). So what else is new?

Comments, complaints? Write now & avoid the rush. -What Rush? How should I know?

Love from Vietnam
Howard

Getting short only 90 days

Dear Dad, Mom, Marilyn, Marv -
      Got your letters of 3/29 & 4/1 today. But still haven't received any packages. I haven't given up. I think some packages are coming though now so maybe mine will be (I'm expecting 6 now). I probably won't get your can opener for awhile but that's O.K. I'm used to my P-38 (that "scrap of metal") & I'm almost as fast with it as with a civilian opener (especially when I'm hungry). Oh-well, as they say it's a hard-ship tour. I hope my packages get here soon. The ones going to Co A may take a little longer since my boys are involved in that operation (which I'm sure the news covered) around Khe Sahn. They assaulted Khe Sahn (the town) at 0200 two days ago. They're at a firebase now a little ways from the marine base.
      Did you check on my insurance & make sure that Allstate got the check? I'm going to try to get through to finance & ask if they mailed the check & what happened to my W-2 forms.
      Don't worry about the Allstate bill, I'd rather take care of my big bills myself & not put you through any big expenses. Especially since I have the money easily (?) available.
      I may get that S.A.M. package before the others. Were the other packages over 5 pounds? If so I may deros before I get them. Did you send me horseradish with the gefilte fish? (Ha Ha)
      If I ever get travel orders, I'll be going to that Passover service & Seder this week. While I'm at

166

China Beach (Da Nang) I'll check the PX for cameras.

I'm going to ask my 1st Sergeant for R&R in Australia in July. I've decided against Hawaii, its too difficult (financially) & illegal to go home for Marilyn's wedding and also unlikely that I'll get the right days. Sorry Marilyn & Steve.

I may go to Hawaii just to see it later on by taking a 7-day leave.

Here is some interesting news, Hanoi has issued another statement that it will meet us on an ambassadorial level in Cambodia or some other place. Sounds promising!

Everyone says something good about the proposed peace including Russia & that does sound good. No, I'm not getting my hopes up. I won't be able to go home even if the war was over tomorrow because my unit, being one of the best - actually, "the Best", would surely be the unit left here for security.

How's things at the hospital school mom? Shakespeare says "Get ye to a nunnery" in Hamlet. It's said by Polonius to his daughter because of what she did? What did you do Mom!!?? Ha Ha Ha Ha Ha (I'm really laughing this one up) - Remember Mom when I get home DON'T HIT! I break easily.

Enough of my bull -till my next letter!
I wish you all a HAPPY & JOYOUS Passover.

> Love from a Jew in Vietnam
> Without a mezuzah yet!
> Howard

The getting short statement refers to my sister's upcoming marriage.

167

The army can opener, the P38 is a small folding "scrap of metal" as my dad called it.

Once again my unit is in the thick of it n Khe Sahn. We really did have great esprit de corps instilled in us and firmly believed our unit was the best.

For all of you Shakespearians, I did not know then what I know now about what Shakespeare meant by a nunnery. Fortunately, neither did my family. At the time my mother was working with nuns and hence the joke. Now that I know what a nunnery is, the absurdity of that statement makes it even funnier.

---

11 April 1968
Time: 0200

Dear Dad, Mom, Marilyn, Marv -

Received a letter from Marilyn today & a package (surprise) containing newspaper articles & I see you found my mezuzah - where did I drop it? (Ha Ha). THANK YOU!

I was going to get a replacement myself in Da Nang but somehow I thought you might do something like sending me an exact duplicate. Actually I was hoping you would since part of the significance of my last mezuzah was that it was sent from home by my family (that's you like it or not - Ha). Now I'm feeling happy again. I think I'll get the ring soldered or better yet welded closed, if I can. That way I can't lose it.

As far as the newspaper articles, the only ones I want are those in which the candidates make policy statements (about Vietnam & treating Negros right) or campaign promises. It's too expensive to send all those articles you've been sending. I occasionally get the Army newspaper & I only want these articles to make sure I'm reading actual statements & not what the Army wants us to think.

168

I haven't got orders yet for Passover but I'm pretty sure the Captain will let me go even without orders. He can give me travel orders to Da Nang where I'm sure I can get a copy of my orders for the record. My Captain is DEROSing next week & I have a new Captain, Captain KASPRZYK (& you though Kalachman was hard). He's a nice guy as are most officers over here. Being a college man I get along very well with them.

Marilyn, Hope you don't mind if I don't write you a separate letter to answer yours, but I'm pressed for time. Marilyn besides the copy of the presidents speech Dad sent me, I also have a copy of the, "Stars & Stripes" (Army newspaper) & I heard it 3 times on the radio. I almost know it by heart! Seriously - thanks for keeping me informed. I had thought about the possibility of him not running but I didn't think he had it in him to withdraw. He's a better man than I thought he was.

Marilyn you have some nerve falling asleep while you're writing me (Ha Ha) Sorry can't send you my right ear, it's the left one or nothing. (Also it's PPS not PSS).

Thanks again Dad & Mom for the mezuzah.

I probably won't write you again till I come back from Da Nang (If I ever go) so until my next interesting & informative letter

HAPPY PESACH!

Love from a <u>new Jew</u>
in Vietnam
<u>Howard</u>

My family has responded to my not so subtle hints and sent me a new mezuzah (which I still have).

17 March 1968 (actually it was 17 April)
1600 - Time

Dear Dad, Mom, Marilyn, Marv-

Just got back from Da Nang (China Beach), from the religious retreat (as the Army calls it). I started back on the 15th but military travel isn't exactly the best so it took me two days to get back here.

When I got here I found <u>Beau Coup</u> (pronounced Boo-Koo) mail & several packages. I got Aunt Molly's package, one from Lou & Eve, your package of 28 March and a package from someone who lives at 161 St. but the name is washed out so I don't know who to thank. I still haven't gotten your first two packages (Jewish food & Italian food) or Janet's package. I don't know if I'll ever get them if they're parcel post.

I had a real good time & went to two Seders. The first one (Friday) was also attended by two Generals & several newspapermen but I don't think my picture was taken. I am sending you a little "Dictionary" of some of the terms I use & am likely to use (like beau coup above).

As I said I got several letters from home. I'll try to answer as much as possible. Thanks again for the mezuzah, it's just beautiful. I sure hope I don't lose this one. I check it every morning (that is afternoon) when I get up since I'm very fidgety at night. I tried to call you while I was in Da Nang but couldn't find the MARS station till too late, so it'll have to wait until July when I expect to go on R&R. You know they gave me a cheap "Star of David" at the Seder; it's the way out type in gold color so I'm holding on to it. If Marilyn or Marv wants it write me & I'll send it since I can't wear it right now (as long as I have the mezuzah).

I also tried to get a camera but was unable to since all they had, even in the 3 largest PX's (Army, Marine, & Navy) was the Swinger & I don't want that. I like color so I didn't buy anything. Hope I can do better when I go on R&R.

Mom, I'll be looking for my dancing niece when the next USO show comes over, I'll be able to recognize her by the animal crackers her "big grandma" bought her (Ha-Ha).

Dad you sure do have a lot of insight into the Vietnamese philosophy. I haven't heard any rumors about N.V.A. except that my unit didn't make much contact at Khe Sahn & that may be a sign, or a "diplomatic maneuver" to show sincerity on the part of the N. Viets. Of course there's still plenty of action all over the Nam. My unit moved out of Khe Sahn after they had it under control & another Cav unit has moved in. I don't know where my unit will be going next or if I'll be going (S-1 that is) with them. There's rumors that we're going down to the Saigon area but so far just rumors.

No Pop, I haven't decided who I'm going to vote for. I really don't know each man's ideas on ending this Vietnam thing & stopping other wars those guys who DEROS go to - that's the racial war at home. So far as personalities go I like Gene McCarthy. If Kennedy does choose his sister-in-law Jackie as his V.P. running mate as that article in the "News" suggest, then he may become #1 for me since Jackie Kennedy would definitely do good for our foreign relations & she's probably a good politician having been wife to John Kennedy. Her statement at the time of King's death was more meaningful than most (including R.F.K.'s).

Thanks also for those articles. The AFRS (Armed Forces Radio Station) did mention some rioting in NY & LI. Where was the LI rioting?

Dad, every one of your suggestions is welcomed. If I had listened to you a year ago instead of being bull-headed, I wouldn't be in the Nam writing you this letter now. I definitely respect & look into your suggestions, only sometimes my ego gets the better of me & I choose differently (like when I pushed up my draft).

Thanks for the subscription to Motor Trend. Dad, the salesman in Da Nang (at the PX) gave me very good prices for a 6 cyl Olds but he says I have too many accessories for a 6 & I should think about an 8 (about $100 difference in price). I'm still not sure of certain accessories like power windows (which are nice to have on a convertible) & console (feels comfortable with stick on the floor even an automatic stick). What do you think? So far my maximum with all accessories I'm thinking of looks like this: Basic (6 Cyl Olds Cutlass S Conv inc bucket seats & power top) $2399.46; Auto 170.79; PS 83.09; PB $36.46; AM Radio 60.93: console (floor shift & instruments in center) 50.78; Rally front suspension (stiffer shocks & stabilizer bar) $7.39; Reclining Seat (right side only) $27.70; Shoulder Belts 30.00; Remote Control Side -View mirror 8.31; Lamps (Trunk, Hood, Courtesy, Ash tray) $7.94; Power Windows 87.70; New car service $60.00; Processing $15.00; Freight to N.Y. $76.00; D&H or EOH (I don't know what this is probably dealer preparation charge) $161.00 -TOTAL -DELIVERED Price $3282.55

($3240 at Ziegler). Any suggestions Dad? Of course the Rambler is still a distinct possibility, without console & power window, which are only offered on 8 cyl models, their price (Rambler 500) is $2985 or with all equip on an 8 cyl $3267.00 (or $3309 with cruise control).

Marilyn, just to answer the question in your letter: No, my unit moved out of Khe Sahn but another Cav unit is taking it from the Marines. There's been no action there since my unit took over & gave it to 3rd Brigade.

Marilyn, be sure to let me know how your apartment hunting is going. Did you get the one in Flushing? Marilyn, does Steve know you're sending a picture of yourself in a bikini to the drooling guys in Vietnam (Ha Ha). I guess you combed your hair different or something since I didn't recognize you. You usually look better than that (that's suppose to be a compliment silly).

Marv let me know how you do on the job. Thanks for the info on the car & college. M&M auto is much more expensive than my place so I'm not considering him. As for the colleges I'm interested in entrance requirements as a TRANSFER student not a freshman. Were those averages you gave me for transfer students? Let me know when you get the info on the other colleges. O.K.?

Sorry I couldn't write separate letters to everyone but as you can see by the size of this letter, it's difficult. Xin Loi.

Hope you have a good Passover & to Mom - HAPPY BIRTHDAY TO MY FAVORITE, SWEETEST, Most Loved, Most Beautiful, SMARTEST MOTHER -YOU. (No wise cracks Marv!)

Love from Nam

173

Those last lines were my feeble attempt at humor about the size of this letter. It was prophetic, as here is the book.

I left in the price info about the cars for comparison to today's cars. Big difference. Isn't it?

DEROS was the date of expected returned from overseas service, or something similar.

Xin Loi translates to something like, "Sorry about that."

That dictionary appears later.

I went on the Passover religious retreat with Jeff, a friend from my unit. I knew Jeff since AIT (Advanced Infantry Training). He told me one of his friend's from home was the civilian manager of the PX, so we went to the PX together. That manager invited us to his civilian hotel. As I recall it was called something like, "The Newspaper Club". Many of the newspapermen & women as well as USO performers stayed there.

The hotel was a castle compared to our quarters, even at China Beach. There, we were introduced to several USO performers including one woman with whom I became friends. She was beautiful and I was somewhat nervous being in my Army clothes, sitting on a real sofa, and not having spoken to a beautiful American woman in quite some time. She made her stage name memorable for me when she told me to just remember the old TV show "Our Miss Brooks". Her stage name was Arlene Brooks. She was very sweet, down to earth, nice California girl from Santa Barbara whose real name was Sandy. I really liked her and had many erotic fantasies about her. After I left Da Nang, we stayed in contact via mail. Her name will come up again. Wish I knew where she is now.

A humorous incident I recall at the hotel was when I needed to use the bathroom. Once in the bathroom, I did not see a commode or urinal. Embarrassed, I went out and ask where the urinal or commode was. It seems there was a small hole in the middle of the floor of the bathroom and that is where you urinated. It should not have surprised me that much. On the base for a urinal, they stuck pipes in the ground. We lovingly referred to them as "piss tubes".

We were invited to spend the night at the hotel & we did. I got to sleep on that sofa, get a real breakfast and a hot shower in the morning before going back to the facilities at China Beach.

The lovely Sandy at hotel in DaNang:

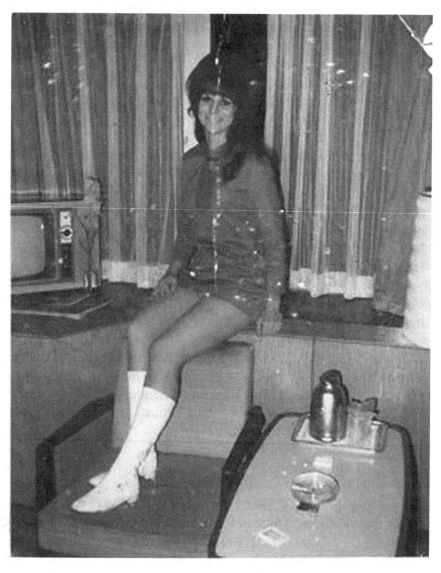

24 April 68
Time: 0235

Dear Dad, Mom, Marilyn, Marv –
 Haven't been getting much mail last few days.
I believe this is just due to a screwed-up APO system.
 I did get a card from the N.Y. Board of
Elections but it was addressed to Dad at my address.
When did you join HHC 2/12 Cav, 1ˢᵗ Cav Div (AM),
Dad? I hope it was just a typing error & they got my
name as the Voter and possibly you, Dad, as the
person making the request for me. They say they'll be
mailing me my balloting enrollment blank &
military ballot on or about 1 October.
 Other than that, nothing new. It's been
unusually quiet here the last few days. Too quiet, my
unit hasn't made contact on their sweeps.
 Not hearing any rumors about moving
anymore so I guess that blew over. I hear 1ˢᵗ Brigade
went south instead.
 What's new at home?
 How's things on the job Mom & Dad?
 Really can't think of much to write. Guess I'll
just close for now.

Love from Vietnam
Howard

P.S. - One suggestion as far as election goes - if
Senator Javits runs this year do your best to see that
dirty S.O.B. doesn't get into office. He's the S.O.B. that
didn't even bother answering either of the 2 letters I
sent him requesting his help way back when.

28 April 68
Time: 2230

Dear Dad, Mom, Marilyn, Marv -

Received yours of 21 April today. That's not bad but I know it's just an accident and not an indication of how the mail is going to be. I see your end is as bad as mine. The Army APO is a S-O-R-R-Y unit!!! Still no other packages. Oh well I still have 6 months in country.

Starting yesterday I'm back to day duty. - (So that's what the Sun looks like). I hope I'm being taken off awards completely but I can't tell for sure.

Unfortunately due to some bad ice cubes in this part of Vietnam, almost every soldier from the General to me & below has the G.I.s. I've spent more time in the latrine then in the S-1 shop. The Doc (who also has it - Ha Ha) gave me some pills, which seem to be working. They say if the gooks attacked us now, "all we have to do is turn around, cough, & S__T all over them." This is a pretty stinky situation (Ha Ha).

I look forward to sleeping in my new bed at home. I can't believe half my tour is over. Hope that the next six go as fast.

Do me a favor & next time you get the Sunday Times, send me the new car ads (They're in Section 5, the Sports Section). I want to compare prices with those I have.

As far as bonds go this is what I should have:
1 Bond - July August   1 Bond - Oct Nov Dec
1 Bond - Jan (started Bond a month)
1 Bond - Feb   1 Bond - March   1 Bond - April
1 Bond - May (This will be the last bond you should receive unless they don't cancel till June).

177

There's a slight chance that my allotment may end this month if finance got my request in time in which case the 6 bonds you have will be all I get. At any rate I'll let you know as soon as finance sends me a confirmation.

What's new at home? Have you been working any overtime Dad? I hope it's not necessary. You know I sure miss your home cooking Mom. You're still worlds greatest cook.

Got to get some sleep so I'll end here.

Love from Nam
As always
Howard

G.I.s = dysentery and contrary to what I wrote, not a laughing matter!

Chapter 11 – Changes

It is said that the only thing that doesn't change in the Army is change. You have seen that already and it continues.

I was starting to be more comfortable in my new MOS but still constantly worried about my friends in the field and my family at home. I even worried about my family worrying!

---

1 May 68
Time: 0920

Dear Dad, Mom, Marilyn, Marv –

First of all before anything else, let me clear up one point. I've spoken to the Sergeant Major (He knows everything) & he's informed me that all I need do is send a note to finance & they will send you the check just like I did with my life insurance. I want to wait for my voucher to figure out how much I can send. I want to keep a reserve of about $300 for my R&R, the $100 down payment on the car won't be till early September since I want to see what each car is offering. So since I will be getting my voucher this week & will be sending out the note to finance this week, I don't want to be upset by any more correspondence about this loan. The next time you should mention it is when you write that you've received the check. Don't bother writing me that you won't accept it because by the time you get this letter & could write me, finance will already have initiated the request. Also, by sending this money home I have it out of figuring for my car since I'll need it for my Profit Sharing & some clothes, which I will have to buy when I get home. I'll let you know in advance how much I'm sending - it should be between $4-500. THIS TOPIC IS NOW CLOSED BY ORDER OF THE NON-Commissioned OFFICER in

179

charge (me!). (Sorry for pulling rank but it was necessary)

To answer your question, I don't know if both of the Generals at the Seder were Jewish. I think they were but one may have been a guest since we were in his area.

I wish I knew what happened to the Jewish & Italian food you sent. They're probably lying in some APO warehouse somewhere in Vietnam. By the way packages to Vietnam can be insured. We receive insured packages every day.

I was amused by the stories of my niece & nephew in your letter Mom.

Tell grandma that I love her very much also. Also tell her that I don't think it's right that while her "boyfriend" is away fighting a war, I don't think it's right for her to be making eyes at another man (Dad). That should give her a little laugh. With those blintzes being kept warm for me I'm just about ready to go AWOL to get them.

There's been quite a bit of AWOL lately and the battalion is cracking down. They don't want to realize that the troops are beginning to suffer from battle fatigue. I can't believe that this is America's Army, it's so sorry in its treatment to the field troops.

I'm enclosing a short letter to Marv & one to Marilyn with this general letter,

Till my next.......

Love & stuff from Nam
Howard

That loan I talk about was my way to give my Dad some relief from the expense of my sister's wedding. I called it a loan to make it more palatable but, at the time, never intended to collect on it.

Once again my grandma and AWOL humor were not that funny but it said I was O.K. enough to joke.

---

1 May 68

Dear Marv (good old Brother type)-

Thanks for the car info & brochures. Did you find anything new about the colleges yet? Also see what you can find out about Human Factors Engineering as far as the duties & schools offering a degree in it. I think this is the field I've been interested in but I can't be sure till someone checks the duties.

Also if you can get a paperback copy of it get the book called (No wise cracks) "The Art of Erotic Seduction" by Dr. Albert Ellis & Roger O. Conway & published by Lyle Stuart. It's a spoof on seduction, which should be amusing for me over here. If you can get it send it without reading it first (Ha Ha) & let me know what it cost you.

So what's new? Haven't had a letter from you in a while! Hope you don't mind if I cut this short since I'm pressed for time.

Stay well & write soon.

Your Favorite Brother
Howard

This letter was marked personal and sealed. I don't remember which of my buddies had that book I requested but one of them did. Was I serious? It turns out it was not so much a spoof as Dr. Ellis's writing style. I learned a few things.

---

1 May 68
Time: 1100

Dear Marilyn,

Received your letter of 22 April last evening. Glad to hear you got an apartment. That's a good price for rent with G & E, & a good location.

Steve's parents sure are generous. That's because they really like you a lot. It's easy to see that. Don't tell Steve but I sometimes got the impression that they like you more than even him.

That wedding invitation is beautiful. I wish I could go but it would take a small miracle now.

I finally got a picture of you with the rest of the family from Vic. As for that picture of you in a bikini which you sent me.. WOW - I'm still trying to find my eyeballs, they popped out when I opened the picture.

Don't taunt me with any more news about Anna (Ha). Wish her luck for me. Her boyfriend will only have to attend 2 weeks summer training for the next 3 years. Same as me when I return & get out of the active duty Army.

I'll be looking for my diploma. Thanks again. That's all for now.

Love & stuffin from you know where
Howard

P.S. Frisky will be your brother in law too!! (Ha Ha)

Even before I was in the army, many of my friends wanted to meet my sisters. Both are beautiful. My humor about my younger sister's bikini pictures was my humorous way of telling here how great she looked.

Anna was one of her friend's whom I had danced with at my sister's sweet 16 party and had taken an immediate like to. She was an attractive blond with a great figure.

Frisky was my brother in laws dog.

Dear Dad, Mom, Marilyn, Marv -

Guess who's back on night duty. Yours truly & quite annoyed over it. Also they got another mail clerk so I'm not getting that job. I laid my cards on the table with the Captain & asked him to do the same. He said he forgot he offered it to me but that I could become the Company Clerk for the new company being formed, Echo Co. I told him I'd think about it but that I preferred to stay in S-1.

The mail situation seems worse then ever but you'll never guess what came today. The package of Italian food from you & Janet's package. Yum-yum.

This afternoon everyone got 5 CCs of gamma goblin as a preventative against hepatitis. With all the dysentery going around Dr Palmer though he'd play it safe & get everyone the shots. Because of the large quantity of serum, the shots were not given in the arm. Would you believe I'm standing up writing this letter? (Ha Ha). Well it's not quite that bad & it's better than risking hepatitis.

Hope to get some letter mail soon - it's getting ridiculous. Going to close now. Thanks again for the chop-chop.

Love from Nam
Howard

One of the things I learned from a few veteran soldiers was to befriend the cook, which I did. Whenever food arrived from home, he'd cook it up for me and we would share it. In our talks he told me he was gay but respected that I wasn't. He identified other gays on the base including a medic we both knew.

Dear Mom, Dad, Marilyn, Marv-

In today's mail I got a letter from home & your package of vitamins & a LI Press mailed 9 March. My 1ˢᵗ question is did you send me the newspaper by itself? The envelope was torn open at one end (from wear & abuse) & all that was in it was the newspaper. I didn't think you pay $1.05 just to send me a newspaper. I did receive my April car mags & 2 editions of the Daily News yesterday.

Thanks for checking out the cars for me Dad. Sorry you got stuck with that pressure seller at Rambler. Actually I sought of expected you'd like the Olds better. I liked it when I rented it from the rental agency around the corner from us.

Dad, I also worry about the fakers in the military car racket. I'm considering three places. If I can I'll check with the legal office before I buy. I'm sending you the literature from Zeigler & Sons for you to read, check with the Better Business Bureau if you want & then _return it to me_ in one of your next letters with your opinions. This will probably be the place I buy from if I don't hear any bad reports about them. I just hope the 69 prices aren't more than 2-3% higher.

Don't send 500- vitamins. I have enough to last me a while now. I only have 182 days left & not all of that is in country. I'll let you know when I need more.

Actually I should fill out City Tax form as long as they owe me money but it's not worth the effort so I'll let them get away with it this time.

Glad to get news of home in your letters. I too hope that the next 182 days pass like lightning.

Well I just don't know why I started this paragraph as I'm just going to end this letter.

Love from Nam
Howard

---

12 May 68

Dear Dad, Mom, Marilyn, Marv –

Well I'm on day time duty again. The biggest news here is that this battalion has been chosen for the Adjutant General's Inspector Generals Inspection. It's going to be held on 15 May Sooo – we've been breaking our backs to get into shape. The colonel said heads will roll if we don't pass it. Actually, S-1 is in pretty decent shape. Yesterday we put in 18 hours.

Today I got a new ID card since my old one is mutilated. The picture came out great. I'm enclosing a few extra copies of the picture for you & my old ID card for you to hold for me (Don't you dare show my old ID to anyone). The new picture makes it look like I haven't shaved in a week. Actually I do have a moustache but I'm clean-shaven on my chin.

I'll let you know how I make out on our inspection.

I also have a "Pay rule" which allows you to figure out what I'm making as an E-4 (It should total $255.90).

That's all that's new. I got my May car mags & was lucky to get them because again the envelope had worn open at the end.

Please use tape or something on my mags, I wouldn't want to lose my next few issues, as they'll have the new car previews.

Guess things are pretty hectic now with planning & financial arrangements for the wedding.

Guess what? I finally broke 6 months I now have 178 days left - maximum.

What's everybody been doing at home? Who's raiding the refrigerator now that I'm gone?

If you ever send me another package (I don't need one yet), there's a few things I'd like: a few cans of _Champale_, chopped herring if you can get it canned, EZ Pop type Pop corn, cheese spread (like Velveeta), synthetic sweetener like Sweeta. All the foods you sent in your first package were well chosen also. Remember to send small packages via SAM for quicker delivery. There's supposed to be a special rate for mail going from you through an APO to Vietnam.

Going to close now please write soon.

Love from Nam
Howard

I included the page below with this letter. Unfortunately the pictures deteriorated.

DESTROY AFTER READING!!

13 May 68
Time: 2200

Dear Marv –

Guess what I got today? Your letter dated <u>14 March</u> and N.Y. Times. I wouldn't say the mail is f—ked up, but it is, even if I didn't say it.

To answer your question – Yes, monsoon is over, no more mud just Hot, Hot & Dust!

Let me know how you're doing on the job. Dad tells me your thinking of buying a car. What do you want to get? If you can wait till after I get home I might be able to lend you a couple of hundred at 0% interest, you can't do better than that. Of course your best bet is a compact & since you're young & want something sporty I'd advise a Corvair. It's the only car that's been proven safe in court (thanks to Ralph Nadar). Since they put in a stabilizer bar it's pretty good & you should be able to get a 62-64 pretty cheap.

Try to hurry up about getting me that information about school & job. I'm getting short enough to start writing for admissions books soon so I need the info A.S.A.P. (As Soon As Possible).

As far as what I don't tell Dad – make sure you don't read this where someone might see it & get worried. We got mortared early this month & last week was the first time I witnessed incoming Recoilless rifle fire (That's a kind of artillery). Of course the targets are the chopper fields & artillery batteries but I still got in my bunker.

Yesterday was a winner, we got artillery fire almost all night, which is unusual & they were

188

landing in this area instead of the chopper field. I was surprised to see artillery fire coming in all night even after the gun ships were up. Well guess what, there's a half assed marine base near here & it was them firing on us. They made a mistake, they say, in figuring the coordinates for fire. As if that wasn't enough, two of our companies set up ambushes last night & ambushed each other! Several men were wounded in the ambush but fortunately there were only minor wounds here at LZ Jane from the marine artillery.

Got to get back to work now.

Love from your favorite soldier
Howard

My brother was no longer employed in NYC so I now had to send his letters to him at home, which was more risky. Of course my brother did not destroy that letter. This time, I'm glad he didn't listen. I did not tell him all the facts or the complete truth.

Now that the monsoons were over we had to deal with the insidious dust. It was everywhere and ruined several of my pictures. To deal with it on the roads the army put something called petaprime on the roads. It was an oil based compound that made the roads very slick. It was not uncommon to see vehicles slide off the road after it was put down.

Every so often we got a few incoming shells. Bad news was getting incoming all the time. Normally we just went to our bunkers when we had incoming rounds. The depression was hitting me hard. The day we had a lot of incoming rounds, I just stood outside watching them explode until ordered into my bunker by an officer. It later turned out that the fire had come not from Charlie, but from the US. Marines. There was an investigation after that incident. When the marine officers came to our base for that investigation, some guys in my unit painted our 1st Cav crest on their chopper.

17 May 68
Time: 1930

Dear Dad, Mom, Marilyn, Marv -

Hi! Remember me, I'm the guy who told you he'd write after the big AGI. Well we had it on the 15th & my office made it with an "Outstanding" rating & of course the whole unit did well.

In the midst of the inspection who walks in but Captain Kausch, a good friend & the battalion Chaplin & who does he have with him but a Rabbi (Jewish Chaplin) who he brought over to see me. It was one of the Chaplain's who was at the Passover retreat & he's holding a service at the 1st Cav Division Chapel tomorrow, which I'll be going to. No, I haven't suddenly turned religious but a few prayers don't hurt.

What's new at home? Mail is normal - all fouled up, it's SNAFU (Situation Normal All Fouled Up), actually it's not "fouled" but the other usage is not printable.

I just thought of something. Today finishes my 1st year in the Army since I was drafted on 18 May '67. Remember?

Going to keep this short since I expect some mail to be coming through in the next few days.

Marilyn, you're getting short you only have 49 & a wake up & a walk. (Ha Ha). Hope you don't get bothered by my teasing you Marilyn.

Till my next action packed letter

Love from Nam
Howard

P.S. - Rumor has it that we may be getting fresh fruit & ice cream regularly & possibly even fresh milk! Now if we could get back our beer rations we'd be set.

190

This is quite different from what I wrote my brother. Much was intentionally left out. I cleaned up SNAFU for my Mom's sake.

In teasing my sister about how long before she would be getting married, I used G.I. jargon. Of course "short" means short-timer. In the Nam if you had 24 days left, you said you had 24 & a wake up. The "world" is the US. As opposed to the "Nam" which, of course, is Vietnam. Lesson over!

---

20 May 68
Time: 1830

Dear Mom, Pop, Marilyn, Marv –

Got your letters of 5 May & 13 May. It's about time the APO decided to send me my mail.

Mom, your idea about "Grandma D's Products" sounds O.K. to me. Let me be among the first to buy 63 cases of blintzes. Now if we could only figure out how to get sour cream. I haven't seen any of that since I left the world. As a matter of fact when I get home I don't want a big roast turkey meal, instead I'd prefer either Italian food or dairy like blintzes & sour cream or Deli (Kosher type) but, I have 5 months before I worry about that.

Mom, I guess you never lost your touch with kids. You related the tale of stopping Doug from crying by talking to him. Well you used to put us kids to sleep when we were babies (remember way back when), so there's no reason you should have lost your touch.

Glad to hear Doris' dog is digging up her flowers, maybe she'll get rid of the mutt. Does he still bark a lot?

By the way do you (Dad & Mom) think I should write a letter to Doris? Maybe if I write she won't

191

raise the rent as much since I'm sure to overcome her with my charm!

Dad thanks for the insurance invoices. I wrote to Mr. Flynn to send me rates for car insurance to see

1) If his rates are cheaper
2) If Allstate will give me regular rates in Nov or do I have to wait till I'm actually 25 (on 5 March) as I do with Liberty.

As long as I'm talking abut cars, the Rambler literature has been thrown out. The car I expect to get is the Olds unless I find a $3-400 difference in price, which I doubt.

In answer to your question about fighting near my location. Yes, there is fighting near my location but not ground fighting. I already told you about the jet air strikes outside the perimeter about 3 miles. The ARA ships (that's Aerial Rocket Artillery - a huey chopper fitted with 48 rockets) are always pulling strikes but that doesn't mean there's anything there. They fire at all likely hiding places.

If you still haven't received my bond for April by now let me know & I'll put in a pay complaint. Also let me know when you receive my check & if the amount is correct ($400.00).

By the way although I outrank a Private First Class & am a E-4 pay grade like a corporal, I'm not a corporal. The only difference is that I (a SP/4) don't push troops. Specialist Four is a proficiency rating. Just for not knowing that drop & give me 6 ½ (Ha Ha).

The weather here is ridiculous, it's 102 in the shade & there's a foot of dust all over. Every time the Colonel's choppers flies over it kicks up a cloud of dust so thick you can't see 10 feet & it does come over

192

pretty often. I hope no one gets TB from all the *!@? (Censored) dust. I hear that it will even be getting hotter yet. Oh-boy I hope the next 5½ fly by.

Well that's it for now. Write soon & send chow (small packages).

Love from Nam
Howard

---

22 May 68
Time: 2000

Dear Marv -

How are you_ got your letter of 10 May yesterday. Today I finally got some mail from Janet & a few friends so I'm going to keep this short.

How's things on the job. What is the "Singer Company", not the sewing machine people?

I'm not a dirty old man, I'm a dirty young man but try to get me that book anyway. Actually, would you believe it -all I want if for is scientific reasons? - You wouldn't! Oh well.

Yes, Dad told me about the new bedroom set. If you get a chance to, send me a picture of them. I hope Dad didn't get us new mattresses since ours were new.

As far as rooms go, since I'm bigger than you and trained to kill (Grrrrrrrr) I'm sure I'll get my choice of rooms (Ha Ha).

Nothing happening here at LZ Jane, but Evan (the last place I was at - in March) was badly shelled on the 19th from the NVA. They used rockets, artillery, mortar, you name it. But, it was only a shelling attack no ground attack followed. That was probably in honor of Ho Chi's birthday, which was on the 19th.

193

Write soon Marv. Also tell me what you've decided to do about a car.

> *Your brother (see - no wise cracks)*
> *Howard*

My brother did go to work as a singer salesman. Yes, the Sewing machine company.

My "would you believe " line is dated and may be familiar to those of you who remember the "Get Smart" TV show.

Because I was no longer at LZ Evans, I felt comfortable also sending this info to the rest of my family, as you'll see in the next letter.

---

23 May 68
Time: 1830

Dear Dad, Mom, Marilyn, Marv -

Got your letter of 15 May today. Glad that you've gotten my check already. I just today got a letter from finance saying you should have received it.

Although I didn't get the mail clerk job I do want to make one point & that is that the mail clerk job is an S-1 job not a P.O. job. The only thing it has to do with the P.O. is picking up & dropping off mail.

I also feel I'd be better off staying in S-1 but if I'm told to go to another company I have to go, but so far I haven't been told too & I don't expect to be.

Make sure any packages you send are very well wrapped, plastic & twine are especially useful Remember it's almost 3,000 miles to Vietnam.

You may be right about me not getting all my mail but I doubt it. I think it's just slow & I'm over anxious to get mail.

194

You know I forgot to mention it but you could have called the Better Business Bureau instead of writing to them though I don't know if the place I want to check on is within the area covered by our local BBB.

In my letter of 8 May I guess I had 182 days left. Well now I have 167. Not bad. I'm getting there. Don't worry about me, all these prayers you people at home are saying must be working.

I guess you heard that LZ Evans, my last base, was hit pretty hard by rockets & mortars on the 19th, probably in honor of Ho Chi's birthday. There weren't too many casualties but there was a hell of a lot of property (like choppers) destroyed. So far we've been lucky that LZ Jane hasn't been hit. The jets are making strikes a few miles outside the perimeter here just about every day & the other 3 sides of the perimeter are all flatlands. I guess that's why we haven't had any incoming. Also, all we have here is about a dozen choppers & our artillery batteries as potential targets. I guess Charles doesn't like to mess with the 2/12.

Nothing new in the office still doing much typing as Battalion clerk. It's very hot here I think it's been 102 or higher in the afternoons Phew-Pant-Pant.

That's all for now - write soon.

Love from Nam
Howard

27 May 1968
Time: 1815

Dear Mom, Dad, Marilyn, Marv -

Got 3 letters dating from 20-22 May. It's good to know you're writing so often.

Will be happy to get your package of goodies. I received Swiss Night Cheese in one of my friend's packages & it was still good. I think it remains good as long as it's sealed. Don't worry though, I will check it out before I eat it or should I say, "we" since we all share our packages here in S-1, even the Captain. I'll be looking for my mail in the package when I get it.

Dad, your friend in the post Office is right, the bad handling of the mail is at this end but unfortunately there's not much we can do about it. I'm glad to hear that he gave you a tip on wrapping the mags since the new car previews will be starting in the June issues.

We did very well in the I.G. and only had to snap to attention for a second when the Colonel walked in. He gave us an immediate, "As you were" so he could watch us at work.

The army doesn't take very good pictures. I'll try to make up for it though with the Instamatic Marilyn sent me, all I need is film which may take a while to get. As soon as I get some I'll send you some pictures of me & my base. You'll have to get used to the moustache for a few months. I'll probably keep it till I go on R&R in July.

You're right Dad, the Army didn't allow moustaches for us. Recently (like 2 months ago) that rule was changed. Mainly because the guys over here like to grow them it's sort of a sign that you're in the Nam.

196

You say that I'm like a prisoner counting days. You don't know how right you are!!! I have 163 today.

A term off for Marv won't hurt him much. As a matter of fact it will give him enough time to see for himself that very few people make it without college. He's smart enough to know he'd make a mistake (I agree he has). It's too bad that neither myself (as far as the Army) or now Marv has taken advantage of your experience & wisdom Dad. I guess that he feels as I did when I pushed up my draft, that things can't be as bad as you said. I just hope Marv comes to himself & realizes his mistake soon. Of course it is possible that he's the 1 in 10 who can make it without college but the odds are against him.

About how many people are you going to have at Marilyn's wedding? I hope you've got most of the replies by now.

You asked if I changed the location of my HQ, No, I'm still at LZ Jane, just outside of Quang Tri.

Now, I have questions for you. Do you save my letters? Do you have all my letters since November? If you do I may use them to write a book when I get home. If not, don't sweat it, it's just a whim which I'll probably get over before I get home.

Don't worry I think I'm on day duty for good now.

Thanks Mom, for checking out my ballot & making sure its O.K.

That sure was funny about Grandma & Aunt Molly. Your mother has a wonderful sense of humor Mom. That's one of her strongest attributes (besides her cooking etc). How do you (all of you) like Molly's new car? It sure sounds nice.

Annette seems real anxious not to be left out of the dress showings. She's a real little Miss America.

Douglas sounds like hard-core, the way he smiles when he punches & pulls your hair. We need his type over here. Ha Ha.

You talk about weather. Well the temp here has been measured at 120° & 113° in the shade & believe me that's hot!!!

They have something new here, scrambles for the gun ships. They use the siren to sound the scramble & every time they do, I have to check it out to make sure it's a scramble & not an alert. They're getting better. They can be airborne & really do bring smoke in less than 4 min.

When you send the next package, send me a small box of soap powder & Borax. I mean the real small ones like you get in the Laundromat. Since I'll only use it once. I can always let you know if I need it again.

Nothing much new here. The workload has decreased at least for a little while so I'm biding my time.

I'll close with a joke the Chaplain told me (The Battalion Chaplin- a protestant Chaplin not the Rabbi type).

A man was at the beach when he saw a bottle in the water. He retrieved the bottle & in it was a note saying, "The finder of this bottle will be granted 3 wishes." Of course he didn't believe this but figured he had nothing to lose so he wished for a brand new pink Cadillac convertible. There was a flash of light & there on the beach was a pink Caddy convertible. The man wished for the car to be full of $1,000 bills. There was a flash of light & the Caddy was filled with $1,000 Bills. The man thought of his *third wish - should he wish for a woman or a new house - no, he could buy all that with the money he has wished for so he decided to save his third wish. He got into his car & started driving.*

The man was so happy that he put on the car radio & began singing with it----"Oh, I wish I were an Oscar Meyer Weiner"

With that I'll close.

Love From Nam
Howard

In one of his letters, my father had advised that my brother had decided to take time off from college to find himself and try out the job at Singer. He knew I had some influence with my brother and wanted me to use that influence to get him to go back to school. Being very bright, social, and a good talker he quickly became the top salesman in his area, much to the chagrin of more seasoned (read that mature) salesmen. He thought that might be a career path for him. I knew that once he saw what real life was about he'd go back to college. However, this issue was not resolved for my father and would appear again.

My reply which I knew would be seen not only by my father, but my brother as well, shows my confidence that my brother would make the right decision as well as my brotherly advice. There was no need to worry; he went on to college and even a graduate degree.

My comment about the gunships getting airborne & bringing "smoke" in 4 minutes meant that these ships had multiple "miniguns" capable of putting out so many rounds per second that when they fired they sounded more like a lawn mowers than machine guns. They smoked Charlie's ass. In the Nam we just cut that to brought smoke.

In this letter I first indicated a "whim" about writing this book. Fortunately my parents & my brother had kept most of the letters I had written. But something slowed me down, life. It was not until my daughter had grown up and I retired that I was able to sit down to write these memoirs.

31 May 68

Dear Dad, Mom, Marilyn, Marv -

Hi, what's the latest scoop on the home front?

Not much new here, as usual, though it did rain long enough to cool it off a little bit at least for a few days.

The Sergeant told me that I'm going to be recommended for SP/5 next month. I hope I make it I could use the money. I'll let you know more when I know more. For now, don't say anything till I'm sure of the rank (In money it's $46+ more a month).

Hey Marv, write soon about your job.

Dad, in my closet, in the Important Papers file, is a letter from the Bank, which I got right after I paid off my loan. You know the type - Thanks for doing business with us. Look us up if you need further assistance (= more money). Please give this letter to Marilyn as I've asked her to send me a photocopy of it to use in writing for info on my new car loan.

That's it for this letter. Write soon & often (as usual).

Love from that place
Howard

Marine Chopper Inbound

Painted with First Cav insignia!

Dust at liftoff (In bacground)

Picture of author ruined by dust

Off road, literally: Truck slid off petaprimed road

Napalm Bombing raid at perimeter:

The LZ and perimeter

Mortar or rocket damage

205

More action on the LZ

Hueys in attack formation

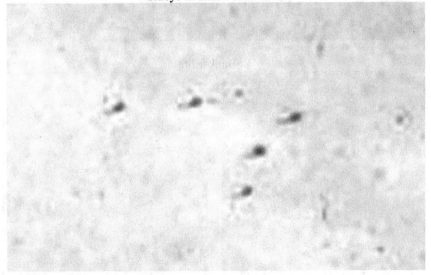

Our House a/k/a Bunker

Bunker life

Inside Bunker

Supplies – Mostly from home

Chapter 12 – SP/5 and beyond

June 1968 was the month I made SP/5. The changes continue beginning with my new jeep. I was also looking forward to moving beyond the borders of the LZ and out of Vietnam for my R&R (Rest and Relaxation) vacation. My first letter of 8 June below (which I accidentally dated 8 May) tells of one of those changes. Unfortunately that Polaroid picture I refer to has long since faded.

Another problem on the base was the living conditions. Flies were a constant annoyance and health issue. There were so many you could often catch more than one in midair by moving your hand quickly through the air. Their presence sometimes made eating disgusting. The flies were stupid enough to eat army chow. We had to constantly shooo or kill them. Since we could capture and kill more than one at a time we made it into a game or competition. We had to invent sick things like that for fun. My record was 7 flies in one quick sweep and slap of the hand on the table or wall. We thought of and laughed at my tale of seven at one blow. Humor is a healthy way to deal with an unhealthy situation.

---

8 May 68

Dear Mom, Dad, Marilyn & Marv

The reason I haven't written this week is that I'm in Da Nang to pick up my new jeep. Didn't have but 1 day's notice. That's why I didn't let you know.

Hope to call you via MARS later this evening. At any rate I won't write again for at least 3 days when I get back to the unit.

Tell Janet that I haven't written her for the same reason.

I will write when I return but this letter will remain short.

Sending you a Polaroid of myself. How do you like your bronzed, blond haired son?

Love from Nam
Howard

The bronzing & my blond hair were due to long days in the sun and the fact that most days we only wore cut off fatigue pants, socks, boots, and nothing else. Yes, that's right not even underwear. Titillating isn't it? Wearing underwear would increase one's chance of getting "jungle rot".

I did get to call my parents using the MARS system. It was great talking to them and seeing South Vietnam's biggest city. There were lots of scooters, rickshaws, and hookers all across the Da Nang area.

---

11 Jun 68

Dear Mom, Pop, Marilyn, Marv -
   Gee, it sure was good speaking to you via MARS. I'm glad Dad was home this time. The voices were clearer that the last time I called, only this time my connection was not so good & there were several things I was not sure of. Did you "Roger" my transmission about getting Marv to hurry up with the college info? Since I intend to use it in my stateside assignment in New York or near the college I chose I need info so I can choose a college & make application by August at the latest.
   I was down in Da Nang to get S-1's new jeep - it's really brand -new!
   It's a ride of 90 miles & takes 2 days via convoy. All the towns & villages are off-limits but I got to see them & take some pictures from the Jeep. I'm sending the film home separately. There's 2 rolls so far one is Kodacolor (12 Exp) & the other is Kodachrome (20 exposures). The Kodachrome makes slides & that's the type of film I'll be sending home for a while. Will try to get pictures of my working & living quarters & of "Howie's Raiders", my mob at S-1.

I got both packages. They arrived while I was at Da Nang. Yum yum -looks good. Yes, the cheese is O.K. Haven't tried the Velveeta yet. I put it in the cooler but it should be O.K. also.

I got Beau Coup mail in the 8 days I was gone so I'll have to keep this letter as short as possible. Will just write answers to your letters.

Mom, I sure enjoy reading of your experiences with Annette & Doug. I just can't wait till that freedom bird takes me for that long ride home. By the way don't think I cracked when you see that I took several pictures of freedom birds at Da Nang (Pan Am type).

I wrote you my location in my last letter didn't I? If not ask again & I'll tell you where on the map to put the "X"

I know there's more I wanted to write but I can't think of it now so I'll just end here.

Love from Nam
Howard

P.S- I may be a SP5 soon if we get enough allocations.
P.P.S.- R&R allocations for July haven't come in yet. They're late. I don't know what's going to happen with them. Will write further on this next time.

---

15 Jun 68

Dear Dad, Mom, Marilyn & Marv-

I've been informed that it's definite now that I'll make SP5 this month. All I have to do is await orders to be cut. That means I've got the same rank as a Sergeant E-5. More important it means another $40 a month. If you still have that "Pay Rule" I sent you, you can figure out my insignia (Specialist 5) & my pay.

I also got orders awarding me a CIB (Combat Infantryman's Badge) for my time in the field. Since they screwed up on giving me this originally they had to write my old MOS on the orders. I'm sending home a copy of the order for you to hold for me.

Have you received the film I sent yet? I'll be sending home roles of film from time to time.

Still no word on R&R for July though as long as I have a week advance I can get the necessary orders.

Mail has been slow this week again!

I had a million things I had wanted to write you but I can't think of any other than what I've written. I'll probably remember after I drop this letter in the box.

The chow here is steadily getting worse and it's a fight to eat your food before the flies get it. This country has more flies than sand and it's dammed annoying.

Marilyn & Steve are getting ready to walk "the longest walk" (I thought that's what they call the walk to the electric chair). Ha Ha-That was intended to be a pun, I hope it was punny. (Ha)

Marv – W-R-I-T-E.

Love from Name
Howard

HHC 2nd Bn 12th Cav
KALACHMAN, HOWARD US52...........SP4 E4 11C10

---

17 Jun 68
Time" 1630

Dear Mom, Dad, Marilyn, Marv -
   Finally the R&R allocations came in. I'll be
going to Sydney on 1 July (I leave here on the 27th
for processing) & return 9 July.
   As far as the two checks you asked about, I
could use the $65 but I doubt if you could get it here
by 27 June. Send it by Post Office money order
anyway. If I don't get it in time, I'll just deposit it in
my accrual. It might get here faster by registered
mail (Special Delivery isn't faster to Vietnam. As a
matter of fact it's slower). At any rate if you get this
letter after 22 June don't bother paying extra
postage I won't get it in time but send it regular
mail as I can use if for my car.
   I'll be calling you again when I get to
Australia. I'd like to call at the hall but I don't know
the number. I'll probably call Janet also. Mom, I also
got tongue tied on the phone so don't worry. I use a
radio very often & still I got confused. At least when I

214

call from Australia it will be a regular phone call, not a radio patch.

If you don't get a chance to mail my money before 22 June only send $50.00 since I'll charge the phone call to you but I insist that I pay for this one myself. It will probably cost $13-14 for the 1st few minutes.

No, Helen & Irv didn't write me about Harvey's 3rd child. I guess the dental business is profitable.

I mentioned that I got my SP5. All I have to do is await orders. The Capt. signed the papers yesterday, not without teasing me first. He said, "Oh no, not Kalachman making Sp5" & threw the request for orders in the garbage pail. Then, when he thought he had me thoroughly confused, he retrieved & signed them.

Dad, to get back to Marv, don't worry too much. He's an excellent salesman & this looks like a good opportunity. If he's wrong he can always get accepted by college if he wants to return. Also he will be getting experience, which I can tell you is more important than getting education. Believe it or not, most personnel men will choose a more experienced man over a more educated one. Thus Marv will not be dependant on this firm.

As far as fighting goes here, at night or during the day there's been no action here at all (near the perimeter) for several months. The Ashau Valley thing took a lot out of the gooks. It's usually quiet here anyway. We've never been attacked though we were once surrounded by gooks according to intelligence reports (that was back in April). It's not quiet here though. The Cav has a policy of firing "harassment & indignation" during the hours of darkness. In other words, they fire all night placing

215

the rounds outside & near the perimeter. Also, we have 8 inchers (range approx 38 miles), which are called on to fire for troops way out in the boonies.

Yes, I heard abut Kennedy but can make no further comment.

Remember you won't be getting any mail for two weeks beginning 27 June (my mailing date). I will write before then several times for sure.

Love from Nam
Howard

P.S. HAPPY BELATED FATHERS DAY TO MY FAVORITE DAD!

G.I.s in Nam always referred to the cong as gooks. By definition it means invaders in a foreign land, so in fact we were the gooks! Be that as it may, that was our lingo.

The hall I refer to is the wedding hall where my sister was to be married.

Radio use was a part of my jobs both in the field, where I was the radio operator for a time & back in S-1 where it was one of my ongoing responsibilities. The radio in the field was the PRC25, lovingly referred to as the Prick 25.

"8 inchers" were 8-inch guns that were big and loud! On one of my bases I slept right under them. Every time they fired my air mattress was lifted off the ground. First night did not get much sleep. By the second night I was so tired I slept thru it.

Left out the part where a few of the guys brought a prostitute on base. I never had been with a prostitute and did not want to start now. Tried to refuse but the others guys would not accept my refusal. The room we used was an empty Conex container with an air mattress for a bed. After, I spent an hour in the shower rubbing my privates till they were raw. The Army had told us that all the Vietnamese prostitutes spread V.D. and I believed it.

The Kennedy assassination was not something I could deal with. I had heard about it. Was too angry and upset about it to comment. Was a little more demonstrative when I wrote my brother.

18 June 1968
Time: 2150

Dear Marv -

Congratulations on the new job. Hope it turns out to be all you expect from it.

Got your letter today with your comments about the training course. That hotel looks nice, especially the cocktail lounge. I imagine you got a few chances to get down there though the drinking age is 21 in Jersey. Xin Loi (Sorry about that). If you want to drink a cocktail to be sociable with a business associate or client, I'd suggest a Manhattan, it's very strong & without bragging, I can hold quite a bit of alcohol (or at least could back in the world). I would begin to feel my 3rd Manhattan. It's straight alcohol, a mixture of rye & vermouth with a cherry (love that cherry). One word of advice, though I'm pretty sure with you it's unnecessary; even one drink doesn't mix with driving.

Marv, what's happening with that college info for me? I need it as soon as possible to make application to a college for Feb so I can get an assignment in the states near the college I want to go to. Also find as much as you can about Human Factors Engineering.

I hope you can do this without too much trouble. I realize now that you're a big business man it may be difficult since you'll be pretty busy.

Marv, I wouldn't suggest the 65 Impala Conv. I heard it leaks badly. Although I'm a Chevy man myself, I'd suggest an Olds Cutlass. It's slightly *smaller though not a compact and handles very well.*

Marv when I get home for leave I have big plans for <u>us.</u> You're old enough to fit into my crowd now & you're a good friend as well as a brother. I want you to go all over with me.

Maybe you'll even get to drive my new car (just maybe!). Marv, depending on where I get stationed I'd like to take a trip to Florida when I get home if I get stationed on the east coast. Do you think you could take a week off late in Nov for that?

Marv, you're a good brother & I think we should definitely do more things together.

As for the assassination of Kennedy: Fuck the bastard who shot him. I'd like to have one minute alone with him without a weapon. I'd change his face so much his own mother wouldn't recognize him.

The U.S. is really going to pot with assassinations & riots.

To get off that subject, I'm going on R&R in two weeks. Like Wow!

Who are you taking to Marilyn's wedding? I'm too cheap to write another page so I'll end here.

> *Love from Nam*
> *Howard*

Even from the Nam that was good brotherly advice on drinking.

All that college info that I kept nagging my brother and family about as well as the stateside station stuff would soon become moot.

23 Jun 68
Time: 1930 ?

Dear Mom, Pop, Marilyn, Marv –
Well things are moving along OK here. Not much happening (so who's complaining?). A few days & I'll be leaving here for An Khe to prepare for my R&R 1-8 July.

I should have about $300 to spend, but about $100 of that will probably go for a camera. I should be down to $150 or so after hotel costs which should be enough, I hope. If I get the $65 I requested, before Thursday, I'll have that much more.

As you know I'm now an SP5. But just to keep in tradition, I'm sending home an SP5 insignia just as I did when I made 4.

I've got some papers & stuff I want to send home but I think I'll wait till after R&R. Also I want to return to Marilyn, the Silver Dollar she sent me for luck just when I got out of the field.

Haven't had much mail lately though its been coming through to the other guys. I don't miss it as much as I did earlier but I still miss it. Hope it will be back to normal after the wedding.

Anybody got a case of nerves yet? Mom? Dad? Marilyn? Or maybe Steve? I can remember the night before Janet's wedding everybody seemed to be getting it.

Again I wish I could be there but unfortunately due to circumstances beyond my control....

Marilyn & Steve, be sure to let me know your address as soon as you get back from your honeymoon, even if it's only a temporary address & remember to W-R-I-T-E.

Have you been getting my films? How are the pictures & slides coming out?

Am out of material for now. Things are a little bit easier since we changed Col on 12 Jun & the XO has an appendix attack (poor man. I really feel sorry for him, almost as sorry as I feel when I see a sick dog). He was sent to Japan & out of our hair. So for a while at least I'm somewhat relaxed.

What's the latest on the home front?

This may be my last letter till I come back from R&R but you can write me still, the mail clerk will hold my mail for me.

Love from Nam
Howard
SP5 TYPE

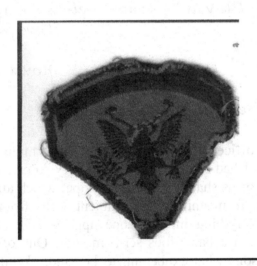

24 June 68

Dear Mom, Pop, Marilyn, Marv –

Got your insured package & letter of 18 Jun 68. It came just in time for me to get it before I leave LZ Jane. I'll be going in on the 26th. Thanks for sending that checkbook. I hope I can cash a check in

Australia. I may buy a camera at Cam Rahn Bay. Thanks for getting it to me in time.

Did you say that I lost weight? I think I gained, at least that's what everyone says.

I'm really looking forward to the day I get to ride a freedom bird.

This will probably be my last letter till I get back from Sydney. I will try to call the hall between 12-1 AM your time if I can find the phone #.

I didn't know NY state income tax was increased. I don't get much local news here. Just national & international. Do you know which of the state candidates we vote for this year if any? I definitely won't vote for a man who feather's his own bed at our loss.

Well, till you hear my lovely voice again.

Love from Nam

Howard

P.S. - Another roll of film is enclosed.

That officer I wrote about on the 23rd might have been the crazy S.O.B. I had some words with. Every so often I pulled guard duty. A few of us shared a Starlight scope, which allowed us to see in the dark. It magnified the ambient light from the moon or whatever. Everything in the scope appeared an eerie green like something from a bad fifties sci-fi movie. One of the officers in charge was somewhat exuberant, to be kind. While on late night guard duty, flares were fired throughout the night. The flares deployed from an artillery shell and floated down slowly on a small parachute so we could get a clear view of the perimeter, while the empty shell fell to earth. As occasionally happened, one of the empty shells fell on a trip wire setting off one of the claymore mines which were also part of our perimeter defense system. We all clearly saw this with our naked eyes due to the light from the flare, but that officer yelled, "incoming", initiating a false alert, and ordered us to fire, which we did. I had my 45 at the time and was content to fire off a few rounds. That officer's eccentricity was known through the camp. When I tried to explain to him what had really happened he cut into me hard and deep. It was just the wrong time. He knew he was wrong and I had had enough of his Bull Shit. Somehow a "FUCK YOU" slipped out of my mouth,. When he asked, "What did you say?" I knew I had to show him proper respect, so I said, "Excuse me, Fuck you sir!" He could have written me up but probably figured I'd say something about his false alert, and there were witnesses. He thus thought better of it and forgot about the incident as I hoped he would.

My weight had definitely redistributed several times, more muscle and less fat. Wish I could do that now without the Army!

In case I failed to mention it, any aircraft that took you home from Nam to the World was a "freedom bird". I know I'd be seeing them in Cam Rahn Bay so they were on my mind.

An incident occurred on the chopper field when I was on my way to Cam Rahn Bay that I never wrote home about. I was anxious to get started on my R&R. a chopper came to transport us from LZ Jane but it was almost full. I tried to pull rank on a PFC who was also waiting for the chopper so I could get on it but a sergeant who outranked me, saw & prevented this. That copper was shot down and all aboard were killed. I saw this as proof again that someone up there was protecting me.

Actually I was shot down three times during my tour in the nam, twice in a helicopter and once in a C-130. Both times in the Chinook helicopters which were used for transport, we auto rotated to the ground. The first time I heard clinks that sounded like the fan blade of a car hitting the radiator, I was told we had been shot down. We landed hard but safe. The next time I heard that particular sound I didn't have to ask what had happened!

The C-130 was another story all together. Same sound but only one of the four engines was disabled by ground fire on take off. We were told we'd have to go to the Air force base for repairs. We lost the 2nd engine on the same side a few minutes later and a 3rd soon thereafter. The pilots were so accomplished they landed the aircraft with one engine. Had we not heard the clinks, or been told what had happened we might never had known. Turned out to be a good thing as we got hot showers, hot meals, milk, ice cream etc while we waited for repairs to be completed or another airplane.

Convoy stop

One of the major roads

Children were always there to sell us something when we stopped

Change of Command Ceremony:

Return to base with prisoners:

Watching bombing

Love those Kids

Also Love those Freedom Birds:

Vietnamese Tomb of the Unknown Soldier:

Author with Sp5 insignia on collar:

Chapter 13 – Return to Nam

My time in Australia was phenomenal. While I was in Nam, micro-miniskirts came into vogue in the world. They made mini skirts look long. I had not seen those before and they made quite an impression.

When I got to Sydney I was thrilled and amazed at the friendliness of the people. No doubt that was due to the fact that Australians were fighting along side us in Vietnam.

I had a great hotel room overlooking the bay bridge. The first thing I did was take a four-hour bath-nap in very hot water!

Although the language was English, there were a few differences. I learned my first lesson when I went to a restaurant with one of the guys I'd met at Cam Rahn Bay. I ordered a burger & fries. When I asked the waitress for Catsup, she smiled at the stupid American and said, "You must mean tomato sauce." When I asked for a napkin she became hysterical. It seems a napkin is what you use for babies, and what we call a diaper! What we call a napkin, they call a serve-it. To me with their Aussie accent, it sounded like "cervix", which was funny to this American.

We went for coffee. When that waitress asked if I wanted black or white coffee, I decided that black or white had to mean with or without milk. So I ordered white and got a latte. That was a nice learning experience. I've been drinking latte's & cappuccinos every since.

At the disco we all met girls. I spent some time with mine and then asked if she'd like to go for dinner. To my amazement she said, "You can knock me up at 8:00". My first thought was "Thank you God! Boy these women are fast!" Unfortunately for me, all it meant was I could come pick her up at 8, oh well.

That evening when I returned to my hotel in the wee hours, a young woman approached me and asked, "Do you wanna go?" Being somewhat naive, I asked, "Go where?"

"To bed" she promptly replied. Embarrassed by my naivety and to save face I replied, "Yes, but only to sleep" and quickly walked into my hotel lobby.

Australia was a blast and I did get to call the hall where my sister was getting married. I bought a bottle of fine champagne before calling the hall. My family came to the phone. I asked them to each get a glass of champagne and then toasted my sister & brother–in–law over the phone. I spoke to all for several minutes. While I was in Australia I also called my older Sister & spoke to her family. An amusing story I was told when I got home was that after I spoke to my 5-year-old niece, she wanted to know when I was coming out of the phone. What a great feeling it was to speak to my family! From this point on you will note my younger sister's name missing from the salutation of my letters home. I wrote her and my brother-in-law separately.

The last night we were in Sydney, we were invited to Sydney's most exclusive private nightclub. The other G.I.s I went with were even less sophisticated that I was. The waiter brought over a bottle of fine wine. He popped the cork and drew a small amount in a glass. Every one just looked, but I knew what to do. I motioned him to bring me the glass, which I quickly sniffed and tasted. It looked good but, at that time, I had no idea what I was sniffing or tasting for. It was just something I'd seen on television or in the movies. However, the others were impressed.

After that meal we went back to the girls apartment and I never left. That night I was in bed with two attractive women. Don't know if I was more excited or scared. If you think I would not write home about that, you'd be right.

But all good things must come to an end. Before I knew it, the week was up and it was back to the Nam.

Upon return to the Nam, I heard of an interesting new Army policy called "Early Out". If you had less than 5 months left on your duty tour when you returned home from Vietnam, you got discharged out of the army at that time with no active reserve requirement.

Cam Rahn Bay on way to Australia

Buddies going to Australia

First View of Australia

The hotel

My first view of new micro-miniskirt

Whiskey A Go Go Disco

Girl met at Whiskey with author

Harbour Bridge from Hotel window

Buddies at Park

Famous Queen Victoria Park

Back in hell at LZ – Prisoner being escorted away from camera (center)

11 July 68

Dear Dad, Mom, Marv –
    Got back to my unit today & as before it's
depressing. I had a great time in Sydney, plenty of
good food & drink & plenty of beautiful women. I am
going to try to get a 7-day leave there if I can. I'm
entitled to a 7-day leave but the colonel has been
disapproving all of them so far. We change colonels
again next month.
    I've been checking with that 5-month drop &
its pretty good. I only have to extend 43 days till 18
Dec & I can come home for good & say good-bye to
Army Green. I'm waiting for the official regulations
to come down from Washington. The newspaper had

the story pretty fast. I'll write you again when I make a final decision.

I'm glad you & Mom are taking a vacation this year. Hope you enjoy yourselves kiddies. Will be waiting to her from you.

Now that the wedding is over you can relax a little. Well 2 down & 2 to go!

Let me know how all of my films came out.

Dad, I agree with you that I should return my checkbook to you for safekeeping. I'm going to send you several items besides the checkbook. A box of slides I developed in Sydney, my driving certificate for the U.S. Army, the brochure from the hotel I stayed at in Sydney... There is also some film (2 rolls) I took in Sydney but I'm not sure I'm sending those home for developing since I have a small viewer here & want to see how these came out right away. If I do send them please send them back as soon as they are developed.

Mom, you can tell Annette I'll be looking for her letter.

Give my love to Steve & Marilyn. Tell them to write as soon as they have an address where I can write them. Till that time I'll write them care of you

I'm really busy & lots of writing to do so I'll close for now.

Love from Nam
Howard

No Dad I didn't Forget   Happy Birthday

There's a check for $15.00 to pay for developing my film (not more than $5.00) & the rest is your birthday gift Dad. Use it in good health & buy yourself something.

That was a very important letter, the one in which I first tell my parents that I might extend my tour for 43 days to get that early out.

----

14 July 1968
Time: 2230

Dear Mom, Pop, Marv -
Had to write with today being my favorite dad's birthday. What are you 21 or 22, dad?
Still haven't found out much about the new program for early out. It will probably come down as a change on the old reg allowing early out with 3 months remaining. I won't put in my 43 or 44 day extension until I know the whole scoop. If you got the newspaper article handy send it to me.
Have also been trying to find out about getting a 7 day leave. Supposedly each man is entitled to an in country & an out of country R&R and if he wants it a 7 day leave. Lately my unit has been having requests for leave turned down by the colonel. I don't know if he's authorized to do that. I may have to check it out with the I.G. next time I'm at base camp. I definitely have to go back to Sydney. The people & place made a very favorable impression on me. They definitely feel for the G.I. & treat him right.
As for your worrying about my job here, don't. It took 3 men to do my job (& at times 4) while I was away so I have no problems there.
Got your letter of 8 July which was postmarked Flushing, NY. I thought you were going on a vacation. What happened? As ranking member of this family I order you to take a vacation & I further order you to enjoy yourselves. So there.

I was wondering if anyone was asking about me at the wedding & what they were asking? Did Sol & Florette know I am in Nam?

Mom, your description of the wedding is almost enough to make even me cry (sniffle). I could tell Marilyn & Steve were nervous when I spoke to them. Steve sounded so bad I asked him if he was drunk. Hope lots of pictures were taken so I can see what it was like.

Have any more of my pictures come back? I hope most of them came out.

It was great speaking to you on a regular phone without the "Over" bit & without security regulations. Hope I didn't run you up too much of a bill. My bill for two phone calls (to Janet & Vic and to Steve & Marilyn -person to person at the hall) was a little over $20 but it was worth double that.

By the way Marv, there's a few things I want from you kiddo. Next time you're in the village in NYC, see if you can get me a copy of the NY Free Press. It's a hippy paper but I want to see it out of curiosity. Also check, if you haven't already (you can call on the phone) & see if the two organizations I mention below can give you any info on schools offering an undergraduate degree in Human Factors Engineering (also called biomechanics, psycho-technology & several other names). Also ask if they have any suggestions as to curriculum (courses to take). "They" are:

1) SOCIETY OF MECHANICIAL ENGINEERS; 345 E 47th St; NYC 10017

2) SOCIETY OF AUTO. ENGINEERS: 485 Lexington Ave.; NYC 10001

One more thing Marv. About a week or two after I get home I want you to take a 2 week

*vacation if you can so we can go traveling together.
I won't know the exact date I'll be home till I find
out about extending. But think about it in the
meantime, O.K.?*

*By the way Dad, did you get my insured
package yet? & Marv did you get the package I sent
you? Well will close for now.*

*Love from Nam.
Howard*

What I didn't say before about Sydney was that the first
woman I met there came back to my hotel and then asked me for
money for sex. I didn't like being duped like that and asked her to
leave.

One of the next girl's I met, I liked and that may be at the
root of my wanting to go back there for leave. That return trip never
happened.

What I wrote about needing 3 or 4 guys to replace me was
true and came directly from the sergeant in charge. I guess it paid to
be a type "A" organized person in that disorganized environment.

Yes, we are back with repetitions. Did my film get
developed, etc. I wonder how annoying this might have been for my
parents or my poor brother. It was not a one-way street; my family
often repeated themselves in their letters to me.

Being a parent myself now I can understand that no price
would have been too much for my father to spend to speak to child
he hadn't spoken to in a while, especially one who was in, and going
back to, a war zone.

Didn't write home about another incident at the LZ. We were
awakened by what sounded like AK-47 fire. Were there VC in the
compound? Almost all the other pussys in my bunker sought
shelter. The firing was coming from a billet area where I had several
friends. Myself and only one other soldier grabbed weapons and ran
to that billet area. The billets were sometimes bunkers constructed of
ammo boxes filled with sand & sand bags, or as in this case raised
tents with wooden sides and a door.

My heart was pounding out of my chest, I was so scared, but
even knowing the possible consequences; I couldn't hide & let my

buddies get killed. Having jumped out of my bed, I was in my cut off fatigue pants, barefoot and wearing my helmet. I looked like a VC.

I actually did say to myself, "What would John Wayne do in this situation?" I quietly motioned to my friend for him to go left & I'd go right. Then I kicked open the door (a la John Wayne) and we dove in to a hysterically laughing soldier who had set off firecrackers. He was lucky we didn't shoot him right then and there; either thinking he was the enemy or because we were furious at his very stupid and potentially dangerous prank. I explained to him in my best Army language what a stupid fuck he was.

The way I was dressed I was also lucky not to have been shot as a VC. With so many pussys around I really had little to worry about. My heart didn't stop pounding for a while. We wanted to pound that G.I. It was like something out of a movie. Hmmmm, when the make the movie about this who's going to play me?

Some months later, when I was a short timer and quite nervous, we had real incoming rounds. It was not the same base. I again ran out wearing my cut off fatigue pants, and the VC style slippers I had purchased off base. I looked even more like a VC. This time I ran into the S-2 (Intelligence) tent to find out what was going on and right into the barrel of an officer's drawn .45! I was lucky he didn't shoot first. I stopped short and nearly shit in my pants!

Because of my concern for my parents' well being, especially my Dad's heart I really wanted them to take some vacation time. You have seen that I use humor or whatever to try to convince them to take that time off. Now, as a parent I understand even more the difficulty of dealing with, and the constant stress of having a child in a war zone. My heart goes out to all the parents, sisters, brothers, husbands, wives and children who have loved ones in a war zone. God bless you all and may your loved one return home to you safely.

24 July 1968
Time: 1900

Dear Mom, Pop, Marv -

Got your letter of 18 July today & was very happy to hear that you took a vacation. I guess you'll be home by the time this reaches you. How much of a vacation did you two get? I hope it was at the very least a week. Did you enjoy & relax - I certainly hope so. I still would like you (Mom & Dad) to be able to take a vacation in Florida. Someday I hope to be able to send you on a vacation to Florida or some exotic place. You deserve it.

I haven't heard from Marilyn & Steve about the apartment yet but I expect to hear from them within a short time.

That stationary you sent was "cute". The Army PX has similar type but with Army jokes & cartoons.

Well, I'm famous & made the newspapers - well almost. Remember I told you about a Captain whom I drove into town with when I was at An Khe. Also you know I was working on awards for my unit. Writing them from notes of what happened, adding a little spice, & typing them. Well, I wrote an award for Capt Kronh, the one I went into An Khe with & he was given the award at the Pentagon where he is now stationed. The article appeared in the paper here with the quote from the award, which I wrote. I'm enclosing the article for you to look at.

The rumor is that we're going to have a typhoon tonight. That will mean I can stay in my bunker & catch up on some sleep. I hope it lasts 5 days or so if it comes.

Well that's all for now. Write when you can.
Love & stuff
Howard

P.S. - My unit name was changed to 1ˢᵗ Air Cavalry Division (The article I spoke of appears below. I believe it came from the Army Times)

Assistant Defense Secretary Daniel Henkin (left) presents a medal for valor in Vietnam to Capt. Charles A. Krohn (center) and a medal for World War II action to his brother James R. Krohn. (UPI)

Acts Were 23 Years Apart

Brothers Cited for Heroism

WASHINGTON (UPI) — Two brothers were honored at the Pentagon Monday for military acts of heroism 23 years apart—one in the Normandy invasion of World War II and the other in the battle for Hue in the Vietnam War this year.

James R. Krohn, 42, of Saginaw, Mich., was belatedly awarded the Bronze Star and Capt. Charles A. Krohn, 31, also of Saginaw, was presented the Silver Star.

The older brother, a Saginaw business man, was an Army staff sergeant during the Normandy fighting, during which he twice escaped from the Germans.

A Pentagon spokesman said a search of the records showed that James Krohn had been entitled to the medal since 1944 and that through oversight it had never been awarded to him.

The citation accompanying the Bronze Star said James Krohn showed "exemplary conduct in ground combat against the armed enemy, on or about Oct. 1, 1944, in the European theater of operations."

Capt. Krohn, an Army intelligence officer, was cited for conduct during the battle for the old imperial capital of Hue last Feb. 3.

His citation said "when his unit became heavily engaged with a large enemy force, Capt. Krohn exposed himself to the enemy as he moved to the forward fighting positions to gather sufficient intelligence. His courageous action contributed greatly to the successful completion of his unit's mission."

27 July 1968
Time: 1950

Dear Dad, Mom, & Marv

Got your letter of 21 July today & was happy to hear from you. Was real glad to hear of your vacation, you sure deserve one.

Sorry I was AWOL from Marilyn's wedding, I plead guilty to the charge. Glad that my telephone call to Marilyn & Steve had the desired effect as described in your letter. It was worth the $11.00 if it made them happy. When Marv develops the pictures I sent, there's one I'm going to make a duplicate of for Marilyn's wedding album. It was taken by my buddy as I actually toasted Marilyn & Steve with Champagne.

Thanks for sending me the newlywed's address. I'll be writing them shortly.

Sounds like there's quite a bit of new furniture in the house. Can't wait to get home & use it.

By the way did you get my letter explaining my extending for 43 days (till 19 Dec) to get out of the Army 5 months early? I expect you did & before this letter reaches you I'll get a letter with your reaction.

I hope you got my checkbook & that Marv got the package I sent him & took care of it for me. Tell him to write. He's my favorite brother & I'd like to hear from him more often. Unfortunately I've been so busy lately I haven't had a chance to write as much as I used to.

Today I went to "Evans" to Jewish Services. The Chaplain wasn't there so the Asst conducted the service. I found out Rosh Hashanah & Yom Kipper services are being held in Da Nang. I hope I can get released for them. The way the Capt. & Sgt are speaking it seemed doubtful, though I think they are just teasing me. The Chaplain's asst said they can't stop me from going.

At present no leaves are being granted but we get a new C.O. in 2 days & possibly he'll have a leave program. I hope.

That's it for now. Got to go have a steak for a celebration. The Capt. is leaving in 10 days & we're having a little party for him.

Love from Nam
Howard

P.S. Hope you can read this letter I'm writing fast so I don't miss out on the steak.

---

30 July 1968

Dear Mom, Pop, Marv-

Thanks for the magazines you sent but I still haven't made a final decision as to a car. It's not even on my mind so much as it was before.

I don't agree that I'm "built great", I'm gaining too much weight just sitting on my, you know what & typing 15 hours a day. I hope to get back into shape before I get home but it will take some doing. I guess running is the best exercise but there's not much time or room for that here. It should be at least a mile a day.

I also can't wait till I get back into civilian clothing for good in December. Only 142 days from now.

Dad, of course I couldn't forget any important event & that includes family celebrations such as birthdays.

No, don't send me any other slides, I can see them when I get home. I should be returning the two boxes Marv developed for me with some slides to be reproduced. By the way, yesterday I sent home another roll of prints to be developed & there will be others following shortly. I hope the cost of developing these films isn't too much.

As for my R&R in Australia goes there's not much more to tell that what I already have. Mostly I slept till about 3 in the afternoon then either went downstairs or walked through Kings Cross - which is the area where I stayed. About 5 or so we'd take in a meal & start clubbing till the wee hours, 3 or 4 in the morning, sometimes later. I met a lot of people I liked & was very impressed. I saw several live show including a strip tease where the girls took just about everything off. I did a little shopping & went to the department stores downtown. That's about it. It's more exciting doing it than writing or talking about it.

I got a new job in addition to my present duties. I'm number one CHEF. Last week we got hold of some steaks & conjured up a grill & I was asked to grill the steaks. Thanks to a little training from Mom & Marilyn, while a civilian, I did very well. All the invited officers & men were complementing me. My head grew so big it almost burst. Now, tonight we are getting some steaks again & I expect I'll be asked to barbeque them, Oh well - you got to expect that when you're a great chef (Ha Ha).

As you probably know by now Co. C of my battalion was hit pretty hard yesterday. As if that wasn't enough Capt Steuer, a good friend, was taking his company on a "routine combat assault". As the area was being prepped by our artillery a *piece of shrapnel hit him in the chest. He's suppose to be in good condition at Da Nang. He should go back to the world with that type of wound.*

Well going to close now so I can write Marilyn & Steve.

> *Love from Nam*
> *Howard*

I had put on a few pounds as a clerk but did start running again and continued to do so for a while when I got home. When I was in the Army and right after I was in the best shape of my life. My weight had redistributed and what little weight I put on was muscle.

I hadn't mentioned those small matters about Australia before. Surprised I wrote home about the strip club?

For a bar-b-que grill in Vietnam we took a 55-gallon barrel, cut it in half the long way. The metal on top was a grate. We had plenty of wood to burn; the ammo boxes, and we used very many each day. As for the steaks we'd trade for them. Sometimes one of the guys would get a captured AK-47 and trade it to a cook or supply person for a side of beef. Even the colonel came down off his hill for my steaks. I mostly taught myself how to BBQ.

Capt Steuer was Lt Steuer when I first met him. He had quite a sense of humor and often had me in stitches. Once during one of the three monsoons I experienced (I seemed to follow them around the country or vice versa), I received a call in the S-1. I answered with the usual required sophistication, "Headquarters Company Sp5 Kalachman speaking sir. Can I help you?" The voice on the other end asked to speak to the Colonel, although I recognized the voice I was required to ask who it was. The surprising response was, "This is God!" Playing along I said, "God, I've been meaning to ask you why all this rain?" His response which may not sound funny now, just floored me then. He said, "Cause I'm pissed off at you". I missed him when he left and hope he is enjoying his life. He is wished the best wherever he is. He is another person I would like to have kept up with.

That was not our only humor. We sometimes created our own. With the usual Army misguided precautions, they sent us a huge supply of unlubricated condoms. We were not near any town or city and our guys in the bush certainly didn't need them. We blew several up like balloons and sailed them in the winds. As luck would have it one of them flew into the colonel's tent. When he came down to ask us about it we all suddenly became very stupid. We were amazed and had absolutely no idea of who could have done such a terrible thing! Could it have come from a chopper that was flying over!? Don't think we fooled him. When he left we burst into laughter. I believe we also saw a smile on his face as he left. You find humor where you can.

Another time we had a colonel who was a real hanging judge and S.O.B. Every discipline case that came before him got the maximum penalty. That was just about the time I learned how to tie several different knots including a hangman's noose. As I raised the flaps to prepare the tent for his trials one hot day, I tied all the tent ropes into nooses. He noticed them when he was in the midst of a case and did not enjoy my social comment! Fortunately, he also did not know who had done it or I'd have been the next one hung.

----

30 July 1968

Dear Marv -
Thanks for developing the film for me. The broads in Australia-Wow. Some time was spent in bed though not sleeping. I personally met quite a few nice girls & some not so nice girls who I promptly sent on their way. The Aussies call them pro's we in the states call them prostitutes. I don't want anything to do with them.
One girl I was doing pretty good with, was a beautiful (& I mean beautiful) blond haired, blue eyed go-go dancer at the Whisky-A-Go-Go. But, just as I was getting her to accept my invitation to "go somewhere" after she got off at 2AM one of my fellow

248

GIs said she was a pro. I don't know if he was right but I wasn't taking any chances. It's too bad she really was the most beautiful girl I saw there. I'll tell you more about my experiences when I get home. OK?

Dr. Tichauer is wrong. I do want Human Factors Engineering & I am well aware that it's a field of Psychology, that's why it interest me. Maybe I'll contact him when I get home. In the meantime I wrote yesterday to "Action Line" in Car Life magazine asking them to get me information possibly from GM's Human Performance laboratory. The Society of Automotive Engineers is still a very large organization. I guess they just moved to another location. If you should find their address let me know & I'll write to them. They are very active in many of the current safety specifications. They are known by their name or initials (SAE).

Marv as far as rooms go, of course I'd like the big room where I used to sleep before I was drafted. But, this isn't fair to you since you will be spending more time at home. How would you like to do it? Remember the one who has the big room will have the desk in it & has to let the other use it. As far as preferences go I prefer our room. I want to be fair Marv so in return for all that you've done for me, I'll let you choose. Let me know which you've chosen

I'll be looking for the times Sect 5 & Free press in the mail. Thanks.

What's been happening with you business wise? What are you doing?
How are you doing at it & do you like it?

Marv, do you think you could get a few weeks off when I get out of the Army (December), actually sometime after New Years to go on a forget Vietnam

249

trip with my new car to Florida and maybe also Canada? Don't worry about money, I'll help you out there. What do you say or is it too early to say?
Write soon?

Your brother in nam
Howard

It is almost certain that the GI who told me that beautiful go-go girl was a pro was lying, jealous, or mistaken. Either way it seems strange that I gave her up so quickly. Did I believe him or was I just scared, or stupid? Either way I should have pursued it to see where it went. I did a disservice to that girl allowing a G.I. to besmirch her like that without any confirmation from her or personal experience.

Needless to say, the way I wrote about it, my brother gave me the big room when I got home. Before I left we shared that room but with the vacancy left when my sister married, we each now would have our own room.

Don't know why I kept repeating my offer to spend a week or two vacation with Marv when I got home. I think he had not yet responded to my offer and thus I kept repeating it. Sorry, but I have not yet finished those repetitions.

---

1 Aug 68

Dear Mom, Pop, Marv
I got another letter from you today so I am writing again though I only wrote a few days ago.

You're right Mom, there are some very pretty girls in the states but unfortunately I haven't found any that knew how to treat a man the way the Aussie woman do but since I probably won't get a chance to return to Sydney I'll have to take my chances with stateside women.

I'm glad Sol & Florette worked out well at the wedding. Dad, do you think there's anything wrong

250

with writing them a letter after 9 months of being in Nam & not writing them?

By the way remember I sent you a contest form & you couldn't find it in any store? Well I'm trying again Mom. Supposedly you've won something. If you win the car, I'll take it O.K.? (Ha Ha). Tell me what you won. It's probably a $1.50 size "Instant Conditioning Lotion".

Well I got to end now - No I don't got to end but I will anyway.

Love from Nam
Howard

Lots of Kisses

P.S. Enjoy the summer weather. It's cold compared to 120 & above.

Not having been with any occidental woman in months, of course I thought the friendly and outgoing Aussie girls were great. I'd of though that no matter what country I had gone to, just as I found that American girls are the best in the world when I returned home.

Uncle Sol and my Dad had issues some years earlier. My uncle had not written me in 9 months so my question was moot. What I was really doing was making sure my Dad would understand and be O.K. with my writing to them. I worded that question in a way he'd have to respond positively.

Of course I knew I hadn't won anything in that contest but you are more superstitious in nam. Remember my mention of the value of religious artifacts? This was all about the same belief system.

Dear Marv...

Got your letter & Sunday times auto section -
Thanks for that.

Marv, it's too bad you won't be able to get two
weeks off when I get home. Do you think it would do
any good if I wrote your company & said I'm a
soldier coming home, back from the mean war in
Vietnam & that you don't know anything about this
letter? I could write a letter that will make your
bosses cry!

You didn't say what you do. Do you sell Singer
products? If you do I'll take a dozen sub-machine
guns. You know, of course, that Singer makes a 45
caliber automatic sub-machine gun for the Army?

Do you get to use the Singer truck on your off
hours? If you really want to save on a car you can
get a Renault R10 & from what I've seen it's worth
the $1900 with auto trans if you don't mind getting
a sedan. I was going to get a Renault R8 before I
decided on a convertible. Meanwhile you got dads
car. If you can hold off for a while & wait at least till
I get home (136 days) I'll help you pick a car &, if I
can, I'll even help you financially.

I put in the paperwork for my early out &
extension to be eligible. I extended a few more days
(3) than necessary just to play safe. I extended to 22
December. If my plans go right we should be able to
go on our vacation about the second week in
January. It depends on the extension getting
approved, my car being delivered on time, & a few
other things. I should be able to give you about 2
months notice of when to ask you boss off. I hope
that's enough. If you can get two weeks off, even

252

without pay, do it. I plan to have enough money for both of us. Also practice up on your driving, I'll be expecting you to do part of the driving on my new car whatever it is.

Marv, there's a place on LI called "Volvoville" which converts the sports model Volvo (I think its called P1800) into a convertible. I asked Lou to check it out for me since he's near it. I want to find out the price & if that model offers auto trans. Though all I drive now is a jeep, I still like automatic.

I haven't given up on the Oldsmobile yet, I'm just checking a few other possibilities. Got to have a good car for our trip to Florida.

As you probably know they are expecting a larger than ever offensive by the gooks so my unit, as a Quick Reaction Force is on 24 hour standby. In other words we could move anyplace where the action is on 24 hours notice.

There's more I want to say Marv but I can't think of it. Keep praying for me.

Your friendly brother
Howard
Of Howie's Raiders fame

P.S. No, I don't need a red book my black one's just fine but thanks anyway.

With the few dollars I made I wanted to help everyone in my family. As previously noted, my concept of money was skewed by the fact that I had never had this much saved before. As it turned out I barely had enough to buy my own car!

Dear Dad, Mom & Marv -

I sent two more rolls of film to you this morning but they were both prints instead of slides. It's all I have now.

My friend from AIT, Jeff Segal, you remember you spoke to his parents. Well he said he's going to have a leave in a few months & was going to stop in & say Hello. I told him if he does he should take his parents. I'm sure you'd hit it off fine, his parents are real nice people. Jeff was about the best buddy I had in A.I.T. He lives on Long Island & I'm sure when I get home we'll be good buddies. He plays the guitar real good & has promised to teach me how to play when I get home. If you remember I told you he got lucky & was assigned at Folk Polk.

Dad don't worry about my shotgun. I'm sure that Sam will protect my interest. That article you sent me tends to indicate that to register my shotgun I have to be finger printed which is impossible over here & I want it registered in my name so you can't do it for me. Don't worry about getting in trouble about having the shotgun in the house. I'm sure the police won't make a house to house search for weapons. If they did the improbable all you have to say is I'm in Nam & it's my weapon, therefore you don't posses it. If it makes you too nervous tell me & I'll ask Lou you store it for me in his house till I get home. I don't think there is any problem though, I have 3 months to fill out my tax forms when I get home, by law. So, I'd imagine I'd have a period of grace to sign up any weapon.

Dad, do me a favor. In my closet there is a folder marked Automobiles. In it should be a list of about 8 or 9 addresses including Cornell Lab in the folder, if there is copy it & send me a copy. I don't want the list with about 40 names of auto safety places, which is a copy of a page of an auto safety book. The list I want if it still exist is either handwritten or typewritten & should be near the end of the folders. If it's too much trouble forget it. I just wanted to write for some information about Human Factors Engineering.

I doubt I'll get that leave but I won't stop trying till it's too late to go.

Dad, you misunderstood me I said I was extending 44 days to DECEMBER 19, not November 19, actually I put in paperwork a few days ago & extended 47 days till 22 DECEMBER 1968. That will be my adjusted DEROS and my last day in the Army. I extended a few extra days on the advice of several people since I'll probably get a few days dropped off my deros & I asked for the exact day I'd lose my eligibility for early separation. Now I can accept up to a 3 day drop. As long as I don't leave here & arrive in the states on the 19th (It's a 12-21 hours ride home but you gain ½ day so you reach the state the same day you leave here). So actually I have a maximum of 138 days left in the Nam & in the Army & a possible 3 day drop to make 135 days. For safety sake we will say my Deros is Sunday 22 December 1968. Believe me Dad, when I say these will also be the longest days in my life.

Well I've written quite a bit so I'll close or now & let you ponder these thoughts.

Love from Nam
Howard

138 *or as they say 137 & a wake up.*

Jeff & I kept in contact for a short while but then we went our own ways. No, he never did teach me how to play the guitar.

Before I went to Nam I had been hunting a few times with that shotgun. Had never bagged anything. They were mostly just male bonding trips. After the assassinations at home, the gun laws became stricter and all weapons had to be registered. That worried my father and he wrote of his concern. That was the gist of my comments to him. Shortly after I came home I sold that weapon. I wanted nothing more to do with weapons of any kind for years after that.

You've been reading of (and are probably sick of) my interest in Human Factors Engineering and ergonomics. Had always been interested in vehicle safety. However, that career path was difficult for me to follow. When I returned home I pursued an undergraduate degree in Psychology.

My explanation of why I extended the extra three days is somewhat convoluted but basically came down to not trusting the Army to do the right thing. I covered what I hoped would be all my bases by extending the extra days.

---

6 Aug 68

Dear Marv

How's my favorite brother doing? I haven't received your poster yet. I haven't gotten any mail in two days - nobody has. We've been having a very bad tropical storm. It's been pouring harder than you can imagine for 3 days now & nothing except Medevac is flying. This morning a man was found dead in a collapsed bunker. It collapsed sometime during the night from the rain soaking the ground & sandbags. Several bunkers have collapsed so tonight no one can sleep in their bunkers because they're afraid others will collapse. My bunker is well reinforced but still I can't sleep in it for a few days.

I just hope that poster comes in dry - but I doubt it. It might be a good idea to put everything in plastic even the letters you send me. I think I'll suggest that to Dad. Tell everyone to put their letters in baggies or something since monsoon season starts early next month or late this month.

Now back to the poster. So you think it looks like Nancy, that girl who's pants I'd like to get into.

Marv, your idea for a New Year's Eve party is groovy as long as you know who to invite. There are a few people who aren't on that list whom I'd like to invite. For instance there's two of my buddies over here who live in Queens one who goes home in November & one about a day after me. Then there's a pen-pal (female) who I might want to take. You'll have to invite people early since New Years parties are plentiful. Probably the 1st or 2nd of December.

Yes Marv, I'm still pretty much set on the Cutlass unless I find the Volvo is cheaper which I really doubt. I'm now waiting for a reply from the U.S. Navy purchasing Dept, China Fleet Club in Hong Kong. I wrote them 11 August for prices of 69 Olds. They advertised that they had 69 prices. One of the officer's here, Capt Steuer bought a 69 Olds station wagon & his prices with accessories were about $2-300 less than my place in Jersey. I'll let you know as soon as I put in my order. I hope they hurry, I still have to find out if I can get a loan from my bank but I won't know how much till I see my total price. I figure it'll take about two weeks from the time I mail my letter to find out if I can get a loan. It'll probably be $1500, that will leave me about $1000 cash in the

bank. If I can't get the loan I'll have to pay cash &
get fewer accessories.

The major offensive hasn't taken place yet but
there has been increased activity.
There's something else I want to tell you, I'm sure,
but I can't think of what it is so I'll just close now.

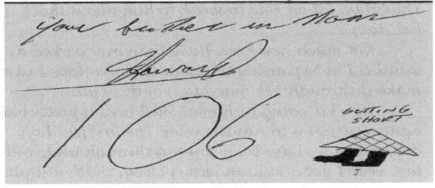

Had to include that sign off & cute picture I sent home, even
if I did write the wrong number of days left. It was 136 not 106.

I was wrong about when the monsoon would start. It had
already started!

We did have that combination welcome home and New
Years Eve party. It was a blast and we had a New Years Eve party at
my place for many years after.

---

10 August 68
Time: 1815

Dear Mom, Pop, Marv -
Got your Katz Salami Package & another
package with some Italian food & Chow Mien. A few
more things I'd like for my next package. We don't
often get "flavor aids" at the mess hall though we
can really use them, so I'd like a small bottle (or can
Of mustard & one of Ketchup. If you can find a Pizza
mix that doesn't require refrigeration, I have a
friend in the mess hall who has offered to cook it on

258

the mess hall stoves. I'd also like lots of potato sticks or cans of potato chips. I always have a taste for salt with the heat here.

Spoke to the Chaplain today (he always visits the S-1 shop) & he informed me that Rabbi Breslau (The Jewish Chaplain) will be on the LZ next Thursday. I'll be able to speak to him about the holidays.

Not much new here. Have been overworked as usual & I'm beginning to resent it more. Hope I can make it through 134 more days of this bull.

How's it going at home? Mail here is pretty bad again - it seems to run in cycles. The last few days only packages have been coming through while only last week I got a million letters (Well, that's a slight exaggeration).

Will close for now.

Love from Nam
Howard

Having a friend in the mess hall was great. You may have noticed that my letters home frequently had requests for food from the world. If you've ever eaten Army chow, especially in a war zone, you fully understand those requests. Even thinking about Army chow now can cause loss of appetite. Have you ever tried Army SOS (Shit on a Shingle) for breakfast? Ycch!

Two things soldiers do are bitch and complain. When finished with that, they start complaining & bitching. It was almost required to maintain ones sanity. This was true whether we were on the forward LZ or in the field. Sometime we bitched so we didn't have to think about our plight or our comrades in the bush who were going home mangled or in bags. I often bitched about the treatment the brass gave the grunts, my buddies in the boonies. I wanted them to get to our field camp and chill with us more often than they did.

We were often just on the verge of telling some over exuberant officer or non-com to "Fuck off" but common sense usually prevented that. I understood that I had a better situation than those out in the bush, notice I didn't say in the field. Technically we were in a forward LZ, which is the field. I was not back on a base camp.

We tried to build a Monsoon proof bunker:

Chapter 14 – What's happening?

I was counting down the days. Obviously, I was really looking forward, more and more to being home with a new car, a great New Years Eve party and a vacation trip with Marv.

Unfortunately at this time mail from home slowed down considerably and I was getting deeper into depression. I feared either that no one cared enough to write, or perhaps someone was sick or injured at home. Of course the problem was in my head as a result of our situation and the Army's poor mail service but that didn't make me feel better at the time. As noted in one of my letters the shorter I became the more I wanted a letter everyday from home.

To complicate maters more, the monsoon was taking its toll on our morale.

Then, all hell broke loose...again!

---

11 August 68

Dear Marv -

Got your letters of 4 & 5 August today. Sure was glad to hear from you. It's the first letter mail I've had in 3 days.

Thanks for thinking of me & sending me that catalog of Gov't Publications.

No, I haven't ordered my car yet. I'll let you know when I do. I'll probably get it delivered on or about 27 December, a few days after I get home. I'm a little nervous that the new car could get wrecked if I pick it up right away after driving for a year in Vietnam. Will let you know when I order, probably in a letter to Mom, Pop, & you!

As far as that trip to Florida goes, I'll let you know what days to take off as soon as the paperwork on my extension comes back. It should be approved but just in case I did it wrong or something, I'll wait (about 2-3 weeks). If it comes back approved I'll be able to give you dates for taking our Vacation.

I'm really interested in those B.S. stories of yours. Ha Ha.

NOW HERE THIS - PVT MARVIN since I'm older than you & outrank you (& will beat the shit out of you if you don't listen to me -Ha Ha). I have some directions for you! You take the big room now & when I get home we'll worry about which room I want If at that time you have decided to still let me choose & I do choose the big room I'll be able you help you move. So there! (Is that O.K. with you??)

You sure have been doing a lot of driving. Hope you're remembering your big brother's advice about driving (Do what I say not what I do) and are driving safely.

As for the shotgun I told Dad what I wanted done in my letter but if you think Dad is worrying too much & he doesn't call Lou to hold my shotgun for me, then I guess you can go ahead & register it for me. I'd rather you wait till I got home to register it but I don't want Dad worrying unnecessarily.

As for the pre-induction, the reason you haven't been called is that due to the budget cut the number of pre-induction physicals has been cut!

If you do get called remember what I said in my earlier letters

Well that's all for now. Take care & write again real soon

Love From nam
Your best brother
Howard

16 August 1969

Dear Marv –

Your letter is the first mail I've had from family in over a week. I sure wish the family wrote me more often. Now that I'm getting short the time goes by more slowly & I miss my mail.

O.K. I won't write any letters to Singer. You could probably do better on your own. The way your sales are going you might become so valuable to the company that you'll TELL them you're taking 2 weeks off & they'll be afraid to say anything.

I sure wish you luck in your promotion contest. You always were a good salesman. Is there good money in it? Do you work on straight commission or salary plus commission or what? If you don't mind my asking – how much commission do you make – figure it's between 15 & 25% right?

That week's vacation in Florida for two sounds groovy – but remember you're just starting out with Singer so you've got a lot of competition from more experienced salesman.

I still haven't gotten the paperwork back approved but tentatively the weeks I expect we'll be going will be Jan 4 (a Sat) to Jan 19, a Sunday or for one week Jan 4 to Jan 12. I should get official word in a week or two & I'll write you again at that time. The reason I picked Jan 4 is so I'll be home on 1 Jan. I hope one of my friends will be throwing a New Years eve party.

Marv I always have been honest with you so I won't stop now. Yesterday the part of my unit which is at LZ Nancy was attacked & there were quite a few causalities. One of the guys I know here who drives back & forth from Jane to Nancy all the time was Killed In action. We expect to get hit here at Jane also in the next few days. Of course that might be another wrong prediction like all the rest, but I don't think so. I think we'll probably get some mortar rounds & rockets. I doubt if they'd try a ground attack here. I sure hope it's a wrong prediction again.

By the way do you remember Arty, Lou's brother in law? He'll be coming to Nam in early September. Too bad! I wish he could get deferred.

By the way do you still have the list of friends I sent you "for emergency use only"?

That idea of a welcome home party sounds great.

When I get back to the states & get back to my job, I'll jump in John's shit (the lawyer) & get him moving on your case. He's one of the best lawyers in the city but like some lawyers procrastinates on cases.

I expected about a $100 rise in car prices for '69 so your news article confirmed that.

Well Marv, keep those prayers going. Tell everyone to write. I'm getting a case of the ass & only writing letters when I get one. That's probably a bad attitude but I get tired of writing 3 letters for each one I get.

Enough of my Bull shit. Be well.

Your favorite brother
Howard

P.S. I hope you're able to read my letter without too much trouble. I write fast and sometimes illegibly.

Most of my letters had legibility issues, not just sometimes as I wrote. Possibly because I am a southpaw, my handwriting, or if you will penmanship, grammar & spelling were atrocious as my fifth grade teacher loved to tell me. As previously noted, that's one reason I transposed most of these letters.

I didn't tell Marv all the facts about LZ Nancy. The unit was attacked by sappers and other ground forces. Sappers were the Vietnamese equivalents of Kamikazes, except they were on the ground. The VC strapped explosives on themselves and then tried to take as many G.Is with them as they could when they exploded them. It was a horror and somewhat successful in killing our guys. As I've been saying, we were at a forward position and not on a safer base camp. Our perimeter protection consisted of trip wires connected to Claymore mines or flares, several rows of barbed wire and posted centuries; guard duty if you will. We used artillery and flares every night to see, and put "smoke" on anything we saw moving.

If you can read between the lines you realize I was more than a little concerned. Did you get that when I asked if my brother still had the emergency list of friends? I'm pretty sure he did too.

---

17 Aug 68

Dear Mom & Pop –

Like what's happening man? Haven't had a correspondence from home in over a week. I did get your package (the 2ⁿᵈ) today. Actually that's the 3ʳᵈ package I got including the Katz salami. Is all well at home?

I wrote away a few days ago to a military club in Hong Kong which has an automotive department... [Another paragraphs of car stuff left out –no need to thank me].

There's been a little action here. An LZ about 10 miles from here was hit yesterday. One of our companies was on the LZ & we suffered 9 KIAs & 27 MIAs. One of the KIAs was a guy I knew pretty well. Now, because this happened so close we got tighter security including everybody in their bunkers by 2000 hours. That means no work after 2000. That's a good point.

My work load has been lightened considerably but as soon as we get the request I have to do at least 10 sympathy letters & they are SOBs. They have to be letter perfect & no erasures. Wow.

I went to religious services today at LZ Evans. The Rabbi was in. I have been going the last few months, once a month, when the Rabbi comes to Evans.

Well that's it for now. Write soon (Please).

Love from Nam
Howard

126 *& a wake up.*

My frustration with not getting mail from home is showing both in my first question and the fact that I wrote home more truth about that nearby action with KIAs & wounded. You'll also note that I addressed this only to "Mom & Dad" as I had received separate letters from Marv.

I would not write home again until I received another letter from home almost a week later! The first few words would tell why I had not heard from my parents in a while. Of course, then I felt like a stupid ass & ashamed of myself.

---

22 August 68
Time: 1900

Dear Mom, Pop, Marv-

Heard about your trip upstate with Uncle Jack & Aunt Lilly. Did you have a good time? I'll bet you did.

Wow, Mom you really won a whole bottle of "New Instant Conditioning Lotion Treatment"? Now, you can be blond too (only the hairstylist won't be the only one who knows for sure). That's O.K., you're beautiful even if you're not a blond. (I don't say that to all the girls - just the ones that aren't blond). I'm kidding you of course.

Yes Mom, it's true that you have to readjust to the states after being in Vietnam. My blood is thinner from the heat & therefore I'll feel cold faster. Also, I have the time difference (13 hours) to readjust to. When I leave here the monsoons should be in season & therefore it will be a little colder here (like 70°).

I got an additional duty of alternate mail clerk. I had to take a mail test to get my mail card. All I have to do is be mail clerk while the regular is on R & R or otherwise unavailable.

I'd like someone to get me the typing correction paper. The one where all you do is type over the letter. One brand is Korrect-type. I need this fast to help with my typing. I am not allowed to erase certain types of correspondence & this would make it O.K. You can even send it with your next letter. I'm sure Marilyn must have some but I won't have a chance to write her tonight.

Dad, did those "lost" pictures ever show up? Have you been getting my pictures OK? How are they coming out? Any request for things you'd like pictures of?

I'll close here. Write real soon or even sooner.

Love from Nam
Howard

121

Now that I received a letter from home I am feeling better as you can tell from the early attempt at humor in the letter.

---

27 Aug 68
Time: 1900

Dear Mom, Pop, Marv-

Got your letters of 20 & 22 Aug. Its' good to get your letters, I hadn't gotten any from 6 Aug to about a week ago. Only packages.

In your letter you say you're sure I'll enjoy my new bed. That's a definite affirmative. I have to fight my air mattress & poncho liner (sort of a nylon blanket) every night & my bunker isn't really wide enough for my bunk so I sleep with my feet & head touching the side of the bunker.

I got my request for extension back today- approved. Now it's official my ETS/DEROS date is 22 December 68.

I have a suggestion for everyone at home. When you write me don't put your name on the return address. Just the address, since there have been a few instances of gooks getting these from the garbage & sending home very distasteful items (the garbage dump is outside the perimeter).

I got a car mag a few days ago. I'm pretty sure now that I'll get an Olds Cutlass S... [Goes on and on again about prices —we can skip that!].

Glad that "lost" roll of film was found. How did my shots of the jets & bombers come out? Are there some pictures of my buddies (You can tell if they're in the S-1 tent)?

No Dad, I don't want the bottle of hair conditioner. If I stay in the sun any longer I can be a natural blond again.

The Army is making an investigation into the action a few weeks ago at LZ Nancy where one of my friends was killed. They said that the perimeter should never have been penetrated since there were sufficient personnel to defend it. They suggest bad leadership or men sleeping or inattentive on guard. Since the attack, the perimeter has been refortified & several new bunkers built.

My battalion is preparing to move again in the next few weeks. It will only be a short move this time. I'll let you know when it happens.

Sorry you had rain on your weekend upstate. The rains should be starting here very soon. The first monsoons are due here in the Northern Province the first few weeks of September. That's next week.

Vic's parents summer cottage sounds nice. Janet told me about it before. Did you go rowing? If so I sure hope you can swim or go with people who can swim.

Annette must have been a riot wearing Mom's under things. You should have taken a picture of that.

Mom, my friend noticed your stationary last time & said it was very cute. I think so too but I bet I could write a few of my own like:

Do I miss you? No, I always go around with this empty feeling.

Do I miss you? - Boy Do I miss you!!!

Do I Miss you? No -I just like counting days. How's that?

Keep those letters coming. Well I have negative
further so I'll break. - This is son to parents. I repeat,
negative further - OUT (That's radio talk, I thought
I'd add it for a little something different).

Love from Nam
Howard

116

If I recall it correctly the VC or whoever was stealing our garbage sent home pictures of decapitated and otherwise mutilated bodies. I referred to this earlier. I really did not have to worry about this as I hand shredded or burned every letter I got right after I answered them.

Finally, I had a real date and a real count of days left. That was a morale booster of sorts. Just under four months and I'd be home! Back in the good old U. S. of A and sleeping in my own bed!

That incident at LZ Nancy was harrowing for those who lived through it, as did some of my buddies. It also scared us, as we were just as susceptible to that kind of major ground and sapper attack and were not far away.

Many of the injured were medivaced out of the bush to the closest Army Medical Unit. Medivacs were ambulance choppers with a great reputation. Some of the medivac pilots had cahones the size of basketballs. Talk about going where angels feared to tread. Bless them all!

---

28 Aug 68

Dear Marv-

How goes it brother? From dads last letter it
sure sounds like you're putting in long hours. From 8
AM to 11 PM! Marv, Singer is taking advantage of
you at $70 + 5%, you could probably do better on a
straight 15-20% commission. Actually, I think that
you should ask them to increase you to 10% plus
basic pay. The fact that you've already won two

promotion contests proves you're good (By the way Congratulations). What type of watch did you get and what show did you choose?

Marv, I seriously believe that if you ask you can get more salary & if not I'd consider another job. Marv from experience I can tell you a good field to get into as far as sales go is either automotive or insurance. Allstate has a pretty good plan for their agents. If Singer doesn't improve your commissions (why break your balls?) by the time I get home, do you think you'd be interested in finding out about the insurance field with Allstate? Insurance is easier to push than sewing machines so I'm sure you can make it.

Marv, if you read the letter I wrote home the other day you know the good news. My extension was approved. MY DEROS/ETS date is now 22 Dec 68. I should be able to get home by the 23rd. so you can now make plans for our trip (I just hope I can get a car in time).

Marv your idea for a New Years Eve Welcome Home party sounds groovy but I've got a few new friends (female). You could definitely invite your friends male & female. I've got two pen pales in the area. One's a nurse in New Jersey & the other a student in B'klyn.

I'll take care of myself Marv, but I'm not an officer. Thanks for the compliment.

Marv there is another thing you can do for me when the '69s come out. Go with Dad to test drive a 69 Olds Cutlass (Try to drive a convertible). You'll have to go with dad since they won't let you test drive otherwise if you're under 21 & any way I'd like both your opinions. You can tell the salesman You & I (in Nam) are buying a car together & since I'm in

Nam I've asked you to do the test driving for me. Also give me your comments on the appearance of the car. [A paragraph followed about locating local Oldsmobile dealers were I could have my new car delivered.]

I've been practicing my driving a little lately. I've been driving the road from LZ Jane to Evans (about 20 miles). I'm really starting to get used to a standard shift. I even like it. The roads are pretty secure during the day & I usually go out with a few vehicles.

By the way my battalion is supposed to move to LZ Nancy within the next few weeks. It will only be a short move & we'll be near a river so I may get in some swimming. Wow.

Well Marv, thanks for the big room. I can't wait to get home. I'm sure you and I can have some good times together. Of course my main interest will be having a good time & that means lots of wine, women, & beds - you know what I mean?

Well kid, take care & write soon.

Your brother in nam.

Howard

114

Did I mention that in a short while my brother became the top salesman in his area? Of course he did, he is outgoing, social and knows how to listen. The other, older salesmen resented him for that.

No, I never was an insurance salesman but worked for the Allstate legal office before I was drafted and knew many of their sales people. In addition to a nice commissions structure at the time, they were part of the Sears profit sharing plan. I did also have a few auto salesman friends who were doing quite well.

O.K, so I left in comments about the car, which I thought, were interesting. Can you believe that back then new car dealers didn't let you test-drive a car if you were unaccompanied and under 21. How many car sales were lost with that myopia?

Interesting that I wrote about my daily trips between Evans and Nancy, the same route I had written about a few weeks before when the driver had been killed.

I didn't go swimming but did go wading. Of course there were no bathing suits. We all went skinny-dipping. It was quite refreshing. We ignored the locals at the river washing clothing and they ignored us. Most of the locals were not attractive to us. Of course I should mention that some of the most beautiful woman we ever saw in the nam were the Eurasians. There were part European and part Asian.

---

30 Aug 68

Dear Dad, Mom & Marv -

Got your letter today postdated the 26th of August. You surmise that I may not be getting all my mail. You're right I never got the pictures of Annette saluting or any pictures of Annette recently.

Tomorrow I'm going to the I.G. if I can find time. We've been very busy getting ready to move & I've been doing the work of several men. For two days I was in charge of the S-1 Section.

Your postal clerk is right that the mails are screwed up here. The mail is screwed up at Phu Bai where there is a main Post Office for this area of Nam. My mail clerk has written letters to their commanding officer but I believe they have been ignored. Now, I'll take over. First I'll see the I.G. & if that doesn't help I'll write to Sen. Rosenthal. Of course it is possible that, that letter just hasn't arrived yet.

I hope you're getting my mail. I mailed letters home on 27, 22, 17, 10, 6 and 1 August. Did you get them all?

I'll be looking for those Pizzas and mags Dad.

How's everything at home? Are you lonely without anyone at home or do you enjoy your second youth?

I know Marv is good. I sure wish I can help him buy himself a new car when I get home. I know how much it can mean to him. I sure hope that he never gets drafted. If he does, so help me I'll bomb the draft board & induction station & take Marv to my friends in Canada. (Boy I sure get mad - don't I?)

Speaking of cars how's the "yellow banana"? I wonder what 3 new cars would cost. Probably about $7500 stripped. All I need is $5,000. Wow.

How's the old TV set working? I wonder how many of my favorite shows are still on.

One of my buddies who lives in Queens went on R&R to Hawaii today where he'll meet his wife. He said he'd have his wife call you when she returns to Queens in two weeks. (Probably pregnant). His name is Rick.

That's it for now.

Love from nam
Howard

For the few days I was in charge of S-1, I was what we called an Acting Jack. That means I had the authority & responsibility of the Captain in charge. That happened a few times.

One of those times I told a soldier to take some papers to another location. Unbeknownst to me at the time, he was a felon who had been given the choice of the Army and Vietnam, or prison. He had chosen the Army. To my surprise and indignation, he said, "I don't have to take orders from any Fucking Jew". I don't remember leaping over the desk, just beating the shit out of him until the lieutenant broke us up. I never was a violent or physical person and think I surprised myself more than him. Of course that was taboo and unprofessional behavior on my part. However, when the lieutenant found out what had occurred, not only was I not charged but he required that soldier to make a public apology to me.

The mail situation never got much better. It was after all the sixties, before the computer revolution and we were in a war zone. Mail was so bad I even received a few letters forwarded to me months after I came home!

My fear and frustration over my brother possibly getting drafted and being sent to the Nam was obvious by the ludicrous statements I made. My brother was and is a patriot and would never do anything to get out of the service, although I would have liked him to.

This letter ran right to the bottom of the page so there was no room for countdown this time.

---

9 Sept 68

Dear Dad, Mom, Marv -

Got your letter of 28 August yesterday & 4 Sept today. The last two days we've been on limited light rations, due to the heavy rains from the tropical storm that just passed. The roads have been washed out and the mogas (gasoline) trucks haven't been able to get through so the generators are only run a few hours a day. I can't even get gas for my jeep. I've been driving to the new LZ almost every day now. Without gas, the trip will be hard to make. We've been working on our bunkers, since we expect to move by Saturday. We are really building a good bunker at LZ Nancy. During the tropical storm 2 bunkers collapsed killing one man so for a few days we couldn't sleep in our bunkers: we had to sleep in the S-1 tent until our bunkers were inspected & passed. Mine was passed so I'm sleeping in it again.

Today we had an experience with some clown flying a LOH helicopter. We were returning from Nancy on the access road to Jane when we saw this chopper flying around the area & what we thought was smoke rounds being dropped to mark the area for artillery. We were driving up the road when this joker buzzes by & drops his "smoke" grenade about 100 meters in front of us. He definitely saw us. It turns out it wasn't a harmless smoke grenade, it was a CS gas (riot gas) grenade used to flush out gooks in hiding. Before we realized it was CS & not smoke we were passing right through it. It chocked us up and had the usual unpleasant (though harmless) effects. I gunned the jeep & made tracks out of there. When we got back to Jane we reported the clown to Brigade Headquarters & our battalion I.G. I hope that joker gets everything that's coming to him. If I ever wanted to bust an officer in the mouth that chopper pilot is the one.

Thanks for the Korrect-Type. I can sure use it.

Don't worry about Grandma Mom, I'm sure she understand that I have several girl friends. She's my oldest of-course and one of my favorites. I like mature women (Ha Ha) Send Grandma my love.

Janet wrote me that Doug can stand by himself now.

Dad, I didn't get any letter from the BBB of New Jersey, not since the post card several months ago saying they were checking. That's the 2nd time you mention something I should have gotten which I haven't gotten. This is annoying, where's my mail going? I hope it is not destroyed in transit. With all the rain lately a lot of mail is accidentally destroyed. Do you know approximately when you sent this letter?

I still haven't heard from Hong Kong If I don't hear from them by the 11th, which is a month since I wrote my request, I'll send a follow up letter & in it

276

include a request for information on the Buick Skylark. What made you interested in the Skylark? A Chevy II or Corvair would be a better car. Is the skylark a full size car? I assume you want an 8 cyl. I'll ask for the price of a 4 Dr sedan & a hardtop. I'm enclosing a copy of their ad from "Army Times" for you to read. It answers your question about delivery in New York (which is still a "major city"). As for additional costs, I'll know that when I get my info, as that was one of the questions I asked.

I haven't received your package as yet.

My head & feet don't stick out of my bunker they just touch the walls.

Dad, your P.S. (Destroy the envelope) struck me as being funny. It reminded me of the "Mission Impossible" show where the voice or letter always says, "this tape/letter will destroy itself in 5 minutes - FLASH" I read the letter real fast before it destroyed itself.

Got to close now, the lights go out in 3 minutes.
Love from Nam.
Howard

103

LOH= Light Observation Helicopter.

As you may have guessed we built our own bunkers. We got together with a few buddies to build bigger ones to share. We were, if you will, bunker mates or roomies.

With all the rain we had lots of small creatures foraging for food. One evening three of us tough, hardened, combat seasoned soldiers were sitting in our bunker, bull shitting when a mouse ran across startling us. We screeched, looked at each other and laughed. However, as this mouse had made us scream like little girls it had to die. I set up a mousetrap using "C" rations as bait. It took the bait within a few hours. We all laughed again saying that any mouse stupid enough to eat "Cs" deserved to die. Our manhood was restored!

"Smoke" was used for many things. It marked an area for artillery but was also used when a chopper was flying in. The man on the ground would pop a colored smoke grenade and as a safety precaution, the incoming pilot would identify the color before landing. CS gas had some very unpleasant effects, in addition to choking you and not allowing you to breath properly, it burns your skin. That chopper pilot, like many, was a warrant officer. We got his chopper ID number. Not only did we report him but my sergeant had me drive over to his area and I am not sure if they only had words or if the serge was more physical. All I know is I'd never seen Sarge so angry.

The barbers on base were locals. Sarge was friendly with our barber. Although we were not supposed to go visit Vietnamese homes, when Sarge was invited to the barbers home I drove him there. Didn't know where I was going till we got there. Sarge knew he could trust me. Once there, we were served something that looked and tasted like a western omelet. I knew enough not to ask what the meat was, in Vietnam it could be anything from rat, to cat to ox. Of course there were no utensils. A young daughter saw me struggling with the chopsticks and said, "Here G.I., I show you how" and she did.

Sarge also has a softer side. He loved cats and adopted a few stays.

That was a twist, my dad asking me for car information. The ad I sent him is below.

Sarge's Strays

Smoke popped on LZ

Capt Steuer in foreground

Sarge with Chinooks above

Chinook carrying damaged observation chopper

Chapter 15 - Less than 100 & a wake up

Was getting "Short", down to a 2-digit number of days left. But that still was over 3 months and there were still a few misadventures and surprises in my future. Still plenty of time to complain.

We were in the midst of moving to LZ Nancy. Yes, that is the base that had been overrun and I'm sure that was worrying my family.

The Jewish High Holy Days were once again just around the corner.

---

12 Sept 68
Time: 2130

Dear Mom, Pop, Marv –

First of all I got two letters, including the one with the Better Bus Bureau letter. Also I got the package with the Pizzas & flavor aids. All the guys in the S-1 say thanks for the pizza. Joe (the mess Sgt) made one big pizza out of them & we really enjoyed it.

My unit is currently in the process of moving & because of that I haven't been able to get anything done. I haven't even been able to write any letters. Today was really a hectic day. The mail clerk left yesterday for his 3 day in-country R&R, so I'm now doing his job also. It's pretty tough doing everything so I just do what I can & if that's not enough (so far it's more than enough) I don't give a damn with only 100 days left. In a few hours I'll break 3 digit numbers and go into 2 (99 days) I must be short, I already have a replacement.

By the way I also got the magazines you sent me. Forget about the potato chips, I wouldn't know what to do with 25 lbs of potato chips.

As for resting when I get home, I intend to go to Florida for a week or two with Marv & maybe to Montreal for a weekend. Yes, I do intend to return to Allstate for at least 6 months so I can get my Profit Sharing.

Once & for all Dad, I cannot & will not be transferred. First of all my MOS is 71B30 which is "Senior Clerk-Typist" & you have to have orders to transfer a man. Also now it is too late to transfer me even to another clerk job. I'm what's referred to as a 90 day loss. So, if I wanted to I could write every Senator & see every I.G. & they can't do a damned thing. (Besides it's illegal to punish a man for complaining to the I.G. unless he lies). But just to make you happy I won't complain officially. Unofficially I mentioned the mail problem to him, he's an O.K. guy & said we all have that problem. I don't think he wanted to be bothered with an investigation so I forgot it for now.

By the way, Bob, one of the guys here says a personal hello & thank you for the ketchup - it makes Army chop chop edible - yeah it does!!!

Got to close now - tell Janet I'm sorry for not writting but with the move & all I'm too busy. You're the only ones I've written to this week

Love from Nam
Howard

Tonight 99

Why a trip to Montreal? For a woman of course. Had met Carol just before I was drafted and we kept in touch via mail. Closet I had to a girlfriend. Funny thing is when I originally met her, she was with her cousin. At first I was interested in the cousin but fortunately Carol was interested in me. We saw each other for a while after I got home.

My father was concerned that by my contacting the IG about the mail situation, there would be repercussions and I'd wind up back in the field. Not only was it as unlikely as I wrote but I was highly valued in the S-1 and I knew it.

19 Sept 68

Dear Mom, Pop, Marv –

Well the move is complete & I'm now at Landing Zone Nancy. It's a pretty large LZ & there will be several units here. As I understand it the 2nd Brigade & all its support elements will eventually be located here. That means the engineers, armor, helicopters, assault ships (Gun ships & ARAs), supply, etc.

Got my orders today for the Jewish Holidays. I'll have 21-24 Sept for Rosh Hashanah & 1-2 Oct for Yom Kippur or the other way around, I'm not sure, except for the dates.

Some time ago, in a letter from home, I was led to believe that certain parties at home still think I got my scar last December from more hostile action instead of the way I told it. Well now I got proof. I took this proof from my files for two reasons. To prove to you that what I said happened, did happen & to clarify it for you and secondly to use in case I have to persue the government when I'm released in December. So keep this paperwork safe for me.

What's new at home? Are you marking off the days till I return? There are 93 as of today.

Well that's all I got for now. Love & stuff.

Love from Nam
Howard

93

P.S. Don't worry about me taking the papers, they are marked for destruction at the end of this year anyway.

When I returned from Nam, I did get disability, but not without a fight. Not only was I left with a scar but also elevated blood pressure. A good part of my medical files were lost along with many others in a fire in the warehouse in Texas where the Army had stored them. As part of that process of getting the disability and resultant benefits I deserved I wrote a letter to the President telling my story and saying something like I tended to loss confidence in a country which was quick to send it's men off to war but then failed to meet it's responsibilities to those men for it's action. I mentioned this to a young lady I was dating at the time who happened to be the secretary for a U.S. senator. She later told me that the FBI monitored her line at work and that such statements could make me a person of interest. I was and still am about as proud an American as one could be so that just added insult to injury and irritated me. It did not stop me from venting on the phone when I spoke to her.

---

4 Oct 68

Dear Mom, Pop, Marv -

Got Back from Da Nang today. Got to stay in Da Nang an extra day to handle a deal with one of the supply people. We have been having trouble trying to get office equipment so I took an AK-47 (NVA weapon) that was captured by my unit & traded it for a typewriter.

The rain has subsided but the clouds may burst at any time since monsoons are about due. I hope they are 3 months late.

We are pretty much set up here at LZ Nancy. My bunker is finished, complete with a ply-board floor & an electric light. It is also big enough to stand in & I can stretch in my bunk. We have sufficient artillery & infantry support here to protect us against any threat of a ground attack.

No reason to get all upset about that accident story. I don't even remember who told me that. It was one of my many spies who I'm sure had been liquidated for giving me erroneous information. I know you trust me as I do you but I was led to believe by certain actions that you might have thought I was "protecting" you from the "painful truth" which of course was ridiculous. So let's forget it.

Thanks for the desk & chair to match my bed and chest of drawers. I can't wait to get home & put them to use.

Vic just wrote me the name of his friend who's in the field I'm interested in. I'll probably get to write him tomorrow.

I doubt I'll be able to attend college in February, possibly in June for the summer. I'm still not sure which college I want to go to & won't be sure till Vic's friend or someone else helps me out with some information & suggestions.

I got your package today on my return to camp. Thanks a lot. I guess you can stop sending packages now since they take so long to get here.

Yes, I did receive some info from the Hong Kong car dealer but Zeigler's prices were cheaper so I'm impatiently awaiting their price lists [As usual, goes on about which car I would buy].

That's all I can think of so I'll close now. While I was in Da Nang I sent a MARS-GRAM. Did you get it?

Love from Nam
Howard

78

The trade for a typewriter was sanctioned by one of my superior's, which is why I got the extra day. I wrote that, "I took an AK-47…" but should have written that I was given one. The Army works in strange ways. An AK-47 went a long way towards getting what you wanted from a supply sergeant who never saw any action.

We spent extra time building our bunker at LZ Nancy, as we knew monsoons were coming and because of the collapsed bunkers which had killed a solider as alluded to in the paragraph about the accident. We put in a floor, ran a wire for electricity, and used lots of plastic sheeting for waterproofing. Pictures appear in an earlier chapter. It was actually pretty dry even during the heavy monsoon rains. As a soldier you are the chief cook and construction supervisor.

I don't think my parents believed my injury was accidental right up until some time after I got home. You can see I tried everything, even humor to convince them, but without success.

---

9 Oct 68

Dear Mom, Pop, Marv -

How goes it at home? Another few months & I can just walk up to you and ask you, "How goes it?"

Had a very satisfying experience yesterday. I made an M.P. "eat crow". I drove to Camp Evans on an admin run to drop off some paperwork. As I got ready to leave I drove up to the gate & told the M.P. I was going to LZ Nancy. Since you have to go with two vehicles anywhere on the roads of Vietnam and one had just left for Nancy, he told me to catch it. I drove up to Q.L.#1 (Highway 1) stopped at the Stop Sign and make tracks to catch up to the vehicle in front of me. The speed limit in Nam is 20 MPH and of course to catch up to the vehicle in front I had to go faster. I was doing 30 when an MP jeep pulled me over. He said I was speeding & took my license and ID card. I explained to him that I was ordered to catch up to the vehicle in front of me but he wouldn't believe me. He started to write a ticket. I told him, "If you write that ticket I'm going to make you look

287

silly" but he still wrote it. When he was done he asked me to sign the ticket. I asked him if I got to see his boss if I refused to sign it & he said, "No" but I didn't sign it anyway. I asked him if I could make a u-turn & he said, "Yes". I went right back to the gate and told the M.P. who gave me the catch-up order the story. He got on the horn and called the sergeant in charge and also called in the M.P. who gave me the ticket. When the Sgt got there I explained what happened to him and when the MP got there, he (the Sgt), told me to go to my jeep. He chewed out the M.P. The MP who gave me the ticket then came over, apologized and told me to rip up the ticket. I told him he could have made things easier by calling the gate when I told him my story. At any rate he was friendly about it and said he didn't mind tearing up the ticket since I wasn't a wise guy.

That's the most exciting thing that's happened to me in weeks but I'm not complaining.

Say Marv, do me a favor and pick up the little NY schedule that Eastern puts out. I'm sending you the old one I have so you'll know what to look for. Also find out if any other airlines have direct flights from Seattle. You can ask any ticket agent this & he'll be glad to give you the info on all the airlines form the master book.

One last request, if you want to still send packages send them to PFC Art Semmig, HHC 14th Engineer BT (CBT), APO SF 96495. That's Lou's brother-in-law who 's stationed right here at LZ Nancy. It was funny. I got a letter from Art saying, "In case you're wondering where I am, I'm at a camp called LZ Nancy." I almost fell down when I read that. He's an S-4 (supply) clerk. I got right into the jeep and drove over to 14th Engineers, just about

¼ mile up the road. Art was real surprised to see me. That was about 4 days ago and since then we get together every night that he doesn't have guard duty. As I once told you Art's parents really like me and vice versa, they write to me as "Dear Son." Also, Eve & Lou have sent me a few packages as I intend to send Art packages when I get home. Until that time, if you like you can send him a package or two. If they get here before 10 Dec I can even help him devour (eat) them.

Well that's all from this end. What's the latest news? Is the car still acting up? Mom, are you still working?

Write soon.

Love from Nam
Howard

73

I love that MP story. It was very satisfying. How many times have you told a cop a true story they didn't believe? Guess you can't really blame them they hear so many stories. Probably about two or three times as many as the number of tickets they write. I have a lot of respect for cops but not for power crazed schmucks like that M.P.

Not only was I dumfounded when I discovered Art was on the same base but when I drove over there, he looked at me and did a double take. He said something like, "What the hell are you doing here?" and I said something like, "The same as you!" It was nice, since I couldn't go home yet, to have a little bit of home come to me. I was happy that he was a supply clerk. We spent a lot of time together until…

---

14 Oct 68

Dear Dad, Mom, Marv -

Did you read about the mid-air collision of the Chinook & airplane at Camp Evans, last week? 24

guys were killed, 17 of them were on their way home—
it proves you're really not short until you step into
your house.

Guess what? I had another experience on Q.L.1
coming back from Evans the day after the Mp
incident I wrote about last time. I was driving on
QL1 at about 15-20 MPH through a village when a
little girl suddenly ran in front of the jeep. Since
there were people on the right I couldn't swerve so I
had to depend on the brakes & tires. Jeep tires have
very little traction and my brakes are scored so as I
was skidding I made contact with the little
Vietnamese girl, but she was quick enough to push
herself off the jeep & she fell. I thought I had hit her.
I had just started to get out of the jeep when she got
up, brushed herself off & ran into her hooch. I went
to the hooch to make sure she was O.K. but her mom
didn't understand. Finally her brother, who spoke
G.I. English said, "No SH_t, she O.K." So with his
reassurance I drove off.

I have two things to tell you. First I sent home
my certificate for my Bronze Star Service award &
some other papers. They were sent registered.
Secondly I sent two rolls of film to Master Color Labs
to be developed & sent to you. Let me know when you
receive them.

Be looking for that package with the Champale
in it, which you mentioned in the letter I got today.
I'll be sure to thank your aunt when I get it without
mentioning the Champale. That's it for now.

Love from Nam

Howard

68

The Vietnam era jeeps had terrible tire treads & brakes. While driving outside the LZ we are not suppose to stop for anything and never, ever get out of the jeep. I didn't mention in my letter that the road was muddy and slick. The sergeant ordered me to keep driving, and to get back into the jeep. I've always loved kids. I was scared, upset & sobbing. Court marshal or not, I refused to get back in the jeep and drive on, until I knew the little girl was unhurt. As you'd expect, that incident remains vividly in my memory.

I received the bronze star for the air assaults I had participated in and my time in the field. My parents did not believe this and thought it was related to my "accident". Maybe I should have just made up a story and been done with it but I could not tell a blatant lie to my parents. Further, it would not have alleviated their concerns.

My father's aunt had given him money to send me something but I doubt she'd approve of Champale (which was a malt beverage that tasted like champagne). My dad had asked me not to mention that if I wrote her.

My Bronze Star Certificate:

THE UNITED STATES OF AMERICA

TO ALL WHO SHALL SEE THESE PRESENTS, GREETING:

THIS IS TO CERTIFY THAT
THE PRESIDENT OF THE UNITED STATES OF AMERICA
AUTHORIZED BY EXECUTIVE ORDER, 24 AUGUST 1962
HAS AWARDED

THE BRONZE STAR MEDAL

TO

SPECIALIST FIVE E-5 HOWARD KALACHMAN US52752433 UNITED STATES ARMY

FOR
MERITORIOUS ACHIEVEMENT
IN GROUND OPERATIONS AGAINST HOSTILE FORCES

DURING THE PERIOD NOVEMBER 1967 TO NOVEMBER 1968 IN THE REPUBLIC OF VIETNAM

GIVEN UNDER MY HAND IN THE CITY OF WASHINGTON
THIS   FIFTH   DAY OF   OCTOBER   1968

GEORGE FORSYTHE
Major General, United States Army
1st Cavalry Division (Airmobile)
Commanding

Stanley R. Resor
SECRETARY OF THE ARMY

1st Cavalry Division
Airmobile

VIETNAM COMBAT CERTIFICATE

Let it hereby be known that SP5 RONALD KALACHMAN has faithfully served his country with the HHC 2nd Bn 12th Cavalry of the 1st Cavalry Division (Airmobile) in the Republic of Vietnam for the period November 1967 to December 1968 is deserving of the honors and respect afforded all members of THE FIRST TEAM whose courageous deeds and sacrifices have preserved the liberty of South Vietnam and advanced the cause of Freedom throughout the world.

The 1st Cavalry Division was organized as a Regular Army Division on 13 September 1921 at Fort Bliss, Texas, and was formed from units whose histories trace back to the days of the frontier expansion, when cavalry troopers fought the Indians and conquered the West.

On 20 October 1944, the Division, dismounted, made the initial landing on Leyte Island, and subsequently moved to Luzon to spearhead a 100-mile thrust through enemy held territory to liberate Manila, thereby earning the right to be called: "FIRST IN MANILA."

On 8 September 1945, the Division, as an occupation force, marched into Tokyo with General Douglas MacArthur to account for its second remarkable "First": "FIRST IN TOKYO."

On 18 July 1950, the Division made the first amphibious landing of the Korean Conflict, at Pohangdong, and pushed northward across the 38th Parallel, capturing Pyongyang, the capital of North Korea, to establish another historical "First": "FIRST IN PYONGYANG."

On 1 July 1965, at Fort Benning, Georgia, this famed unit became the first Airmobile Division, lending proud cavalry traditions to the new air assault concept of the United States Army.

THE FIRST TEAM arrived in the Central Highlands of the Republic of Vietnam in September 1965, and within 75 days had met and defeated the enemy in the historic PLEIKU Campaign. For this outstanding achievement, the 1st Cavalry Division (Airmobile) was awarded the Presidential Unit Citation, for another "FIRST": FIRST DIVISION TO RECEIVE THE PRESIDENTIAL UNIT CITATION IN VIETNAM. Subsequently, decisive victories have been attained in operational areas throughout the I and II Corps Tactical Zones in which the aggressive spirit displayed by the troopers has dominated the enemy and has destroyed his will to resist. These prevailing victories are lasting tribute to the heroism and devotion of each fighting man who has served with the 1st Cavalry Division (Airmobile).

GENERAL, U.S. ARMY

COMMANDING

---

17 Oct 68

Dear Mom, Dad, Marv –

Glad to hear you received my Mars-Gram. It's the first one that's ever been delivered.

Well if you're going to get drafted the Navy is the place to be, but Dad in the Navy? "Nevah hoppen G.I." - I hope.

Something like monsoons are here, unfortunately it's probably pre-monsoons. At any rate it stopped for a while now & the road is pure mud. I got my replacement his license today so he can take over the driving for the most part.

No jack doesn't sleep in my bunker I hardly ever see him anymore. He disappeared again this afternoon just when he was due for shots. I'll have to find him tomorrow, he's probably hiding somewhere so he won't be given his shots.

Arty came over and brought his cassette tape recorder with a tape from Lou & Eve, & his parent which was addressed to both of us. It was nice to hear their voices again. They offered to take Mr. Semmig's recorder to you & play it if I would make a tape. You remember the Semmigs, I introduced you to them while I was on leave, they are Art's parents (Lou's in-laws) & insist I call them Mom & Pop (which I do) since they say I'm family. We'll at any rate Art & I made a tape yesterday so you should be hearing from them in a few days or so. They'll probably come some evening to surprise you.

I intend to get a cassette recorder myself but so far the PX hasn't had any when I was there. It's too late to use it for mailing tapes but I want if for my car.

Speaking of my car I've run into a small problem. I got a reply from Mr. Kelly of Merchants Bank saying he could not give me a car loan while I'm in the Armed forces. That means I have to pay all cash or get my loan from the new car dealer which might prove expensive. I had wanted to save $500-$100 in the bank for general use and emergencies but now I don't know if I can & still get a new car. At any rate I'm sending you my letter to the bank & their reply for my records.

Dad, do you think you could get a loan for $1000- $1500 to be repaid in 36 months? If you can

294

maybe you can get the loan for me then when I get out I'll get my own loan In my name & pay off your loan? What do you think of that?

I got my absentee ballot today & cast my vote. I voted for Nixon as the lesser of the three evils of the candidates but voted against that S.O.B. Javitts. I am still pissed that he didn't even bother with a form letter to answer my 2 letters to him. He's too confident of the vote & I would like to see the (censored) lose.

That's all I got for now.

Love from Nam
Howard

66

That first tape home that Art & I made was not kept for me as it belonged to Art and his parents. We made another and I made a few on my own, as you'll see later on.

Not getting a car loan because I was in the army was a blow to me. Being in a war zone the bank did not feel I was a very good risk. Bummer! Not patriotic! It did however, finally, bring me back to Earth as far as my financial worth. I did not have as much money as I had thought and would not be able to buy my brother or father cars or televisions as I had mentioned I would like to several times .

---

18 Oct 68

Dear Marv-

Got your Popular Science mag yesterday & your letter today. Mom had mentioned one of your friends was drafted. Let's hope your not next. Don't sweat about not being able to write those weeks, I understand.

Glad you got your two weeks in January. Now start checking the Sunday Times for places to stay &

295

send me the ads that you find most interesting. I don't think I can get delivery of my car in time so we'll either have to go by plane or rent a car. I don't think you've ever been on a plane. Have you? O.K. I guess it'll be a jet. Read the ads in the paper carefully. Some places offer a free use of a car (convertible), check them out also the Sunday Times Vacation section always has car rental places in Florida so if its cheaper to rent from then & go to another hotel take that into consideration.

My plans for a car have been screwed a little by the bank. They say they cannot give me a loan while I'm in the Army. That means I either pay cash & get fewer accessories or use the car dealers finance & pay a high interest rate. I asked Dad for some help in my letter to him 2 days ago. I am really not worried. I know I can get my new car even if it's a VW Karmen Ghia (Ha Ha). [Even with my 'Ha Ha" Marv believed that I was considering the VW which I was not.]

Marv, you're probably right about family at the party but I still think Janet & Vic, and Marilyn & Steve should be invited to both a relative and a friend party. Barbara & Sid should be invited to a friend party. Don't worry about being restricted I can handle them. [Our parents] Also, I'll bet most of my "friends" won't be able to make it as New Year's eve is a time when a lot of people like to go out. Lou & Eve already said they will come and are leaving their New Years open so at least they will be there. As for Rick Brower, his wife just moved and he doesn't know his new address yet but I'll let you know when he does. As far as Tom Nelson, he's on R&R right now. I'll try to remember to give you their names & addresses in my next letter.

As for the best time to invite people to a New Years party, its right now or at the end of this month.. How do you intend to invite the people? Are you going to call or send invitations by mail? If you call you should call now and then confirm again about a week before the party. (Don't tell the people you're going to call again or they'll think they can change their minds easily). I may sound worried but I just am trying to give suggestions to make the party a success.

Here's a list of the people & addresses & phone # I would like at the party. (Revised list)

Lou & Eve Berg, 377 - - - - -
Tom (& wife) Dixon, 234 - - - - - - -
Ray Kiernan, 209 - - - - - - -
Jeff Segal (He's in Army but may get off New Year's eve), 1259 - - -
Don Wecht, 211 - - - - -
Rick Brower & wife (address to be sent)
Thomas Nelson   ("   "   ")
Dennis Spring, 9101 - - - -
Janet & Vic - Marilyn & Steve -
Barbara & Sid 983 - - - - - -

On second thought I'll leave it up to you on inviting Barbara & Sid to a friend party. As long as they get invited to one party that should be good. They have written me as much as you or Dad & Mom, or other members of the family.

Also, I will be personally bringing between 1 & 3 girls to the party. Probably just one.

That's it for now. Keep smiling & having fun cause I'll be home to join you soon & we'll show the world what the Kalachman brothers can do.

Your looking forward to

64

Not a word about the Nam. You can tell I'm getting short and for now it's all about coming home and the party. However, life in the Army and Nam is subject to changes even for short timers.

SVA on our base

CHAPTER 16 – Tape at Eleven

As noted Art had a cassette recorder. Art & I sent a tape to his parents, which they graciously shared, with my family. They in turn sent us a tape, which we listened to together.

Buying my own cassette recorder would enable me to send home tapes to my family and receive one from them. It was a great way to communicate. Hearing all their voices really lifted my morale. It also allowed them hear the sound of my voice.

We did have electricity in our hooch but even that was not without incident. Frenchy, our electrician, was asked about connecting our bunker, which he graciously did. However, it only had a bulb socket. I needed an outlet for my recorder and Frenchy was in a cast as he had been knocked off a pole by a shock and broken his wrist. He was lucky to be alive. I decided to try to install the outlet myself, after all how difficult could it be? I had done this before in the world. Of course that was a 120 line that I could pull the fuse out before working. This was a 240 line with no off switch. However, I was feeling pretty confident. I found out why Frenchy had warned us about trying to do anything ourselves. Both wires accidentally touched and the resulting shock knocked me clean off the chair I was standing on. That hurt! I wound up with a black mark and hole on my thumb where I had accidentally touched the wire. Frenchy came and saved the day by installing that outlet.

Finally at the eleventh hour or actually the eleventh month of the year, November, I was able to send home my first tape. It covered the last week or so of October 1968. For some reason, I decided I had to fill up both sides of the tape before sending it home. Fortunately you'll only see excerpts.

Note that for clarity and brevity, I have made cuts and continued to make comments indicated by brackets […] in the body of the tape instead of at the end as done for most of my letters.

As mentioned before, the only thing that stays in the same in the Army is change! Another one came at the end of October.

Some of my letters in this period were typed on that portable typewriter, which typed in script. It is the same typewriter used for a few earlier letters. Those letters that are more legible and are presented as written.

300

20 Oct 68

Dear Dad, Mom, Marv -

Finally I got something I wanted from the PX. There was a PX representative here at Nancy today & I bought a Cassette recorder. It's a SANYO model MR400. It cost $48.50. I don't know if I saved on it or not but now I have my own recorder. The cassette is a cartridge the same as the one I sent the Bergs. I'd send you a tape if I could fill it & thought you could get to use a cassette. The Semmigs have one they would gladly let you use, and the U.S.O. somehow makes them available. The main reason I got this is to use in my car & away from home for music. I imagine the Semmigs would let you use theirs if you went over to their place. Actually I will only be writing another 6 weeks before it's too late to write. In that time I may send one tape. The recorder works on batteries or electric.

Got your letter of 11 Oct 68. By the way have you heard the tape I've sent the Bergs & Semmigs yet? They said they would take it to you (that's the tape Art & I made on his cassette recorder early this week).

Boy, Mike is really doing OK with two cars & all. An Olds 98 costs almost as much as a Caddy. Speaking of cars I'm still waiting for the price lists from Ziegler. I probably won't be able to get delivery till late January or February by the time I get their brochures and get a down payment in. I always think I could write a book but often fall short of even a short story when I sit down to write. [Dad had asked if I sometimes forget what I wanted to write.]

301

*The monsoons aren't quite so bad when you
have a watertight bunker to stay in. I can almost
bear it for the next 63 days (or actually I'll be
leaving LZ Nancy on 15 December to start clearing
at An Khe)*
That's all for now.

*Love from Nam
Howard*

62

Mike was my father's favorite cousin and a great guy. He and his wife, who were Nazi concentration camp survivors, owned a butcher shop in Newark. Unfortunately some years after my return from the Nam, he was brutally murdered when he surprised thugs who were robbing his store. My Dad was devastated by this senseless loss, especially for one who had lived through and survived a brutal Nazi concentration camp. I don't believe that crime was ever solved. Hope those thugs rot in hell.

Dear Mom, Pop, Marv -
*Here's the tape I said I'd send. If you haven't got a
friend with a cassette, you can call Arts parents & use
theirs.*

*Mr. & Mrs. Art & Barbara
Semmig   (Lou's In-Laws)*
61...........
L........
Phone # 516-5.....
Mr. Semmig just retired so they should be home.

The tape covered Oct 23rd thru Oct 25th.
Here are some excerpts:

Tape of 11-1-68
Side 1
DAY1 (OCT 23, '68)

Mom, Dad, Marv, and anybody else who's there. Here I am talking to you from the heart of the Paris of the Orient in the tropics.

Well I wrote you that I'd purchased this cassette recorder and sooner or later you were going to get a tape. Well this tape may take me several days to make but I'm going to try to fill it up before I send it. Today is the 23rd of October; puts me down to 59 days. I'm beginning to think more & more about home. I really just can't wait till I get home. I got a lot of things on my mind .. to take care of when I get home, the most important of which is school.

On that matter I'd like to talk to Marv. If you're around Marv, listen up. *[Several paragraphs about cars and the vacation I want to take with my brother were left out. It ended with...]* They really screwed me up from this bank by telling me they won't give me a loan because I'm in the Army. That's what I call Patriotism. I've grown to accept being a second-class citizen while you're in the Army.

By the way, you know what happened? It was pretty funny. Today I got my DEROS orders, no not my ETS orders. It seems they cut the orders down at orders branch and the cut the orders for me to DEROS on 6 November. Of course they're not worth the paper they're made on because on my record, it says 22 December. But leave it to division to screw things up. I have a better description but that's only among Army people. *[...]*

I've been working a little today trying to straighten out things. We put up a shower. We didn't finish it. It'll be nice not having to go all the way down to the shower point to get a shower. *[Even through we had civilians working on the base, including females, we usually ignored them, walking to the shower point wearing only our birthday suits and a towel over our shoulders.]* We're going to get an immersion heater so we'll be able to heat the water. I might possibly get 1 or 2 more warm showers before I leave this place. A warm shower – boy lately with the monsoons, the showers have been frozen. The water is in a big black tank. During the day, usually, in Vietnam it get pretty warm. You go to the shower point about 5:00 you can actually get a hot shower. But with monsoons of course the sun's not shining and the rain is cold. You go for a shower at 5:30, 6:00 boy, wow it is cold! After a couple of days you just can't take it anymore and you got to get a shower no matter how cold it is. *[When it was not monsoon season we often had droughts with resultant water shortages. When that happened a shower was only possible when it rained. If you never took a shower in the tropical rains, let me tell you it hurts!]*

[More about Human factors engineering and the cassette recorder] Arty Semmig had his *[recorder]* here a couple of weeks ago and we made a tape. I guess you've heard that one by now. The Semmigs said they would take it over to your house (I believe I wrote you about that) and let you hear it. I thought that was very nice of them. They're very sweet people. They just feel like family to me. It's just like I knew them all my life. Same, same with Lou & Eve. They've been great to me and especially like over here in the Nam, I get letters from Eve and packages. It's just nice to know that your friends remember you. [...].

Well Dad, how are you doing in work and everything? How's your health? I hope you're feeling O.K., and the car hasn't been giving you too much trouble lately. I haven't done a lesson in that USAFI course in so long. The next time I do a lesson (I'll probably do one more in Nam), I'm going to ask them for an extension of 6 months so I can finish the course at home. But I just haven't had the urge to do it anymore the last couple of months. For a while I was very busy and I couldn't do it, but now that I got my replacement I actually could do it. Trying to train him for most of the new stuff. But it won't be like that for the rest of the tour because he's beginning to learn. As he learns, I start splitting the work more evenly with him. He's a real good head and I'm sure he'll make it in the S-1 shop. I've already had him promoted once to Specialist 4 and before I go I'm going to recommend to the sergeant that he be promoted again to Spec 5. But, I don't know how far that will go because I really don't have that much say. I can just make recommendations. I mean for a while I did have the say while I was acting in a supervisory capacity *[as an Acting Jack mentioned earlier]*, while the supervisor was in Ah Khe.

There are a couple of guys who were wounded and I think there were 2 guys who were killed in an accident out on Davis hill. Which is the forward LZ from here. That's where the battalion is, in other words the fighting men. They were bringing in a bubble, which is a chopper like the news chopper with the glass front; (they call it a bubble here). It's used for observation. It seems that as they were bringing it in the tail rotor caught a tree. The tail rotor on a chopper controls stability, and as soon as it caught the tree it flipped the chopper. The rotor caught one of the lieutenants in the back of the head, one of the other guys was killed and several guys hurt. That was a pretty big mess so we got to have an investigation to find out what happened. That's all this year has been is a bunch of investigations, and sympathy letters, and reports, and more reports. I really see what they mean about this Army being, wow, screwed up! You know, they say there's the right way, the wrong way, and the Army way; and boy they mean it. The Army way tends to lean towards the wrong way. As a taxpayer, which I'm not this year, but as a taxpayer quote, unquote, I can see that there's a lot of room for improvement in Uncle Sam's Army. The waste factor is completely ridiculous, and when you do need supplies, such as a typewriter, it's absolutely impossible to get, unless, of course you happen to have an AK-47 or an SKS, which are gook weapons. Then you can get one, no sweat!

Well looking over the mail situation. The last couple of days I haven't gotten much. They've come up with one good idea. It's one of the first really good ideas I've seen this Army come up with yet. They have large plastic bags and they're putting them inside the mailbags and putting the mail inside of them so that the mail stays dry during this monsoon. The monsoon should last until early... well the heavy rains should last till December. Then, starting in December, they'll start tapering off till March when they stop. Actually it'll be May before it really stops completely. But March it stops pretty much. So, I can expect these last 59 days to be pretty wet. We've had 2 days of sunshine now, which is almost a record. Actually the way the monsoons work is that every so often you will get 2 or 3 days of sunshine. It's not constant rain day after day. It may rain for 7 or 8 days, maybe longer but sooner or later you're bound to get some sunshine. It's nice to know the sky's still up there and there's still some blue up there.

Getting back to what I was talking about; mail. As I said, well gee, this month I haven't had very much mail. But I'm missing it less & less. [...] I'm really excited about getting a new car, at least the prospects. With this bank I don't know what's happening. I want to save at least a thousand dollars, mainly because I'll need it for school and for other reasons. I figure I'll be back [*at my old job*] about 6 months to collect my profit sharing. After that I'll see what happens. If they give me a good job, such as an adjustor I'll stay with them. If they try to keep me in that same clerical department, well it's going to be bye-bye Allstate, and hello to whoever gives me a better job.

Of course my main goal is going to be to get that degree. I am really hot on getting that now, and the subjects really intrigue me. I think I've always been interested in it but I didn't realize my own interest. If you remember I was interested when I was kid in psychology and then I was interested for a while in automotive engineering. .. off takes of that field. I didn't know what the field is that I was interested in. Now I know. *[or so I thought].*

In that letter from Vic, he tells me that Janet's going to be a model. I always said I have the best looking sisters around and I guess that's sort of proves it. Now, she's probably going to be discovered and they'll make her a movie star, and I'll come home and I'll have to make an appointment to see her. No, I guess it won't get that bad. I know she's very good-looking woman, both my sisters are. I'm glad to say. I don't know what my excuse is. I guess I have none (Laugh).

I keep going off on tangents. It seems that I can't stay on the same subject for 4 minutes [...]

I'm going to have a lot to do as far as learning how to drive when I get back because over here, the top speed limit is 20 MPH. You got to stay with that. I won't say I'm an angel as far as that goes because I know I've done 30 & 40. But, most of the time I try to stay within the speed limit. [...]

Talking about driving, the jeep is a very good vehicle and it can go thru anything but an Army jeep with Army tires on it, boy let me tell you the brakes are just about worthless. When you first get the jeep they're O.K. but the tires are meant for military and they're meant to last. They're not built for traction at all. Boy I tell you, if you depend solely on the tires to stop you when you're in 3rd or 4th

gear, you can hang it up. **That incident I had with that little Vietnamese girl is just a case in point.** I had shifted down to second at that time, no, wait a minute I had it in 3rd. I was going pretty slowly. I was going about 15, which is what you're supposed to be going when you go thru a village. When I saw her I hit the break immediately. It's funny that in an emergency I reverted back to automatic, not thinking to downshift into 2nd. I had to stop too fast anyway; I don't think downshifting would have helped. But slamming on the brakes, I just kept on going. Skidded all the way down and just about made contact with her. She pushed herself off, as I told you, and fell down. Scared me good, boy let me tell you. Fortunately she was O.K. and I didn't have to fill out an accident report. I'm glad because I don't want that on my record. Had that been a vehicle in the world, it would have been no sweat stopping. You step on the brakes and the tires would have grabbed the road. Especially at 15 MPH. You know for a fact that you can step on your brakes at 30 MPH and practically stop on a dime. Not so with a jeep.

I tell you if I had an opportunity to get a surplus jeep in the world, I wouldn't mind getting it . Then, of course, putting civilian tires on it, making a few minor changes on it and I think it would really be a nice little car for hunting and things.

By the way my buddy Bob, my other bunkmate, just walked in and he said Hi, […] Bob is one of the guys I've known for quite a while, since February. He and a couple of us are planning a reunion in Chicago in August of next year. We should all be home at that time and one of the fellas here, Ron, who lives in Chicago, has offered to let us use his home for the reunion. We've all agreed and we got the date written down somewhere. I don't recall what it is. I think it's the 8th of August. […] Bob and [..]Scott are planning to travel all over the states. […] I told him if he comes to New York, I'll show him around New York, both him and Scott and fix them up with a few female types. I'm sure I can spare a few. *[Neither event ever happened and, as often happens, we lost track of each other.]*

As far as female types go I've met one girl here in Da Nang. She's an entertainer, a go-go dancer and singer with a group here. She's a very nice girl. I've also, in a sense met 2 girls thru the chaplain. He gave me the names as pen pals. I've been writing one of then since I think about March or April. The other one only recently, I think in July, I started writing her. I've got a picture of one of them. She's in New Jersey. The other one is in Brooklyn, New York. I haven't got a picture of her yet but she's sending one. So the situation looks good from this end. I never did get a letter from Nancy but that's O.K. She lost her big opportunity in life and she's just going to have to live with it. (Laugh). Seriously, it doesn't bother me at all that she chose not to write. Quite a few people are writing me.

I appreciate the writing. The most letters of course I get from you [...]down to people who write once in a while when they think of me. But I don't really expect that much. I guess a lot of people don't like to write letters, are just too lazy, or whatever, or maybe they don't think they write well. Not that I'd ever evaluate letters. It's the thought that counts! I haven't had a letter yet that I didn't think was well written. *[...]*

Maybe I can get this tape out in 3 days. I don't know. Possibly if I get a letter from you tomorrow it'll give me some more material. I'm hoping you can get a recorder to listen to this and also possibly to send me back a tape. Although I don't know when you'll get this and I would imagine you best mail it at least by the first of December, if I'm going to get it in time. ... It would be nice to hear everybody's voice and possibly even Marilyn & Steve and Janet & Vic. Give them all my regards, by the way, if they don't get a chance to listen to this tape with you.

Say Marv, I got something more for you. I don't know if you've taken your physical or not yet but there's [...] Standard Form 89 report of medical history. It s a form with about a million things to check on it. If you haven't taken your test yet, I've filled one out. Some of the things you could think about, ... I have a few things checked off and little notes next to them why I think you should say that. I'll send you this next time I write you so, you can keep it around and if you ever go down for the physical read this and you'll get an idea of some of the things you can write. Plus this isn't, you know, the bible. You make your own decision on what you want to say. Just remember you got to be able to explain everything you say "yes" to [...] They also have things like hay fever, which you have, [...] things like that, you know? It might help to get you out. Can't promise you anything. *[My brother could not stop me from ranting about these things even though he had no intention of following my*

308

suggestions.] I don't think the Army will take you anyway on your eyesight, at least they better not or I'm liable to start buying Russian war bonds. The Army really isn't really that bad if you don't have to come over here. I would say the worst part about Nam is missing home and some of the hardships that you have to put up with. The main thing I don't like about the army is that there's too many dam bosses around and everybody wants to tell you what to do. I've sort of been able to make it through the year without too much problem. I mean I've have had no serious incident.

Side 2
DAY 1 continues (OCT 23, '68)

Well, how are you Mom?

How's things going with your job, I guess you're still working with the sisters.

I've been getting everybody's mail. I like reading all your letters. Of course pretty soon I'll be able to talk to you and that'll be even better. Well, I'm talking to you now, but I mean face to face. I just can't wait for that day. The closer it gets the more home sick I get. I've made it all through the year without thinking too much about home because that's what makes you homesick but now, as time gets closer, I think more & more about home and how it was and how I think it will be. I hope I haven't changed too much; that's one of the things that's been bugging me. How much I've changed and things I'm going to do that might not be acceptable at home that are acceptable here in nam. I made it O.K. while I was on R&R I think I should be able to readjust myself to living as a human being without too much problem at least I hope so. I think one of my biggest problems is that every time I get excited I'm liable to start using four letter words. I just hope everyone will just turn around and pretend they don't hear. The army sure has given me a beautiful vocabulary.

Well I'm going to close down for tonight. This is spotter one out – Break.

DAY 2 (OCT 24, '68)

Hello again this is your favorite son, or maybe not your favorite, Howard. Remember me? I'm the guy who's in Vietnam

Today is the 24th of October and I'm down to 58.

309

Well in the mail today, as I thought, I got a letter from you and you want to hear a great surprise? I got a letter from the Law office of King & Sobel. Yes, that's right, Uncle Sol wrote me! It's a type written letter and he goes on so & so, so & so, and he even invited me to his office [*Uncle sol just wrote me one time. There were some issues between him and my Dad since the death of my grandmother years earlier. Fortunately they were resolved before his untimely demise from lung cancer. Although the youngest of my Dad's siblings, he was a three pack a day smoker and the first to die.*]

The day started off fine today. I had some toothache last night, [...] So this morning I went on sick call and they sent me down to 15th med, which is the main medical facility here at LZ Nancy, and they had a dentist there. He [...] filled a nice sized cavity. I asked him if I could get a complete check up but he said they're not equipped for that here, so possibly when I go in for ETS I'll get that done. Might as well let the Army do as much as they can before I leave. But, I did get a little silver out of this mornings deal, all free.

I had another surprise this morning right after I got back from the dentist. I was working on the hooch putting some sandbags around it when the guys called me and told me I had a phone call and it was a girl. Of course I though he was kidding I haven't had a phone call from a female type since I've been in Vietnam. The only female type I could think of was Sandy; the girl I met down in Da Nang who's here with a group entertaining the guys. I said, "Nah, what would she be doing up here?" So I went to the phone and it was dead. I figured they were just pulling my leg. I decided to go back and then said to myself, "I might as well check". I went over to the operator, we call spotter switch, and asked him. He said sure enough there was a female and why don't I try to call her back. The call came thru Silver, which is the brigade's call sign.

Sorry I just got interrupted to go up to a meeting of the unit, the S-1. We just had our nightly bull session and I found out there we're going to have movies here.

Getting back, to Sandy. Sure enough I was just about to get on the phone when she calls me back. It seems that her plane had to put down at Evans, on her way to Quang Tri. She told me this and said she's going to be at the airfield. I went over to Evans this afternoon in a jeep. I went looking for her but I couldn't find her. I thought it was real nice for her to call me. **For a while I was the most popular man on LZ Nancy having a female type call me. She's a good looking female too I'll show you a picture when I get home.** *[She was beautiful and made me very popular on the base!]*

What I just found out is that possibly in the next few days they're going to start having movies at the chapel every other day and I might possibly be able to go up there every day, that is every other day.

I got your letter today Dad, [...]. You asked me how I managed to get a clerk job. Well, see my 201 file, which is the main file you have in the army, was loused up. They didn't put down on it that I was working as a clerk and where it's got college degree, he wrote that I have a degree in Engineering instead of a degree in Business. [...]

Marilyn wrote me about getting a new job. Boy that's really great for her. That's a nice size increase and she'll be working with a friend. Gee she'll be making more money than I'm making but I suppose it'll only be temporary. At least I hope so. Not that I don't want you to get raises but I'd like to see myself making in the neighborhood of $200 *[add a zero at the end for today's dollars.]* at least at the beginning once I get my degree But of course as far as that is concerned that could probably be a long way off.

Well this tape recorder really works pretty good. I've been playing it back from time to time to find my place, and change certain thing I say that I don't think I should say and all that good stuff.[...]

I only have 50 days left in this hole before going to the rear area to clear. Another 50 days of this garbage over here and I'll be through with it. I think I can put up with it for that length of time. It's not really that big a thing.

Boy when I came in today I figured I was gonna finish this tape today, but I'm out of things to say right now. Maybe in a few more days and ah. I want to get this tape out tomorrow whether or not I finish it. I don't want to keep this too long a period of time. I had thought I'd get a letter from you today and I did so that helped a little bit.

311

This recorder has a hand mike with a remote control switch and that's the click you keep hearing every few minutes.. I'll turn it off to form my words and turn it on again and say what I thought of.

If you'd like to make a tape to send to me I would very much appreciate it and I'd like to hear everybody's voice but don't feel obligated to fill the tape. I mean just say what you want to say and send it out. I'll be happy to hear your voice whether it's for ten minutes, 5 minutes, half an hour or a full hour tape. If you don't get an opportunity to make a tape don't feel too badly. It will be only something like 58 days before I'll see you again and we'll be able to talk face to face; which I'm sure you're looking forward to as much as I am.

By the way, I don't know if I mentioned it or not but they're changing the money here. They're changing the series. It seems like a lot of the gooks are getting our money. You're not supposed to give the gooks MPC, which is Military Payment Certificates. It's the play money that we have over here, that's what it looks like anyway. Instead we're supposed to use Pia, which is Vietnamese money. You can get it exchanged on base at the piaster exchange office but a lot of guys give the gooks ten dollar bills because they can get about fourteen dollars worth of stuff for it because they're used for the black market. Well the Army pulled a fast one. About 3 days ago they pulled in all the money and today they issued new money and a new series. The colors are different and everything. So old Charlie got stuck with a lot of money he can't use. Sorry about that Charlie.

[…]Lou & Eve have already invited me over for Christmas Eve to come over the house. That'll probably be the day after I get home[…] they are my best friends.

Well … I'll answer Sol's letter and I want to write Sandy to tell her I'm sorry I missed her in Evans and possibly while I'm doing that I'll think of something to say. But, if not, I'll sign off and pick it up tomorrow night. I won't use any call signs right now like I did last night with Break and all that stuff. I figure I do that to confuse ya (Ha) I'm a meanie.

I'm wondering just how well my voice came out when I called you on MARS a couple of times. If I do get to Da Nang again I'll try and call you again on the MARS station but I won't know about getting there for a while. I don't know if they're going to stop me from going. See the S-1 said he wasn't going to let me go because I had gone on the Jewish holidays and I don't know whether or not he was kidding. It's hard to make him out and the only way I can find out is ask. But, as I told you before, the first sergeant said I could go. The S-1 will be leaving in about ten days and we'll have a new S-1 so I can get around that pretty easy.

Till tomorrow night, good night and see you. Write soon.

DAY 3 (Oct 25 '68)

Hello again, this is Specialist 5 Howard Kalachman speaking, sir. Yes, it's your son Howard Kalachman after another day in Vietnam. Down to 57 days today and they're moving along a little slower but they're still moving.

It started raining again today and the weather has turned a little bit colder. Cold for Vietnam is about 70°.[…]

Picked up the newspaper today and all I read about are the strikes in New York[…]

You know I've been wondering, about veteran's benefits. When you return to your previous job, which you're guaranteed plus all raises which you would have gotten had you stayed in the job […] The way I read it, it seems that I should get all my raises. But, I'll see what happens with the company. If I find they're screwing me, I won't stay longer than the 6 months necessary to collect my profit sharing. […] I'll meet that bridge when I, or I'll cross that bridge when I come to it.

I went over to see Arty today. He's pulling K.P. […] at least he doesn't have to pull guard duty in the rain.

I don't know what it is with the mail situation over here. Maybe it is that I haven't been writing enough to get answers to my letters but lately, the last 3 or 4 months, the mail I've been getting is less in volume then when I first got into Nam and the first 7 months. Of Course, right now it doesn't bother me that much.[…]

One of the fellas I work with is Ron Duda. He's over here now and he's going to say a few words to you. He says he's a sergeant but don't you believe him, he's just an acting jack.

"Mr. & Mrs. Kalachman, as Howie had mentioned my name is Ron Duda […] I have worked with Howie for quite a few months. I must say they haven't been the most enjoyable primarily because of the fact that Vietnam is not a very enjoyable place to be working […]. Actually Howie has made our situation here in the Nam much

313

more enjoyable then it might be otherwise. I'd like to mention one thing, that I do look forward to seeing Howie once he gets out [...] It really would be a shame if he would miss this, what we call, a reunion at my house in Chicago. Well I don't want to take too much more tape of your son's so I'll sign off now [...]."

This has been a paid political announcement. (laugh) Well at least you see I have one friend who's not afraid to talk, unlike the others who were asked. I'm sure if Arty were here he'd be glad to say a few words, but he's probably sleeping by now. K.P. takes a lot out of you.

Speaking of Arty, I asked him about packages and he says you could send him anything. He's not particular. I don't know if he gets heat tabs so for a while I'd just stick to stuff that doesn't have to be cooked. [...]

Well now that you really haven't got that much responsibilities at home, Mom & Pop, I hope you're getting out a little more often. Whether to a show or movie or even just out to dinner, I think you deserve it. I sure hope you're getting some fun out of life now.[...]

The mosquito problem here is pretty bad. We all sleep under nets. That's battalion policy. Matter of fact, you can get an article 15 if you are caught not sleeping under a net. You better have a good excuse if you are caught. One fellow who's our battalion courier, caught Malaria. I don't know where he got it, whether he got it here at this location, or at An Khe, or somewhere in transit. All I know is we sent him about a week ago, down to An Khe. He never got there. We were told that he had Malaria, and they took him to some air force hospital. He began showing symptoms in the airport. But it usually takes several days for symptoms to develop. [...] There are several strains. We take Malaria pills. Well they have big pills, which we have a very descriptive name for, and we take those once a week. Then we have little pills, which we call "Birth Control Pills" because they're suppose to have some effect on birth control as a matter of fact. We take those every day and together they're supposed to fight all types of Malaria, or at least prevent them.

Well I'm about out of words again and I was going to send this tape out today but I think I'll hold on just one more day. I've only got about another 10 minutes of tape left and I can possibly fill

314

that up tomorrow. Until then I'll say good night for now and I'll pick it up again tomorrow morning. Good night!

By the way just in case you're keeping track, today is the 25th of October.

DAY 4 (Oct 26, '68)

Hello Mom, Pop, Marv and anybody else who's at home. Well here I am again. I'll try and finish up this tape today. I mean I'm sending it out whether or not I finish it up. Today is the 26th of October and I'm down to five-six days. That's right fifty-six. That means I have between 40 & 52 days left here at LZ Nancy.

Well again today I got no mail so I haven't got that much new to say. […]

I was thinking a lot today about coming home, the plane trip home, and what airline I'm going to take and all that. I don't know how long it's going to take me when I get there for ETS processing. ETS means Estimated Time of Service and that's the time you get out of the Army. When you come out of Vietnam and go to Fort Lewis you can have a steak dinner if you want. But I'm going to try to get out of there as soon as possible on the first available flight. Of course if I find I have a lot of time I'll take the steak dinner but I'm sure I can have plenty of better steak dinners at my own home, cooked by mom. I miss your cooking mom. Boy do I miss it! The food here is terrible. Can't expect much in a combat zone though. It's enough to survive on.

Well it looks like I finally did it. I reached the end of the tape so I'll say good-bye to everybody. Good-bye to Dad, and Good-bye Mom, good-bye Marv. I probably won't be sending you another tape. Be sure to let me know when you get this one. That's the date you receive this one. Since it's being mailed out on the 26th, it will actually go out tomorrow which is the 27th, so I can get an estimate of how many days it took & mention when I sent it out since I don't keep a record here.

By the way I forgot to mention you can use this tape to rerecord on, just record right over it and if you like that is and send it back. That's it over & out, etc etc. *[Fortunately they did not use the tape to rerecord but they did send me back a tape. More on that later]*

315

29 Oct 68

Dear Mom, Dad, Marv -

Guess what - remember I told you that the Adjutant said that we'd be at LZ Nancy forever or there abouts? Well right now I'm on the U.S.S. Point Defiance on my way to Saigon where we will disembark and move by vehicle to the Cambodian border or within approx 3.5 miles of the border. The move was a real quickie, that's why I didn't get a chance to write sooner. We got about 24 hours notice (from the time I first heard the rumor to the time we were packed and moving). The adjutant said we were getting too comfortable and that's against Cav policy.

I haven't been able to receive mail in two days now & won't until this move is completed in a week or ten days. I probably won't be writing again before that time.

I told Art before I left & he promised to write & tell his parents & Lou & Eve. He doesn't know if he'll remain with us or not. I kind of doubt it.

This may be the only letter I get to write so tell Janet & Vic, Marilyn & Steve, & anyone else who asks. No, my address will not change, it will remain the same.

What do I think of the move? I liked it at LZ Nancy and the area we are going into is more active, but I am enjoying this short stay with the Navy. Boy- I really hurt when I remember my saying No to that Navy NCO who called our house & asked me to join the reserves after I passed the tests. They have bunks with mattresses, good chow, hot water & showers etc, etc.

316

Some of the guys asked me if I'm sorry I extended now since if I hadn't I'd have been able to go in two days. Well it's still worth it. I figure by the time we get set up, I'll only have 3-4 weeks left in the field (that's what we call the forward LZ). I've gotten this tour of Navy life & I'll get to see Saigon. Of course going into a new area I'm always apprehensive since I don't know what to expect. We may be lucky enough to get an LZ with barracks & bunkers already build but knowing the Cav, I tend to doubt it.

There's a lot more I want to tell you. I'll do it when I get set up at my new location. Have you heard anything on the move of the Cav over the news?

Did you get the tape I sent you? I may send you another short tape after I get set up - if I have enough to fill it at least on one side.

That's all for now. See you soon.

Love from Nam
Howard

THE ARMY STINKS
53

Half my unit moved south by air and the other half, my half, by ship and convoy. The ship I was on was an LSD, which we thought was funny as it was the letters of a hard-core psychotropic drug. We joked about the alternate reality of the Army. In the Navy, LSD stood for Landing Ship Dock, which were used for transport of men and equipment.

As indicated in this letter, that few days on a ship were great. We even had fresh milk and real ice cream just like the Air Force!

Before boarding, we had to wait on a loading dock filled with acres of supplies. My unit re-appropriated many cases of Beer. Every spare inch of every duffle bag was filled with cans of that beer. However when we disembarked from that ship, they had mysteriously disappeared from our duffels (no doubt into the many hiding places on that LSD). Easy come, easy go!

That was the least of it. Sarge bribed a forklift operator, and just like that my jeep magically became brand new again. Sarge even had our I.D. numbers & letters painted over in green on the old jeep and repainted on the new jeep. Sometimes getting supplies in the Army was just a matter of opportunity and ingenuity.

This was just about the time we started writing F.T.A. on the envelopes, which stood for "Fuck The Army". Although we disguised it with either First Team Airmobile or Future Teacher's of America, every G.I. knew what it really meant. Note the double questions marks.

As an interesting aside, it was somewhat prophetic that we told officers that F.T.A. stood for future teachers of America. I had not thought of becoming a teacher at that time, however that's exactly what would happen some twenty years later.

Turns out I was worried for naught, my next base would have barracks.

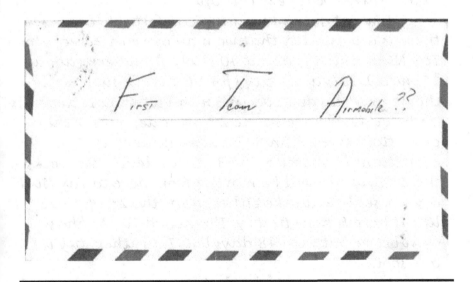

3 Nov 68

Dear Mom, Pop, Marv -

I've been at my new location for 3 days now. I'm at a base at Quan Loi, which is about 80 miles North (?) of Saigon (at least it looks North on my tactical map). This is a base of the First Infantry Division, the unit known as The Big Red One. This base is a rubber plantation - that means millions of trees & real green grass! Also, I'm living in a building!!!! In my own room yet & our S-1 shop is in the building next door. There is a PX on the post as well as an Airstrip. This place is almost like the world. It's better than An Khe.

There's suppose to be 3 divisions of gooks down here, that's why the Cav was sent here. We are not really set up yet. The way the Army works the move was pretty mixed up. We've had 3 buildings in 3 days - but I think we'll keep this one.

I'm not going to get too comfortable because there is a possibility that we may move in 2 weeks to Tay Ninh which is about 40 clicks from here (about 25 miles). It is a big city (for Vietnam), supposedly the 3rd or 4th largest city in South Vietnam. It depends on brigade. We are in the 2nd brigade, but for this operation us & 2nd Bn 8th Cav are under the operational control of the 3rd Brigade. In two weeks - the 2nd Brigade will be moving from here to Tay Ninh & supposedly will take either, us or the 2nd of the 8th. I like it here & hope to stay. I've heard Tay Ninh is even better but with 48 days left, I'd rather stay in one spot.

Mail came in today but it was only packages & newspapers. I expect I'll be getting letter mail in a day or so.

I had a good life on board the USS Point Defiance - LSD31. Those navy people really know how to live.

I have got a million things to say. Maybe when I get my footlocker from the CONEX I'll make another tape. I bought a tape at the PX today - it's a Beetle album -"Sgt Peppers Lonely Hearts Club Band Presents."

I may write Janet & Vic, & Marilyn & Steve tonight. Please keep the other people informed.

We may have the CONEX's (metal storage containers for moving equipment) here tomorrow from their present location at the motor pool. If we do it'll be several days of work setting up & catching up during which I won't be writing much.

Hope all is well at home.

Love from Nam
Howard

47 *? or is it 48?*

Still have that Beatles cassette. It, and everything else came home full of red dust…read on!

My second and last tape home was sent home on the 12th of November, 1968.

Here are excepts:

Tape of 11/68
Side 1 (Nov 9, '68)
DAY1
Well hello everyone, Mom, Dad, Marilyn, Marv, Janet, Steve, Vic, whoever else happens to be around and since I suppose

you're using the Berg's or Semmigs' recorder, hello to them also: Lou, Eve, Mom & Pop Semmig.

Well, here I am at LZ Andy in Quin Loi Vietnam, some 4 to 500 miles from my last location, LZ Nancy. I'm sitting here in my own room with an actual wood frame building which is the frame of a building with a tent flopped over it. It's got wooden floors and wooden walls, and I've got my own little room here. I got a pretty nice set up and I just hope we stay here for the next 32 days. Which is how many days I have left with the battalion. I have 42 left with the Army.

I'll tell you a little bit about the move. It was actually rather secret. It came to us with 24 hours notice. One day I was making a tape to you and then the next night the adjutant told us we're moving tomorrow. I said, "Yeah, that's nice, where to?" He said, LZ..." well this didn't have a name, "We're moving down south near Saigon". We had a lot of planning, and changes of plans and everything – typical Army. It was finally decided that I'd be going with half the group on a boat, the other half would be coming down here by plane. I lucked out by getting on the boat. We spent about a day on the docks waiting to get on the boat in the midst of the garbage and all that monsoon rain. I finally made it, we got on the boat. We laid-to, as they say, for a day. In other words we didn't move, we just stayed; the boat was anchored waiting for the rest of the ship to be loaded. We came over on an LSD, which of course is open for many jokes. Taking a trip on LSD etc etc. The Navy life is beautiful man, let me tell you. They have bunks, and hot showers, and good chow [..] The way it was cooked it has the Army beat 100%. One of my buddies here is a cook and he agrees with me, there is just no comparison. He says the Army has lousy cooks (laugh). Which is true but they also have lousy conditions to cook in. Even here where they have pretty decent buildings, we still haven't got the supply that the Navy has. I had milk every day and real ice cream and all this good stuff. I was really enjoying it. They had movies every night. I got to see 3 movies. We were on the ship for 3 nights.

Then we got on the convoy coming down here. Fortunately that'll be my last convoy. We lost 2 vehicles to mines on the convoy. Some of the vehicles were sniped at. *[including mine]*. It was a big convoy, over a hundred vehicles in it; way over a hundred vehicles!

When we got here, we started seeing about 10 miles of rubber trees. All this area, they say the whole area, about 50 miles, is a rubber plantation, one rubber plantation owned by a Frenchman who has his home here with his wife & child. I believe he has a 19-year-old daughter. At least that's what I was told. Right here on LZ Andy, which is what we now call this place. [...]

We're under the operational control of the 3rd Brigade. In other words, we're regularly 2nd Brigade. For this operation we're working with the 3rd Brigade, which is just a lot of Army gibberish. As I was saying this is a rubber plantation. There are Beau Coup trees –BEAU COUP! If we damage any of the trees we have to pay something like $700 for them.

Yesterday I saw a few gun runs by the A-R-A ship, that's the gun ships. I think they might have damaged a few trees. I just hope that isn't going to be tax money.

At any rate, this base is pretty nice. It's got a PX on it and clubs. The clubs aren't opened yet. But the clubs [...] used to be French chateaus [..] given to the Army possibly by this Frenchman. There are other civilians on post also. It's got it's own airstrip so when I go home, I just fly from here to An Khe. Then from An Khe, (I'll clear there) I'll go to Cam Rahn Bay and get my flight to the states [...]. Probably to Seattle, Washington, where I'll clear the Army [...].

I haven't written much lately since I've been here. I think you noted that Dad, in your letter but it's not that I've been really busy. Although for a while I was, now I'm not as busy as I was before because I have this replacement. I guess I'm getting lazy as far as writing letters.

This will be the last tape I'll send home. In the next month I'll be writing letters though. Of course I expect to get letters also. As far as the last day for writing letters to me, it's hard to say because lately the letters have been taking about 8 days. But I want to give it a couple of extra days. Now, if I don't get orders for ETS, I go in a few days early. So, that means I'd probably be leaving here the 12th and maybe the 11th. I'd say after about the 1st or 2nd don't send any mail. You can tell me whatever you want after that, it's just be 2 weeks or so until I get home. Maybe three weeks. The 22nd I'll be getting back to Washington. I should be home by the 23rd, the 24th at the latest but I expect the 23rd. [Confusing isn't it?]

Let me get back to the base a little bit. **The main problem here is red dust.** Boy it is bad. Usually, you're in the Army over here in a combat zone you don't worry about clothes too much. But, over here you got to change just about every 2 days because that dust gets all over you. It gets all over my work. I've had to do beaucoup of my typing over, and my replacement also has been doing his work over because you can't keep dust prints off it. You get it on your hands. It is really difficult working conditions.

They have a MARS station on post. I possibly will use it, possibly even before I send this tape. *[...]*. I'm not going to keep it till I fill it like I did last time because that will take too long. I'm just going to put as much as I can on it and then send it out.

I finally started getting some mail. I got about 5 letters from you. Let's see if there's anything that requires reply.

Mom, you keep telling me that I'm handsome and all this good stuff. Thanks a lot, it's very good for my morale and all that good stuff. I look at my mirror every day and say, "Mirror, mirror on the wall who's the fairest of them all?" and it laughs. I wonder if it's trying to tell me something. Seriously Mom, you said you're funny. The only way you're funny is that it's funny that you think you're not beautiful because when I had the picture of you and I showed it to my buddies, I swear, they actually thought that you were my girl! They asked, "Is that your girl?"

I said, "No, it's my Mother", and they said, "Ah come on".

I said, "Yeah, it's my mother",

"Really?"

"Yeah",

"She looks very young." You know the whole bit. So that should put an end to that thought.

No, I didn't make a mistake about the sex of my dog. The 2 puppies I have in the picture are not, I repeat, not offspring of Jack. As far as Jack goes he's not with us anymore. He *[...]* was left back at Nancy. He use to run off to a different battalion. Some other battalion probably adopted him.

I'm glad all the papers I sent you are O.K. As far as that Bronze Star Award, let me get this squared away right away. I didn't

323

do anything great to deserve this award. It's just an award for putting in a year of good service in Vietnam. There's two classes of awards and this is the higher class of award. There's an Army Commendation Medal and there's a Bronze Star. I got the Bronze Star. As long as you stay squared away, you don't get any article 15s, you don't get into any trouble, and you do your job, you'll get one of these if you don't get a valor award. This is just an award for service rendered. The certificate that goes with it says it's a service award, that's all it is. I'll probably tell war stories about it when I get home. It'll sound better. But, for my own family this is what its for. [*Did you believe that? Isn't the good conduct medal the one you get for good service? Was I convincing? Was I truthful?*]

Oh, by the way Dad, in the pictures that came in see if there's a picture of me and two other guys in full combat uniform, trying to look real tough. That is Howie's Raiders, in case you were wondering. The guys are wondering if that came out, because I was going to send them copies of it if it did.

I got the East Village paper and mags that Marv sent. That's a pretty groovy paper. Not exactly what I though it was. I just wanted to see what it was like. I've seen a paper called The Los Angeles Free Press which is a bit more interesting paper. I just wanted to see if this was going to be the same thing. It's not. So, now I've seen it, that's it.

Hey Marv, *[…]* I came across these ads for Florida. *[…]*. One of the places I wrote to was the place that Janet went, the Castaways. One of my buddies here lived in Florida for 2 years and he said that's a swinging place. We'll check into that. That might be a good place to stay and if not it's always a good place to visit. They have something called a wreck bar, which I believe is a nightclub.

With all the mail Marv, I got your letter of 21 October. I'm glad you had a good time for your birthday and we'll have a few more drinks to celebrate your birthday when I get home. We'll celebrate a few other things also.

[More rhetoric about cars]

Marv you asked for a good story you could tell your friends about how I got my Bronze Star. O.K. here it goes. There I was alone in the CP *[Command Post]* after everybody had been wounded and there's nobody around. So, I took a bunch of ammo, took the radio on my back, and ran down to get help disregarding the incoming rounds. If this sounds good it's because I wrote about 600 awards back in January and I know how to do it. [...] Leave the B.S. stories till I get home and I'll figure one out by then. O.K.? Till then you could just tell them, you don't know what he did. All you know is that he was supposed to get a Medal of Honor but it was downgraded. (Laughing).

Thanks for the offer to pick me up in Seattle, Marv. But, I don't think you have to drive quite that far. LZ Kennedy would be far enough. I will by all means let you know my flight info.

Dad, you're always saying you wish you were a good letter writer. Personally, I've been getting letters from, I'd say from about 20 different sources. I consider myself something of an expert on letter writing and I consider you a very good letter writer. You keep your letters interesting and they keep me interested in them, which is the main thing. I look forward to all your letters. That goes for everybody from home. Janet's always worried about the same thing, that she doesn't know how to write a letter and she does. She writes very well. I want to get this across to all of you.

I got a letter the other day also from Mel *[my favorite cousin]*. It was the 3rd letter he's written me. Of course he made the usual excuses, which I understand. I know a lot of people just don't like to write letters. I told my buddies over here that I'm not promising any of them that I'll write them because I don't know what's going to happen when I get home. That way at least I haven't promised them. Chances are I will write anyway. I know I'll be writing Art. I'll see what happens as far as writing my buddies. Getting back to Mel, he's got a fireman's attitude, the police are wrong in what they want but the fireman are right. I sort of kidded him a little about that; humored him along.

I haven't read too much about the crisis that has been going on, exactly who's involved, and the issues. Although I think the issue is racism in the school, it also has something to do with the unions and I haven't quite got that straitened out. I figure once I get home I can catch up on the news and what's happening.

I want to say to Vic and Steve; I want to wish them both a happy birthday. Excuse me for not remembering but you know how it is over here in the Nam. There's a lot of things on your mind. But, at any rate, the wish is still there. Dad, if Vic & Steve are not around I'd like you to convey my birthday wishes to them and wish them many more etc. You know, luck and everything else.

As far as where I'll be flown to Dad, [...]. I'll be flown either to Fort Lewis, Washington, or else I'll go to California. There's an entry there. Chances are it'll be Fort Lewis. I'll be discharged from the Army at Fort Lewis and get travel pay. With that travel pay I'll take a commercial airline; the first flight out. It'll probably be to Kennedy, but it may be to LaGuardia or Newark. As I said I'm going to get the first flight out! I'll probably be able to get in touch with you at the stop over because there's no thru flight from Seattle to New York. They all make a stop either at St Louis, [...] or Chicago. When we stop, I'll put in my call and let you know what time the plane will be in. Chances are I'll call you again from Seattle, Washington anyway, to say hello. I don't know exactly what's going to be happening. I might get rushed and I want to try to get through that clearing as fast as possible and get home. Home, boy there's so many things I want to do. Once thing I got to do is get a hot shower for about four hours, maybe a steam bath even. Then, get some good real home cooked chow.

On thing I haven't asked in a while Dad, is how's things going with you at LOFT's? *[Loft candy was my Dad's employer.]* You still got your helpers? Hope you haven't been putting in any overtime lately. I hope you haven't had to.

Ma, you say that Doug is bumping into everything and you want me to figure out something as far as human factors engineering goes. Well, this may seem funny to you but actually that could become a human factors problem. I'll see if I can come up with a quick solution. I have it! [...] There's a system out now, being tested in cars, whereby on impact, immediately a balloon blows up to cushion the impact. All you have to do is put these on the babies clothing. Anytime he hits something, before he falls down, all these balloons blow up all around him and all he does is bounce around. Of course you got to hope he's not on a hill or he'll roll down the hill. (Laughing)

As you also know by now, I'm not bothered by Monsoons here. That's another good thing about this move. Unfortunately, Art is still in the monsoon area. I wrote him yesterday or the day before.

I sent him your good wishes and told him he had a package coming from you. I also wrote him that I think he may be coming down here. It depends. You see, the 2nd brigade remained up at Nancy, but supposedly sometime either in the next few weeks or in January (and I hear a lot of different stories) the second brigade will be moving down to Tay Ninh. If the 14th engineers remain under the operational control of the 2nd brigade, they'll move with them. That means Arty will move down to Tay Ninh and possibly the 2nd of the 12th will rejoin him. Of course that'll probably be after my DEROS, so I probably won't get to see Art again until he DEROSes, but I'll still be writing him.

Yeah, I guess you're right Dad, about this tape recording idea being a good idea. Actually I had thought of it a year ago but I didn't think it was a good idea at the time. I don't know but the price is rather high to keep a tape communication going, but it is nicer to hear voices than a letter. It has more of a personal touch. It brings a person more to you.

No, dad, I didn't hear the president's speech about the bomb halt. I heard about the bomb halt .. I've read about it but I didn't hear his speech. As far as how we're taking it. Well, it's mixed reactions. My person reaction is, I hope Hanoi doesn't use it just as a propaganda move. In other words, say the stop the bomb move is, *[...]* American propaganda and this is our way of telling the world, "Look we're doing something and the North Vietnamese are not". I just hope the North Vietnamese don't do some token gesture and then say, "Now you have to take all your troops out of I-Core and then we can talk peace". Then maybe, "You have to take them out of two-core." This is the kind of thing I think they're going to try. *[An interesting observation as this is basically what they did some years later.]* If the president stands for that, he isn't much of a man, or much of a president. I think the time has come when he's got to put his foot down and just tell them, "Look, this is what's happening. Now we're going to tell you what's happening. You can either cooperate or not. If you don't cooperate, well blow you off the map." We can do that. *[A bit hawkish wasn't I? Can you blame me having seen so many of my buddies die/ I'm not done!]* North Vietnam, contrary to popular belief, does not wish to have Red China in the war with them because if Red China were in the war with them; they would proceed to take over North Vietnam after the war, or during the war. Ho chi Min does not want his country taken over by anybody. That includes the Red Chinese. So, it's doubtful that they'll be able to get into the war, except as a last resort. Even if they do we could still have enough power to blow them off the Earth too. I hope it doesn't come to that. *[O.K., now I'm done!]*

[...] I want to keep at least $1,000 in liquid form for college and other things. Even though I'll have the G.I. bill for college. I also have the trip to Florida that I want to take with Marvin. I'll have to buy a new wardrobe. Well, there's a lot of things I'll have to buy.

Do you remember in my last tape I mentioned to you about this girl I met in Da Nang? Well she wrote me. As a matter of fact I have two letters from her in one day. She told me that she might come to New York. I hope she does. I've already invited her more than once and told her I'd be glad to show her the city. I'm nice that way, You know how that is! No, seriously, I told her it would be very nice to have her come to the city. She's indicated that she will come. She'll be leaving Nam in January, but she'll be going to Australia first. Then she'll probably be coming to the states. I guess she'll be traveling around the states then. At any rate I should know....I'll find out when she's going to visit the states, when she' s going to visit New York that is. She lives in the states. She won't just be visiting the states. *[That too, never happened]*

Actually that's all I have tonight so I guess I'll close up.

Say a few words to the Bergs and Semmigs if they're around. How's everything doing Lou, Eve, Mom & Dad Semmig. I just wrote you a few days ago. *[...]* I'm sure Art has written you about my moving.

How are things going at Allstate, Lou? I have been thinking about going back there and probably will go back for a while. I'll have to talk to Stan *[our office manager]* first because, according to the G.I. bill, I'm supposed to get all promotions and salary raises I would have gotten had I stayed. Knowing Allstate and knowing their personnel management policies, I imagine that I'll have a little trouble getting the raises. But, if they're in as bad a shape as they seem to indicate that they are, as far as personnel, maybe I'll have it a little easier. I'll be talking to you before I go back there about how much *[...]* I can work with you on that, Lou. You'll be able to help me out, I imagine. I'm wondering what your plans are as far as Allstate. *[…]* I don't expect you to stay with them very much longer, unless of course they have something in the pot for you such as a supervisor's job. *[…]* If you think you've got the sales technique, I'd even try for sales. That's a very good field. If not, than this adjustors bit is your best bet. We've been working with the adjustors long enough that, I know I feel that I could do an adjustors work. I've read some good books on the subject and I probably will read more. I've taken a little bit of this mechanics course and that'll help a little bit. At any rate, I'm going to ask for an adjustor's job when I come back and see what they give me.

Well, that's all I got right now. Say, "Hello" to everyone for me. Hello to all my nephews and nieces and I think that's about it for tonight. I'll say a few works tomorrow night, probably only a few unless I get that tape. Then I'll be sending this tape out. It won't be a full tape but I think you can understand that I don't want to talk myself hoarse. Goodnight for now. One more comment, today is The 9th of November and I have exactly 42 days left in the Army. Probably about 32 left in the battalion. That's it –out!

I do have a P.S.

P.S., you'll note that Nixon has won the election as I had hoped for. I hope now that he lives up to my expectations. We've only to wait till January to see. Possibly the fact that he's won the election would also have some effect on the peace talks in Paris before his January inauguration. Let's hope so. That's all. Goodnight.

Side 1 (Nov 12, '68)
DAY2
Hello again, this is your favorite nut in Vietnam. I had thought I was going to send this tape out in 3 days.*[…]* But a few things came up and I never did get to send it out. So today is the 12th of November. I have 39 days left in the Army, approximately 28 or 29 left with the battalion, which is about 4 weeks. That's not bad.

I still haven't gotten the tape that you people sent me. I don't know what happened to it. It's probably taking the same course as the brochures I never got *[More car rhetoric]*

[...] The mail is still pretty screwed up. It's hard to find anything. I'm sending out this tape today right after I finish taping. When I get the other tape (if and when), I'll try and answer it in writing.

I want to thank you Lou, or Bergs, whoever happens to be there, for letting my parents use their cassette. I'm hoping that pop Semmig is enjoying his retirement. From your letters I would say he is enjoying it, and I'm glad of that. I think that's the time when people finally get some freedom. Children are married; well they're not married maybe but old enough to take care of themselves. It gives you some time to be young again.

Marv, I want to thank you again for all the favors you've been doing for me. Remind me when I get home I'll buy you a couple of drinks or something. Really, I'll take care of you when I get home.   *[...]* Since my last tape it seems I'm getting letters from everyone with the same comment. Don't buy a Volkswagen. Well, never really intended to buy a Volkswagen. That comment was mainly made as an indication of my desperation.

To answer your question about Champale; No, I didn't drink it warm. We have a Fridge. Now we have regular electricity. We got giant generators. Before, we had 10Ks, (10-kilowatt generators) and that kept our Frigidaire working.

Dad, you also asked me for some information about when & where I'll be getting out. I believe I explained that all the first day on this tape. The day is still not exactly permanent. It varies anywhere from the 19th to the 23rd. My date on my record is the 22nd, so you can go by that. As I said I will give you a call at the time & let you know.

Well I'm just about thru again. I'll see what I can think of. I'll look up at my walls at all these lovely playmates of the month, Miss October & Miss November, wow, wow, wow. Oh yeah, back to the tape.

Hopefully I'll get to see some more good-looking women when I get back to the world. That's one of the 3 things I've missed. Booze, broads, and er.. buddies? How about cars?

There's a lot of things I actually miss from the world. Seriously, of course I miss family, and miss my freedom. I think that's the thing I miss most, my independence. Being able to do what

I want when I want to do it. Not having anybody tell me what to do, not having anybody tell me how to do it, when to do it, how to breathe, how to act. Of course, as you get more and more rank that's less but it's never completely over. Lately, I've been throwing my weight around more than usual because I know people don't usually mess with you when you're short.

I get along well with everyone here. I made quite a few friends. I've also met several people not in the Army. One I mentioned several times is Sandy, the girl I met in Da Nang. Also at the same time I met her, I made a friend though a fellow New Yorker, who was working in the PX. Those are about the only two; well I've met other civilians thru them. But, those are about the only 2 that I'll probably keep up contact with.

Well, now I'm just throwing the bull around. I haven't really got that much more to say. I don't expect to finish this tape. I'll probably go only another few minutes. I'll try to end with the first ending this time unlike yesterday with PPSes and double PSes, and, "Oh yes, I forgot". I won't say I'm finished until I believe I am finished. *[Don't believe that for a moment]*

I guess the weather over in the states is getting pretty cold now. At least that's what it seems to be from the newspapers. That might take a little getting used to for me. I'll just have to find me a nice warm girl. Wow, did I say that? See, Vietnam is corrupting me. Well actually, there's nothing wrong with that.

I've just about finished now and will say goodbye to everybody. If I do get the tape that you people sent, I'll answer it in writing, as much as I hate to. I'm getting lazier and lazier. Pretty soon I'll just sleep all day. Well I don't think I'd get away with that but...

I was just interrupted. I have to call up brigade and give them the daily strength report. [...] So I'll say take care for a few minutes and I'll be right back.

Just called division to try to get through to 2nd brigade. There's so many switches involved, there's 4 switches you have to go thru. It's really quite a bit of a problem making any sort of a phone call in the Nam. I got about halfway thru my transmission and lost contact with them; started getting a lot of interference. This is on a landline yet! This is a phone type deal. Imagine what it would be on a radio! At any rate I'm waiting now for them to call me back. The switch guy said the only switch they have out to Quan Loi switch, which is the main switch for the area, is busy. As soon as they call back, possibly you might want to listen in. I'll leave the recorder on and you can get a general idea of what this type of thing is that I'm calling in now. This is not one of my permanent duties. ….the man who's permanent duty this is, is on guard duty.

For the first time in quite a few days, matter of fact the first time since I've been here, it really rained hard today. The streets are pretty muddy. All that red dust becomes red mud and it's extremely slippery. All the jeeps & trucks are slipping into the, [...] drains dug on the side of the roads. It's really funny watching them. I drove the jeep tonight as little as possible. The only place I tried to drive was down to the Officers club to pick up a lieutenant. Other than that I won't be doing much driving. Possibly by tomorrow the roads will be dry again. They dry very quickly here.

I still want to try to get a shower tonight. I haven't been able to shower the last couple of nights. I had radio watch last night, which is almost like guard duty except that with my eyes I can't pull guard duty. So I have radio watch, where I stay at the command post and I keep an eye on the radio for a few hours, calling in situation reports and keeping contact with the troops. If I hear any firing or anything I check it out to make sure that everything is O.K. In case of emergency, I'd be the command network. My job would be to get messages out, bring them in, and keep the officer in charge informed of what's happening. Also, to keep division & brigade informed of what's happening, and to assist the troops out on the line with any illumination rounds or support rounds that they may need or whatever support they need. It's not a very difficult job. It's somewhat boring as a matter of fact... You just sit by the radio and watch. I'm not complaining. I prefer nothing happening with only 28 or 29 days left in the battalion. I just hope we have no more trouble. I've seen enough trouble.

By the way I had some films in this package I'm going to send home. I don't know when I'll be sending it home, probably after payday, which is the 15th. Today is the 12th. One or more of the pictures on this roll of film is of Arty. If they should come out, I'm sure the Semmigs and/or the Bergs, probably both, would want copies of the pictures. Be sure they get any copies if you get them before I get home.

"Quan Loi give me Phuc bin.... I see. All right, O.K. forget it I'll call back. Thank you"

Well my switch is still busy I'm just going to go get my shower and forget about it. I have nothing further on this tape so I'm just going to close now and say so long to everybody. *[Didn't I say that already/]* Be seeing you real soon. I guess I should give you one of my typical, silly sign offs but I won't. Not this time anyway. As I said this should be my last tape. You should have two of my tapes at home now. When I get home I'll be making some tapes. I've already bought one tape with the Beatles songs, I believe I mentioned that I my last tape, or did I? No, I don't believe I had it last tape. I bought a Beatles tape at the PX; Sergeant Peppers Lonely hearts Club Band. That's the only one I have right now and I play that quite often. The PX is out of tapes right now. I'm hoping they get some more by the time I get paid. If the do I'll get some more. If not I'll get some when I get home. Of course I'll also be taping my own.

I had a little problem with my recorder. The door, which keeps the tape dust free, one side of it seems to have broken. I'm not exactly worried about it. I got a warranty on it and that should take care of that. It won't affect the way it plays and I keep it in plastic so dust won't be getting in.

Well that's all I got for now. Until approximately December 22nd, when I can see all your happy smiling faces, so long.

November 1968

Dear Mom, Dad, & Marv -

I'm sorry out phone "patch" was so poor. I hope you were
able to hear at least part of what I said. Just in case you
didn't I'll repeat myself in this letter. I hope by now you
got my tape, the second one which I sent out on the 12th
and also the package of things I sent home a few days
ago. I finally got your tape and as I mentioned on the
phone, you sounded like the competitors of Rowan &
Martins Laugh In. I really enjoyed hearing the voices of
my friends and family and it did wonders towards
heightening my morale. By the way in case you're
wondering that MARS station is right her on this LZ.

Now I want to answer a few questions you asked in your
letter. You seem interested in the exact date I will be
home, Well even I don't know that it deepens on how early
I get out of Nam (I can accept a flight up to two days
early) and how long it take me to muster out at Fr Lewis,
Washington. I tried to explain this in my tape.

I still haven't heard from Zeigler but early this week I
wrote them a final letter telling them in a diplomatic way
that they weren't showing the service they advertise and
that if I didn't hear form them by the end of the month
the PX would get my order.
Color TV you mentioned. When do you expect to get
delivery? Did you get antennae yet? I hope you were able
to get a service contract on it/ I don't even know what
model it is or the size of the screen.

I've been reading about all kinds of problems in N.Y.
besides the teachers strike which I heard is now finally
over. I heard you had some very bad weather and that the
Whitestone Bridge was swaying causing many motorist to
panic and abandon their cars which in turn caused a

massive traffic jam forcing the closing of the bridge. Then in todays paper I read of the ticket craze the fuzz is going on in Long Island. I hope you haven't been caused any problems by these situations.

I got your letter of 11 November, yesterday. I'm glad you got to call the Bergs, my latest tape which also has something for the Bergs is as good an excuse for you to visit the Semmigs in Lynbrook.

This will probably be one of the last letters you get in time to answer. I'm down to one month and a wake up tomorrow. The days have started to get longer but I'm getting there slowly but surly.

I know there more I wanted to say to you but I can't remember what at this time. When I remember I'll write again. I'm sending you my last roll of film from the Nam. I may get another roll at An Khe to record my mustering out but I'll carry that one myself.

Hope you were able to understand my explanation of my profit sharing payment or that Lou can explain it to you.

See you soon, and pray that I don't make so many typing errors on my next letter (Ha Ha).

Love from Nam
Howard

PS.* I got a letter from my boss at Allstate inviting me out to lunch when I get home.

30   30   30   30   30

I was not the world's best typist or speller and this was in the old typewriter days. There was no spell check or delete button.

The tape my family sent me was interesting and pretty funny thanks to Steve. I've reproduced parts of it in the appendix, although it loses some of its humor in print.

Not much new here. You can see my concern about getting home. As you'll soon see that was not totally unwarranted.

On the same day I wrote home to my Brother. No, it's not the last letter to him. Most of it has to do with my car but it begins advice to my brother. Disregard the parts about the car; it was not the car I finally ordered. The ad I refer to is a public service ad by the National Auto Dealers Association telling us how important it is to stay in school. It asked the reader to send for a box about careers in the retail automobile industry. I wanted him to continue to make good choices for himself, and of course he did.

---

20 November 1968

Dear Marv,

This will probably be my last separate letter to you and its going to be a short one.

First I want to mention to you about the enclosed ad from the National Automobile Dealers Association. Now I think you should send away for these books. It may have some good ideas, your a good salesman and if you would like to make it your profession or even have a thought of it, the automobile is a good product with a high per item profit and a pretty good turn over. Besides I could get a discount on my next car (Ha Ha). Seriously I think you should send away for it even if its "just for laughs". Lou and I are thinking of going into business together and franchises are good deals with small initial investment good returns and small risk. If you decide to go for this maybe we can work out a deal since I can get a G.I. Bill small business ~~trust~~ loan to start a business.

As far as my car goes, I believe I said on the tape I sent home everything about the car I finally decided on but in case I didn't I'm say it again for you. I'm intending to order a Chevelle Malibu conv with 3 speed console mounted auto trans, power steering, brakes, and windows, bucket seats, Heavy Duty Battery, auxiliary lighting, radio, remote control outside mirror, rear window defroster (first time this has been offered on a convertible), and belted tires (which I didn't mention on the original list). I'm getting it in butternut yellow with a parchment (white) and black interior and a white top (not positive about white top). Haven't decided on heavy duty suspension yet, it depends on weather it includes a sway bar if so I'll get it. Thats it, besides undercoating, and of course the 155 HP 250 cu in engine (6 cyl). How does that sound?

Thats it for now, see you soon. Hope all is well at business and play.

Love from Nan

Happy thanksgiving

30+

23 Nov 68

Dear Mom, Pop, Marv -

Just a short letter to wish my favorite parents a very happy anniversary and many more happy ones.

To all I wish a happy turkey-day. I should have turkey here but I'll be more thankful in 29 days when I'm home.

Marv - did you ever send those airlines schedules I asked for?

Will write again in a few days.

Love
Howard

29

(28 & a wake up)

---

25 November 1968

Dear Marv,

Thanks for all the airline schedules and information you sent about almost everything. I had to take half a day off just to go through my mail. It's too bad you didn't look at the schedules, only three airlines have flights between New York and Seattle/Tacoma; Northwest Orient, United, and Eastern and those were the only schedules I needed. I looked over the other schedules to see the rates for flights to Florida in case we should have to fly. It now looks like I won't have my car in time for our vacation so we'll either have to fly or possibly drive a car to Florida as a service for someone as in the ad I attached to this letter. If as I think you have never been in a plane, and I don't have my car we'll probably go by plane and I think you'll grove on flying as much as I do. If we go by car, I figure we'll make it in two days, my First Sergeant (Head sergeant) is retiring next month and he told me we should stop by his house in Georgia if we drive down and he'll put us up for the night. I don't like any of those travel agency affairs, they are too constricting and as you will find out the prices they quote is a "from" price and is usually applicable only to the cheapest dives. As long as you have some idea of where you want to stay by the time I get home, I'm sure we can call most of the better hotels and make reservations (calling collect of course).

I just briefly went over the N.Y.S. regent scholarship incentive thing, I'll read it better when I get some time. As for the application for N.Y.U., its too late for the fall semester and I have till March for the summer session so I'll wait till I get home before I do anything with that. Thanks alot for sending them.

I check the car ads in the times and didn't find any prices for the 69s, so I guess if I don't hear from Zeigler, I'll buy at the PX it will still be cheaper than the states.

If I see some kid chasing my plane in a blue uniform with a star on his chest, I'll know it is my favorite brother Super Jew ?? (guess who is SJ 1). Don't try to stop the plane before it lands. If you see some idiot trying to get out the window before the plane has even landed its your idiot brother.

339

I have been checking the airline schedules all day and it seems that NorthWest has the most flights from Seattle to New York so its very likely I'll be flying with them though it really depends on the time I get to the airport at Seattle. Theres two rather long periods when there are no flights to New York on any airlines, from 3:00 P.M. to 10:00 P.M. and from 12:00 midnight to 8:00 A.M., watch with my luck I'll get finished at just 3 P.M. or midnight. If that happens I'll see if I can get a flight east that connects with a New York bound flight, at any rate I'll call you either from Seattle airport or any airport inbetween that I stop at and let you know what flight and what time to expect me.

Wow, your own stereo, I bet that feels good. Dad told me that he told you to buy a color tv also. The old home is really shaping up. Marv, don't go over board on the liquor. Mostly get soda, so people can mix there drinks and ice and have a shot glass out. My going away party was small but there were still about 6 couples there and they didn't even finish one bottle of booze.

As for the address and phone numbers of my friends, I gave them to you on the last tape for as much as I had. I don't really have that many friends, the two guys from here both already said they have previous engagements but anything can happen. Tom Goldman, just got married but I'm sure if you call his mother she can tell you there new address and phone number (929-9008). I remember giving you quite a few names but I don't know just what they were. As for Rick Brower (he already back in the states and has [?]et a ready) he said he couldn't come but you might invite him and his wife anyway. (His address is: 212-16 69th Ave, Bayside and his phone no. I don't know). I can't remember any others right now who wouldn't be on my tape or available in the phone book if you have their addresses. Don't sweat it if not too many of my "friends" can come.

I don't expect you'll be able to answer this letter as it will arrive after 1 Dec and with Xmas rush and all I don't expect to get any mail which was sent after that date. As I mentioned several times before and in my latest tape I don't know the exact date I'll be home but I'll let you know when I reach the airport

See you soon, hope you had bout coup turkey and enjoyed it and the booze.

Your favorite brother

alais Super Jew !

340

25 November 1968

Dear Mom & Dad,

Just got finished writing to Marv, he has really done alot for me this year. He's a really good brother and I'm glad he's a member of our family as he is definitely a credit to the name of Kalachman.   Thats the end of the speech.

Got your letter today of 11 Nov 68, yesterday I was getting letters from 16 Nov so you figure it out, actually with the christmas rush started anything is possible that's why I told most of my friends to stop writing about 1 Dec 68. I believe its safe to write till about 4 Dec but why take chances, of course all it'll mean is that my mail will have to be rerouted back home to me.

Dad I was impressed that you couldn't find Quan Loi on your maps till I checked some maps in several publications and saw that its not on many of them. If provinces are on your map look for Binh Long province.   I'll help you find my base on your map, look at saigon, now look at the cambodian border to the left of saigon and above it, you'll notice that Cambodia has two places where it sticks into Vietnam almost forming a point at both places. The lower one points below Saigon if you followed it, the higher one known as the fishhook, is about 100 miles above Saigon, from the point of the hook use the scale of miles to measure about 10 miles east (left) or if it shows roads look for route 13 and that is approximately where I'm at. If you still can't find it wait till I get home and I'll point it out to you. If I get the paper that comes out every week with a map of the Nam I'll send that page home with the spot marked.

No, I'm not sorry I extended, this place is much better than any of the other bases I've been on lately and I got to see a glimse of Saigon on my way up here. This place is obviously safer than my last place as evidenced by the fact that we can sleep in billets instead of bunkers and its much larger having its own air strip. The MARS station closed up yesterday because the rest of the 1st Infantry left this base, its now strictly Cav Country.

Don't worry Dad I'm nowhere near comfortable by world standards and I'm looking forward to coming home ~~xxxxxxxxx~~ at least as much as you are to having me there.

In a way I am sorry I didn't join the Navy, but now that my tour is almost over is no time for me to start thinking about that. The few days of Navy Life I experienced on my way down here from LZ Nancy were enough for me to realize I made an error in refusing to go into the Naval Reserve when I had my chance.

I'm glad you got to speak to Lou & Eve and to the Sonnigs and I'm glad you agree they are wonderful people. You know they got to be nice when you learn that their tenant of the last unteen years moved from B'klyn to Lynbrook with them when they moved and became their tenant there at Lynbrook. I only wish we could be so lucky as to find a landlord like them.

I'm wondering what type of snow tires you have gotten, if I were home I'd have recommended you get radials instead or if you did get snow tires then get studded tires but I guess you just got a regular snow tire. Well it will also serve the purpose and I guess you don't expect to keep the Rambler more than another year or so.

Hope you got my short Letter wishing you a Happy Anniversary. May you have many more happy years togeather.

Thats it for now. I really lucked out tomorrow for Thanksgiving I got radio watch which is sort of guard duty except I'm at the command post and I watch the radio instead of the perimeter. I kind of like to operate the An Pro-25 (thats my radio). Well at any rate I get to eat my thanksgiving dinner early as I have to report to the CP by 1700 (5 PM).

Love from the Nam

Howard

26 & a wake-up

P.S. - Don't think I be surprised that my boss from Allstate the big-shot has invited me to lunch when I return stateside. He sends me a how/weather letter.

You can see from the postscript how bad my handwriting was and why I retyped most of my letters.

----

26 November 68

Dear Mom, Pop, MARV -
Finally I got my order blank & prices from Ziegler.
I ordered my car already, the total cost is $3395, including positraction rear axle & HD suspension which I didn't mention to you on the tape. It was only a few dollars cheaper than the other place I had in mind.
I sent out a check for $100.00 down payment. Now all I have to worry about is getting a loan for between $1300 & 1400 for 36 months. It shouldn't be hard if I put the car up as collateral.
I'm sending you the Buick price list. I have Radio Watch tonight. I'll write more in a day or two. Send you the full info on my car.

Love
Howard

After all, I finally ordered a car. I was so excited about it, I hand wrote this short letter home and you'll notice even forgot my count down! But alas this was not the final on my car order. Zeigler would not be the source of my first ever new car. Was naïve to even order from them when they took so long to get me their literature.

Although the next letter is typewritten, it is 3 pages long and begins with a lot of repetitious verbiage about the car. Therefore, I decided to input the first page:

Dear Mom, Dad, Marv;

Seems like I'm writing more now than I have been in quite a while. I got your letter of 21 Nov today. Actually I'm quite excited since as I mentioned in my brief note yesterday, I finally got my price lists from Zeigler and sent in my order [Repetitious details of my order].

I'm glad to be getting out of this #%! (censored) battalion. Now they have some new bull, a uniform requirement, if you're out of uniform you can get disciplined by as much as a court martial. You have to wear a full set of fatigues, weapons, helmet, boots bloused, and a pistol belt wherever you go. I wish someone would tell the dammed idiots to get their heads out of their rectums and look around, there is a war going on - at least that's what I've been told. For two more weeks I can take this,

I should be leaving this LZ about 11 Dec for An Khe where I will start my processing out of Sam's army by processing out of the Cav. Hurrah, Hurrah !!!

The Frenchman owner of this place isn't all that lonly, he has several french families working and living here with him. I'll bet the last few weeks since the Cav has been here he has been pulling his hair out, the chopper piolts aren't very careful of his trees when they fire bouc coup (yes that means many) of his trees have been destroyed.

Actually beau coup here means many, much, alot or anything similiar. What happened to the dictionary I sent you (a page from an Army newspaper) about four to six months ago? It should have beau coup on it and din LoL (sorry about that) and some other words and phrases I've picked up here. You may have to hire a translator to talk to me (ha ha).

I have heard about Mel being on the list for Lieutenant from him and from your brother wh has been writing me quite often. He also wrote me (Uncle Jack), that he got this new job as a speaker before a committee.

I haven't seen Art since I left and so far the only mail I've gotten from him is your tape. I've have written him a few times and expect to hear from him at any time now. I've heard that he may be moving down to the delta, I also heard that my unit may be moving again to the delta in January. Quite glad I ETS before then.

I'm sorry Dad, I was almost passitive that I've written you before about my Profit Sharing. I was sure that I wrote you about it when I sent you the money for Marilyn & Steve's wedding, telling you that you could pay it for me and out of that money if you had it at the time. As long as your going to take care of it I won't worry.

What do you mean Dad your the handsomest of all, you want a punch in the nose or something (ha ha), actually I'm jelous and I know if I punch you in the nose you won't be the handsomest anymore, than I'll be it. (Never could let anyone have the last say on a joke in their letter - din LoL).

I don't know what you meant by your question of weather it is dangerous to talk on the phone or radio. If your referring to MARS calls, it is, thats why I can only say certain things and its the same on all the phones. Phones which are long distance don't use land lines like in the states the call are transmitted via high freq AM radio. As for the radio, the freq we use are changed pretty

345

often and there are also security regulations governing the use of the radio and special radio procedure to follow using code words and call signs. I'll tell you more about this, if your interested, when I get home.

You say you'll have two well cooked peas out of a can for me when I get home, complete with knife and fork. The way they have been feeding me here two peas are two much for me, I'm not use to such a large meal and by the way what are a knife and fork? The situation has gotten so bad with chow here that I had to go to the PX and buy myself a package, since I told everyone to stop sending them. Now I have enough to last me till I get out of here. Don't think there is such a thing as too much food, booze and females once you've been in the Nam. Especially females - women type, one each as the Army would say. Unfortinatly I don't know the federal specification number so I couldn't order any while I was here.

If I'm lucky I'll get home on the 21st or 22d which is a weekend and I won't have to call anyone at work to pick me up. At any rate most of the flights from Seattle land either early in the morning or late in the afternoon.

See you soon, don't write me anymore, save it for when I get home as you'll probably get this about the 3rd of December and by the time you could write me it would take a minimum of 6 days to get here which would make it the 10th leaving only 4 days grace before I leave for An Khe.

Love from Nan

Howard

24 days

Every once in a while you'd get a C.O. who thought that looking good was what made you a soldier. In a base station that should have been expected but obviously it rubbed me the wrong way. One of the reasons I extended in Nam for the early out was that I knew that after being in a war zone base, being at a stateside base would be very difficult. I did not want to put up with Army bullshit stateside and here we were putting up with the same B.S. in the Nam.

Laying too before boarding LSD

Loading the LSD

Loading LSD 2

At Sea

Captain on bridge:

Author on board LSD

On the Delta.

LD Guns

Old Glory flies above

Lifesaver with ship's Name

Sampan

Sniper fire from hill

Conex convoy leaving base

Chapter 17 – Happy New Year = Happy Days

Finally the time was approaching for me to go home. The days were few, the holidays were near, I had ordered my new car and all was well with the world! My biggest concerns were which flight I'd get home, which accessories I'd should have on my car, where I'd go to finish my education, the homecoming party of course. These were the four "Fs" - family, friends, food, and females!

Mess at LZ Andy (notice wooden billets)

Homes on LZ Andy:

1 December 1968

Dear Mom, Dad, Marv,

Today starts my last month in this place. Only three more weeks and I'll be on my way home. Thanks for the air-line schedules Marv, I have finally figured out which flights are best and chances are very good I'll be coming home either by Northwest (most likely) or United. I got a letter from my buddy Rich, who ETSed about two weeks ago. He wrote me that it takes 22 hours to process out once you reach Ft Lewis. That means I'll be free any time from 21 to 23 of this month, depending in when I get back to the states. There is also another problem, the 21st and 22nd are the weekend and military reserve rates are not in effect from noon to midnight on friday (20th), and from noon sunday (22nd) to noon monday (23d), and also on Northwest all day on the 21st and from the 24th to the 26th. That means on NW I can only fly standby from friday noon to sunday noon or pay full fare for a reservation ($145 coach, or $160 first class). I can still get a military reservation on United and Eastern from midnight friday to noon sunday. That's about 5 good flights (one stop or less) or a total of approximately 10-15 flights. Hopefully I'll get out during this period or get into Ft Lewis on the 20th and leave it the 21st. If I get in on the 22d which is my normal date, I should get out on the 23rd in which case if I get out before noon, I'll either wait for the 1:00 flight via United or if theres a better flight go standby. Also the airline schedules Marv sent may be outdated by Xmas. Most of them only run 2 or 3 months. At any rate I'll get home the earliest way possible even if I have to pay full fare or go by train ("hich I doubt). Mary, maybe you shouldn't warm up the car till I get home. At any rate not until you know what flight I'm coming in on. If you start warming up the car too soon it will run out of gas. Make sure the heater is working, even the though of winter and weather with temp below 50 makes me chilly- Brrrrrr rrr.

That was one of the longest paragraph's I've written since I have been in this place. I believe I told you about the place I wrote to that submits my name to many colleges and the colleges will write me if I qualify. I heard about them from the radio station here, the service costs $15 but is free to GIs eligible for the GI bill. I got there application form and sent it in a few days ago so now I'll see what happens. I'm sending you the form letter they sent me with the application for you to look at if you like.

I hope by now you have received the two packages I sent home, one contained three rolls of film to be developed and some personal items including heat tabs for me to use when I go hunting. The other was a manila envelope containing several car magazines and my Chevelle brochure with my copy of my order and receipt for my deposit check of $100.00.

Speaking of my car I have thought of getting it ever since I've been here and had all the financing figured out. Now that I've finally ordered the car at a cost of almost $3500 with N.Y. tax, I'm worried that I may not get a loan in time. I don't know why I'm worried, I'll be able to put the car up as collateral. The think is the bank may not want to recognize my job at Allstate until I return to it which I don't intend to do until February. At any rate no matter what happens at present the most I can lose is my deposit. I guess Dad, you'll have some advice to me when I get home. One thing Dad, I have thought about the car and each of the accessories I'm getting on it and have decided I should get only what I needed for safety and comfort. I did just that though I stretched the comfort bit a little (bucket seats & console). I made this decision since, barring an accident, I intend to keep this car at least five years and maybe longer since I'll be going to school. Also I expect Mom and yourself will be using it from time to time. Now keep this letter as proof of that I'm going to say. As soon as the car is well broken in you may borrow it any time I'm not using it. Also Mom, I want you to come with me when I pick it up.

Got your letter of 21 Nov today.

Thats about it for now, how do you like this now that I'm really getting short, I'm writing more often (at least to you) than I have since I have been here.

I don't think I'll be writing much more before I get home (do you believe that, I don't).

Love from that place

Howard

P.S. * Notice I didn't mention this place once in this letter, I'm going to start early in trying to forget it.

PP.S.- Karl-Rick Brown sent this new address.
It: 95-20 222d St.
Queens Village, N.Y.
phone: 479-1217

21 Lg Wake Up To Echo Tango Sierra
(3 Weeks)

Not only did I write "3 WEEKS" across this page I also wrote "21 days" in big letters on the back of the envelope.
I was so excited about going home that I wrote "November" instead of December for this letter:

---

4 November 1968

Dear Mom, Dad, & Marv-

Only about a week left here on LZ Andy. In a week I'll be at An Khe, in two weeks Cam Rahn Bay and in three weeks I should have been home several days. Since I don't have any locking luggage and it is unlikely that the PX will get any before my departure, I didn't want to take any chances so I mailed home my cassette recorder via PX which will mean that I should beat it home. I of course insured it for $50.00. If it should get home before me just put it in my closet, I don't want anyone playing it yet as it has a broken part in the door and I don't want it broken further. I intend to find the nearest place and use my warranty to get it fixed if possible. I beleive it was broken by someone trying to open it without knowing how, now it doesn't open the regular way at all and that is why I don't want anyone to use it.

I've typed up a small composite airline schedule and put it in my wallet, now if the flights aren't changed I'll be okay, providing I can get a flight. As I explained last time that may present a problem.

I have nothing new now to write about so I guess I'll just close for now, I guess this typewriter must know I'm leaving soon it is starting to act up. The capitals don't space correctly.

See you all real soon.

LOVE

Howard

SHORT

358

4 December 1968

Dear Marv,

Well, it won't be long now! I just can't wait to get home and see you all again.

Marv, you undoubtedly know by now that I've ordered my new car. I really doubt if it will be ready by the time I get home. It may be ready by the time we go on our vacation though. I've been thinking and I think that we shouldn't spend more than a week in Miami, we should do some traveling, especially if we have the car. You and I both will have to get used to Power Brakes, I got them because I remembered how hard Janet & Vic's Olds is to stop and the Chevelle with all the equipment I got on it will weigh more than that.

Pray that I not only make it home safe but as early as possible and that I don't have trouble with getting a flight. I'll be leaving this LZ on the 11th only a week from today.

I still worry about you going into the Army, while I was looking through the regulations I found the regulation about medical standards for induction and they aren't very stringent. On your eyes for instances if your bad eye can be corrected to 20/400 you can be accepted. I have taken the pages from the regulation that are revelant to the pre-induction physical. I am sending them to you, hold on to them till I get home at which time I'll explain them to you. You of course can read them in the mean time but keep them in a safe place where you won't forget about them when I get home.

Thats it for now. Don't be chasing my bird when it lands but have a chaser for me (Liquid) if you know what I mean.

Love

Howard.

This was my last letter to my brother from Vietnam. This was also my last letter with this portable typewriter. A friend who was going back to the world had given or sold it to me. Now that it was almost my time to go back to the world I passed it forward to one of my buddies.

LAST LETTER

14 December 1968

Dear Mom, Dad, Marv -

Well, I've been here in An Khe for 3 days now. I've already seen a show at the NCO club, and a movie. As far as business I've gotten my ETS orders cut, for 22 December '68 since that's what was in my records. It doesn't look like I'll get any days so you can expect me about the 23rd of December, depending on the airlines. This DEROS center is really something, you spend a year here & then come to this place to clear and you get harassment & get put on details. I'm too short to fight it. So far I've been lucky enough to get out of details but they are sure to catch me sooner or later. Well I just have to put up with this one more week & then------

The last letter I got from you before I left was dated 29 Nov 68. I hope that was the last you wrote.

I sure hope I get home on the 23rd as I want to spend my first day at home but promised Lou, Eve, & the Semmigs to have Xmas dinner with them & spend part of Xmas day with them. Also the 23rd is the last day of Chanukah.

Have a Happy Chanukah, give my love to Janet, Vic & family & Marilyn & Steve & anyone else who inquires about me.

Almost time to go out and get some alcohol in my system - yippee! - The NCO club opens at 4:30 PM.

Well that's it, the next sound you hear may be me!

*Love
Howard*

*7 DAYS
1 WEEK
Ha Ha!*

*Echo
Tango
Sierra*

This was my last letter home but I did include the reprinted letter below. Although the original author is unknown, I retyped it to make it more personal before sending it home.

The army had contracts with various airlines to fly troops back and forth to Vietnam. The plane that took you home was known as the freedom bird. Flying Tigers owned my freedom bird and I had a soft place in my heart for them after that. I was sorry to see their demise some years later.

Dear Civilians, Friends, Draft Dodgers, Etc. -

In the very near future the undersigned will once more be in your midst, dehydrated and demoralized, to take his place again as a human being with the well known forms of freedom and justice for all; engage in Life, Liberty, and the somewhat delayed pursuit of Happiness. In making your joyous preparations to welcome him back into organized society you might take certain steps to make allowances for the crude environment that has been his miserable lot for the past twelve months. In other words he might be a little Asiatic from Vietnamesitis and overseasites and should be handled with care. Do not be alarmed if he is infested with all forms of rare tropical diseases. A little time in the "Land of the Big PX" will cure this malady.

Therefore, show no alarm if he insists on carrying a weapon to the dinner table, looks around for his steel pot when offered a chair, or wakes you up in the middle of the night for guard duty. Keep cool when he pours gravy on his dessert at dinner or mixes peaches with his Seagrams VO. Pretend not to notice if he eats with his fingers instead of silverware and prefers C-rations to steak. Take it with a smile when he insists on digging up the garden to fill sandbags for the bunker he is

361

building. Be tolerant when he takes his blanket and sheet off the bed and puts them on the floor to sleep on. Be patient and allow him to adjust to such luxuries as light switches, flush toilets, running water, and peace and quiet. Don't be disturbed if he yells "Incoming" and dives for the nearest sewer when he hears a car backfire.

Restrain from saying anything about powered eggs, dehydrated potatoes, canned ham, fried rice, fresh milk, or ice cream. Do not be alarmed if he should jump up from the dinner table and throw his plate and eating utensils in the garbage can. After all that has been his standard. And, if it should start raining, pay no attention to him if he pulls off his clothes, grabs a bar of soap and a towel and runs outdoors for a shower. Disregard it if he searches for his steel pot each morning to shave from.

When in his daily conversation he utters such things as: "Sin Loi" and "Choi Oi" just be patient, and simply leave quickly and calmly if by some chance he utters "Di Di" with an irritated look on his face because it means no less then "Get the Hell out of here!" If by chance, during a conversation, he says "No Bic" all he means is that he doesn't understand. Do not let it shake you if hew picks up the phone and yells, "Spotter sir" or says, "Roger Out" for good-bye or simply shouts, "Working!"

Never ask why anyone held a higher rang then he did, and never by any means mention the term "Extend" or "Re-up." Pretend not to notice if at a restaurant he calls the waitress "Numbah one girl" and uses his hat for an ashtray. He will probably keep listening for "We Gotta Get Out O This Place" to sound off over the AFRVN. If he does, comfort him, for he is still living in the past. Be especially watchful when he is in the presence of a woman; especially a beautiful one.

Above all keep in mind that beneath that tanned and rugged exterior there is a heart of gold (the only thing of value he has left). Treat him with kindness, tolerance, and an occasion fifth of liquor and you shall be able to rehabilitate that which was once (and is a hollow shell of) the Happy-go-lucky guy you once knew and loved.

Last, and by no means least, send no more mail or sugar notes to APO 96490 after 2400 hours 1 December 1968, fill the ice box with beer (or Champale), get the civvies out of the mothballs, fill the car with gas, and get the women and children off the streets---

BECAUSE THE "KID" IS A COMING HOME SOLDIER!!!!!!!!!!!!!!!!!!!!!!!!!

HE CAN'T WIAT TO TOCH THE GREEN GREEN GRASS OF HOME!!!!!!!!!!

Howard Kalachman
THE "KID'S" SIGNATURE

COMMANDER OF HOWIES RAIDERS

362

Author at Cam Rahn Bay for the last time!

Flying Tiger Freedom Bird

Next stop the world!

Chapter 18 -Home & Beyond. The End of a Nightmare?

In addition to the Bronze Star I was also awarded the Good Conduct Medal, Combat Infantryman Badge, NYS Conspicuous Service Cross, and others. I had also earned an Expert badge for both the M-14 & M16 rifles. Every soldier in my unit also received the Vietnam Service Medal, Vietnam Combat Metal with 2 Overseas bars, and National Defense Service Medal.

Earlier I had mentioned my unit's motto painted at the entry to the Base Camp at AnKhe. As it was time to leave another motto comes to mind. I do not believe it was indigenous to our conflict but every bit as true. It went something like, "When I die I'm going to Heaven, Cause I've already spent my time in Hell - Vietnam!"

Our Freedom Bird from that hell was run by Flying Tigers and, as previously mentioned, I always had a soft spot in my heart for them and their flight attendants. Most of the guy's on that very long flight back to the world had not seen an occidental woman in quite some time. Many were rude, crude and offensive even to other G.I.s including yours truly. I was offended by the way they treated the girls but the FA's handled them all professionally.

What I remember most about Seattle was that their bums were all Native Americans. To me that was a sad commentary on America.

After processing, I did get connecting flights thru to New York pretty quickly at Seattle Tacoma Airport. They booked me on flights up to Oregon and then to the somewhere in the Midwest and home. My plane arrived at JFK airport at 3:00 A.M. December 24, 1968. Not only were my parents, and family at the airport waiting for me, but also my friends Lou & Eve.

My family didn't recognize me at first. They had sent off a light brown haired Caucasian son, and after almost 14 months half-naked in the sun, a blond, very dark, baked bronzed man returned. It was a great feeling to see and touch them again and one of the very few times I had ever seen tears in my dad's eyes.

The readjustment was difficult. I drank heavily for a while, almost a bottle a day, but that did not last long. However, it was many years before I could even watch a movie about war or fire a weapon again. I even sold my shotgun and never bought another.

I had my emotional ups and downs for a while. During my down times I could get pretty low even contemplating suicide and would occasionally express these feelings by writing poems. A few of those depression poems appear below:

I HAVE DISAPPEARED FROM THE FACE OF THE EARTH

    WHY IS NO ONE LOOKING FOR ME?

DIDN'T I EVER EXIST.

    OR PERHAPS IT WAS A DREAM FANTASY

MIGHT I BE A PRISONER OF THE WORLD?

    OR NEED I ONLY THE COURAGE TO LEAVE OR TO STAY.

EMOTIONS ARE THE CURSE OF MAN, AND KNOWLEDGE.

BUT WHY AM I CURSED?

    WHY CAN'T I EXIST?

FOR HOW LONG AM I REAL,

    OR AM I NOT REAL – OR TOO REAL IN A PLASTIC WORLD

OH WQHY CAN'T ANYONE HEAR MY FINAL APPEAL.

BANG! –WE'RE ALL DEAD

THERE'S NO SUCH THING AS GRAVITY THE WORLD SUCKS!!
ARE WE BUT THE PAWN OF SOME SADISTIC GOD?
OR PERHAPSOUR PERSPECTIVE IS THE PAWN OF OUR MINDS
WHICH CAME FIRST- IS THE WORLD AS WE SEE IT, AND WE Its
PRODUCTS?
OR DO WE SEE WRNG & NIEVLY PRODUCE UGLINESS?
NO THAT CANNOT BE!
THE UNCLES AND FATHERS OF THE WORLD ARE BUT CHILDREN
SOLVING PROBLEMS WITH PHYSICAL FORCE INSTEAD OF
INTELLECT.
LOVERS ARE UNTRUE AND HURT OR BECOME HATERS.
AND FRIENDS TURN TO ENEMIES.
AND THE WORLD CLOSES IT'S DOOR ON THOSE WHO CANNOT PLAY
HER GAME,
I SAY AGAIN – THE WORLD SUCKS!!

I had written home about it but never thought it would actually happen. We were at the dinner table when I asked my brother to "pass the fucking salt". My dad, and brother laughed, while mom pretended she didn't hear it!

In the Nam we had many fear lectures where the Army tried to scare us out of having sexual relations with the locals. They told us there were unknown venereal diseases in the Nam that one could get. If you got one of them they had to prevent you from spreading it in the world so you could not go home. Instead you'd be sent to some unknown island (like lepers were many years before). One of the many (probably bogus) symptoms we heard about was urinating blue. We didn't really believe or heed those warnings, but we heard them. A day or two after I got home I went to the bathroom. I wasn't watching too closely when I urinated but when I flushed sure enough the water was blue. Was the Army being truthful? I was scared. As I exited the bathroom, my mom was in the kitchen. Trying not to show my apprehension or scare her, I nonchalantly asked, "Mom, do you know when I flushed the bowl it was blue?" What I did not know was that while I was in the Nam they had come out with those blue toilet cleaners that you hung inside the tank and my mom had just hung a new one the night before. She told me that and I was relive. Yes, quite funny now, but it wasn't to me then!

I had nightmares about my time in the Nam and even woke up a few nights after my return home, heart pounding, jumped off the bed on to the floor yelling, "Incoming!" I scared the heck out of everyone including myself. Nightmares about having to go back into the Army were a part of my life for many years. They only stopped a few years ago when I knew I was too old for that to occur.

That first July 4th at home, someone drove by in a car and threw a large homemade firecracker in our direction. The explosion caught me off guard. Once again "Incoming!" slipped out of my mouth as I dove under the nearest car. My brother in law laughed at first, then he thought about it and comforted me.

Vietnam Veterans were not welcomed home by all with open arms. With mortars you never know, but to my knowledge I'd never killed a child, woman, or any civilian. We were on a line waiting to get into a restaurant talking about my experiences in the Nam when some bastard who overheard called me a murderer. I was still feeling somewhat aggressive and wanted to take him to task but at the urging of my family settled on a verbal response. Those waiting to get into the restaurant witnessed part of this. A little later when I was in the mensroom, one of the guys asked if I was just back from the nam. He told me he recognized that by the way I acted outside as he too was a vet who had been back a little longer and had time to adjust. Although the current wars are just as unpopular, we have matured and now blame the government and not the soldiers for the situation. Thank the lord for that. The last thing a returning G.I. needs is to be ridiculed for doing his or her duty over which they had no control, and or to be accused of crimes they did not commit.

Marv & I did hang out together, take that trip to Florida and several others. Marv even met his future wife when we were out together. We did have that great coming home New Years Eve party and I threw a New Years Eve party at my place for quite a few years after that. Over time I let my hair grow long and grew a beard. I occasionally hung out with social drug users for a time. Some even called me the world's oldest hippie but I was employed full time and going to school so that title really didn't fit. Even turned down a chance to go with one of my girlfriends to Woodstock as I did not want to take off from work. That I regret.

As to my car, it turned out my order was repeatedly delayed so I cancelled it and ordered my "blood money car" as I called it, from a local Oldsmobile dealer in Flushing, New York. It was the first new car I ever owned, a banana yellow 1969 Cutlass S convertible with a black top. I made the best deal I could for it, very close to what I had from the overseas place. After I had signed to buy that car, my brother in law, Steve went back to the dealer and renegotiated that sale saving me another few hundred dollars.

The car was delivered in mid-February 1969 about two days before the biggest snowstorm I had ever witnessed. It stayed parked for a few days under several feet of snow!

Forget about Human Factors Engineering or any engineering. As I had an associate's degree from Queens College I just went back there for my B.A. in Psychology. Went on for an M.S. in Counseling Psychology, a Professional Diploma in Educational Administration & Supervision. Never really stopped going to school in some form or another.

When I went back to school there was unrest on campus and some organization, I think it was the SDS (Students for a

Democratic Society), claimed there were going to close Queens College and not let anyone in. Being a combat Vet I made up my mind that there was no way they were going to stop me! I suited up in my army fatigues and told my family I was going to go to class. As usual, the media had blown things out of proportion and no one even tried to stop us but I looked cool in my fatigues.

As they did not offer me a better job I did not go back to work for Allstate, but was able to collect my profit sharing. Instead, I went to work as a claims manager at an airfreight forwarder near JFK airport some eight miles from where I lived. When that big snowstorm hit, I could not dig my car out, and besides the roads were not drivable. In the morning, as no buses were running, I walked the eight miles to work. That was no big deal for a soldier just back from Nam. The only other person who made it in was the operations manager in charge of the facility who lived right in the area. When he saw me he asked, "How'd you get here?" He was amazed when I told him I walked and let me go home early. By that time the buses were running again.

I spent 23 years in the business world mostly as a middle manager in law, airfreight claims, collections, personnel management for a Fortune 100 company, hypnotherapy, and counseling. I then found my true calling in education and never looked back. You get what you give with kids. Give love & affection, you get it back. Saw that with my lovely daughter, as well as with my 1000s of other kids, my students. Retired from the NYC Dept of Ed after 22 years of service as an Assistant Principal, computer & math specialist, and teacher. I really had become an F.T.A (Future Teacher of America)!

When I first arrived home from the Nam, I was idealistic and politically active. I supported a man who was running for city council member. I used to don my class A uniform and go out speaking with him on a crime in the streets platform. I'd say something to the effect of at least in Vietnam I could carry a weapon to protect myself. I was a little discouraged when people came over to him, not about that important issue, or finances, but asking if he'd fix the hole in their street if he were elected. People were so myopic and self centered it was just amazing. I did a lot for Jim and he ran me for a minor job of alternate delegate to the Judicial Convention. After the election I received a letter from the Board of Elections that

I had won. Of course, as he lost, that was unlikely. A few days later I received the corrected letter. I threw away the corrected letter but kept the one that told me I won!

A disability allowance was awarded to me after almost a year of letter writing. Because my medical records had been lost along with many others in an Army warehouse fire in Texas, it was difficult to prove the extent of my injuries. My sister's employer at the time was a very active disabled vet whom was admired and respected by all. It was his intervention that got my claim recognized.

With a friend I explored various veteran's organization including the Veterans of the Vietnam War but found none that interested us. After I received my disability rating I did join and become a life member of the DAV (Disabled American Veterans). When I first went to one of their meetings, all I saw were a bunch of old men so I did not go back. The last few years I have been an active member of the American Legion. Joined when I saw a few members my own age. My current rank at my local post is Commander. I have also become a life member of the Veterans of Foreign Wars (VFW). I have always been proud to be an American and I would stand up and defend her still today!

For one of my birthdays some years back, my ex-wife had my name inscribed on the Vietnam Veterans Wall of Honor (wall number 39) in Eisenhower Park. I always joke that my name is in granite and I'm not even dead yet.

While I was in Vietnam I kept a notebook. The notes refer to people I wanted to remember like the lovely Sandy of Da Nang & California (as if I could ever forget her), potential jobs & school thoughts and ideas I wanted to pursue. Although these were thoughts that I felt I would write about or change the world, not all had to do with the military. I decided to end this book with a few of those notes. Remember these were written some 40 years ago. See if you can figure out what was going on at the time....

"Idea for congressional paper: Draft not voluntary, therefore draftees should not be forced to fight a war which is not our war. Vietnam Specific

Example: If U.S. to stay in Nam should only be volunteers. If insufficient volunteers GET OUT!!"

"It would be cheaper, better if Army had better physical & listened to individual complaints so that 11B or 11C etc would not have as many people reclassified due to profile after they reach combat zone. Possibly ask man when he is classified if he feels he is physically able."

"Twiggy popularity could be repressed homosexual tendencies"

"Is overuse of horn causing accidents? First you hear the horn then crash. Do drivers depend too much on horn to prevent accidents? If they didn't have horn would drivers develop different defensive measures, which might prevent an accident?
Factors to be considered: Reaction time to sound horn, next movement, order of events such as depress brake, horn, swerve, etc. How much security horns gives. Does security help or hinder reaction to accident?"

"Each unit pushes off personal action to next one"

Still true today & on that note I'll close.

Dad & Mom!

Got ya Marv!

Author at home

Author & his dad wearing author's other uniform

Author's sisters

Neice:

The Bergs

The Semmigs

The "blood car"

Appendix

Cast:
Mom & Pop – My parents
Marilyn – My kid sister
Marv- My kid brother
Steve My Brother in law (At that time)
Lou & Eve Berg – My best friends

Marv: I'm not even going to say anything on this tape for one reason, because by the time you'll get this tape I expect you'll be home. Well I guess I got lost for words. Goodbye.

Lou: Well Howie I guess you know where we are now. It's Friday October 25th. I guess it's around 10:30 at night and Steve has a couple of words for you. Here's Steve right now.

Steve: How come I had so much to say till it was my turn? Seemed so easy when everybody else was talking. Well this is your newest brother in law and hopefully your best. Don't let Vic *[my other brother in law]* hear that. By the way, Oh, Marvin's still here. He's peeking through the banisters rail like a little prisoner. He looks like he's in his play crib. Think I'll take him over tomorrow to play with Doug. *[my infant nephew]*. Doug might be too smart for him. I don't know. Oh, by the way your singing was really great. But what happened to my song about the F.T.A.? Really it was a good song. Your captain liked it, didn't he? …. The only reason I'm pausing is I'm waiting for Marvin to get out of here so I can you the truth about the no good blank blank. Marvin's got a date with a V.C. Real cute! He's about 4 feet tall.

…Another point. I'm reading from a sheet so I have a lot to say. Too bad I didn't start taking notes on the first side of your tape. By the way you've got a big mouth. I never knew you could talk so much. Why didn't you say something in all that time?

Cutlass doesn't have a six it's the F-85. So the choice, if you're thinking of a 6 is an F-85 vs. a Chevelle. If you want to get any options….

378

I was just hit by some ugly guy needing a shave. I think it's a Viet Cong Santa Claus. Now he's grabbing my knee. We saw Marvin for about 8 and a half minutes before he left. He's living in the back of a Singer truck with about 18 other hippies. *[My brother worked for Singer and often brought the truck home].*

Don't worry about your language when you come home. I'm married now and I've gotten used to it since I met Marilyn.*[sound of a smack]* That little sound you just heard was me being hit by Marilyn. They call her, "Heavy Hand" around here. Now she's going thru your mail. I'm almost finished until I think of some more notes. I just want to know if it's true you're reenlisting for another tour over there? Hey, watch that language, you're coming home soon. I want you to get rid of that. I think I'm going to invent a 10-minute tape. It'll make people feel a lot easier. I feel like I'm in a peanut gallery with 5 peanuts. They're all staring at me. I'm lying in the middle of the floor. They want me to give it to the next one. Who volunteers? See they all want it until it's they're turn. The next voice you hear will be your father. Duhhhhh...

Dad: Hi Howie and Artie. This is dad talking now.

Marilyn: Hi dad talking now.

Dad: I heard your voice for the first time in almost a year.

Steve: *[Calls out]* Still rotten.

Dad: Still sounds very good! It's almost like you're home. I also heard the monsoons in the background.

Steve: He's really in a go-go joint those are strippers taking it off.

Dad: You hear the voice in the background? Don't mind it, its dirt. I also received your letter today from the 20th of October and I believe it's a little too late for that recorder. Though, that would be good in your car when you do get one. But I understand you've been taken for a sucker out there. Out here I understand it's about $35.... I understand there's different models and different prices, so I may

379

be wrong. It's a real nice gadget to have. About the 2 cars that you mentioned Mike has, don't worry. He can well afford them. Plus his $50,000 house. When you come home, he'll probably come here to see you. It'll be a good time for a get together.

Art, I remember meeting you once and probably if I saw you again I'd remember you.

Marilyn, Mom, Lou, and his wife are next to me. I'm sure they want to put in a couple of words so I'll end right there. Try to squeeze in another tape.

Mom: Hello Howard, this is mom. It sure was wonderful hearing your voice. It really did sound like you were right next to us when you were speaking. That's really a funny incident about you meeting Lou there. Did you have all your clothes on when you went to see him? Arty I meant...Did you put on all your clothes when you went to see him? *[A question only a Jewish mother could ask seriously.]*

Steve: If you didn't have all your clothes on, what kind of friend is this Arty?

Mom: Howard, I hope you've been receiving all our letters. We've been writing quite frequently. Dad writes about 2 or 3 letters a week; and I write quite frequently too. I don't know what to tell you about the cute things that the kids are doing right now cause, as I said. I'm suppose to see them this week. I'll have more to tell you. I don't know if I wrote you that Doug got a haircut, so he really looks like a boy now. Not like a hippie anymore. Ah...I must sound funny that Ah...like I got stumped for words. But I am, that's the truth I am. You know when you called up that time Howard, I had so many things to tell you. I felt so stupid because I didn't know what to say to you. I was stumped for words. I guess that's the way it usually is.

Marilyn: Hi Howie, this is Marilyn. How are you? I just got a new job and I start on Monday. I'm a nervous wreck. I hope I'll do O.K.

We heard your tape and it was really great. We heard you singing. Steve's still under the coach, he hasn't' come out yet. I'm sure you appreciated the song.

As far as Queens College goes, they decided to cut out their school of general studies. It's pending. The made the decision but we haven't heard it yet. If they decide to go thru with it they'll start next term. You're eligible for day, it's only for the night students, so don't worry about it. If you take psychology courses, that's what I'll be majoring in so we can take them together. I have 12 credits in it so I can help you out.

Steve: We look like a bunch of dodos here sitting around taking notes and then grabbing the mike to say something, and then going back to the next person. But, you know, anything for you Howie. I wanna ask you how the food is there. I hear you're an excellent cook. Is it true your kitchen consists of a can opener and that's it? Marilyn's getting all ready for you, so hurry home the lasagna is getting stale. She made it last week. I'm still taking notes but I can't read them.

Marilyn: By the way if he doesn't sound too great it's because he had a piece of my apple pie last night

Steve: Ehhhhhhhhhhhhh. I need protection. Well at least you'll be able to take her food. It'll be just like home. We'll at least home for the last year and half, whatever it's been. Marilyn, I have to be nice to her though. Monday she starts a new job, she gets a raise and I quit Tuesday.

You know if you go to Queens, you have, I guess it's close to 90 credits. You don't lose anything like you do if you go to another school. You could stay there. Take the rest of the courses in your elective or your major, which I guess, would be Psy and finish up in a year. I hope you don't stay in night. Like you made the mistake the first time. Just go straight thru and get it over in a year. Then go back to work and get a better job. P.S. I just thought of something else. When do you intend applying for school? It's getting closer & closer. Has anybody sent you any applications? If they have, you better get them out soon. I know the applications for Queens I think are due in November. The end of November. So you better hurry up and do something about it because I've got to apply to. I'm getting a little fed up with Queens. They haven't sent my transcript out to

Hofstra from Summer School yet and Hofstra won't give me my degree. I just spent another half-hour on the phone today like I did 2 weeks ago. Everything was ironed out 2 weeks ago. We're starting all over again.

There are now 21 minutes or 12 hundred and 61 seconds to go of something ... anybody else want to take over? O.K. here she comes, ready?

Mom: [singing] Here she comes...

Steve: O.K. Now for our next guest speaker. I can't stand this I'm getting beat all over. I came over here for a meal. Then they make me use up as many calories defending myself. Marilyn said the food wasn't worth even coming over. Now I'm going to get hit from the other side. Right?

Marilyn: No you're going to get it tonight.

Steve: I'm going to get it tonight, I want to rush home. *[sound of smack]* Ow, that one hurt Howie. (laughing)You probably heard that one in Vietnam without the loud speaker. I'm not sure I think this button is still up.. My shoulder is down but the button is still up. Hold on here's you mother.

Mom: What I was going to say when I was so rudely interrupted (laughs) was... (singing again) Here she comes Miss Mother America.(Laughs). Anyway Howard you look very good in the pictures.

Steve: You just thought that was your mother, that was Frisky *[Steve's dog]*.

Mom: Howard, it's mom back again. I say, you look very good in the pictures. You look like you put on weight. Those are cute puppy dogs that you have there. I wrote to you that I think you might have made a mistake with the dog, Jack. If those are his puppies, or her puppies. I didn't get an answer. I'm thinking maybe they're from a local area.

Say Howard, you know in the picture where you're in the jeep? You look like an Australian Bushman. Especially with that mustache.

Marilyn: Oh Howie, by the way, you asked me to get Arty a pen pal. There was nobody in the other place. But now, this new place has 31 floors and I'll find someone. Signing off. I won't sing for you because you know there's no place to hide around there.

Lou: Howie, your sister Marilyn really doesn't believe all those stories that you've been sending Steve & Arty about these girls you've been running around with. We do believe you, but you really got to send some proof. You don't have to send the kids home but just save a little bit for us when we go over there.

Steve: Forget the kids, the empty penicillin pill bottle will do Howie.

Dad: Now that I got this pest next to me, I got to be careful. This is dad now speaking. About my car, it's O.K. now. All it needed was a battery. It's not in perfect condition but then again it's 5 years old. I'm doing very good. The other day I got some printed matter from a LaSalle University, if I'd be interested in any books that they want to give me free. They had something on traffic management. So, what the heck, it doesn't cost anything. So I sent away for the traffic management book. Maybe you'll be interested. Being that you once mentioned something about it.

How about that last package I sent you. Did you get it? Did you and Art finish that Champale I had in there? Of course, don't let the post office know Champale was in there.

Now about that Bronze Star. I'm still waiting for a letter explaining what you did for it; or who you paid off to get it.

Steve: Howie, I told him the truth about the Bronze Star. That's for public relations and I hear you've had more relations over there then anyone else in the army. Bye Howie. Howie, I'm not really this bad. It's just that when I speak to you, you bring out the best in me. I don't know what it is. Anyone else want to suffer through another

383

round on the reel? Watch carefully, Marilyn's dancing for you. Is that Douglas over there...da-da-goo-goo. I'm not kidding I've regressed about 23 years. I just had to get even with Marilyn. I tell you Howie, you're lucky I got into this family or you'd be getting a blank tape. You better appreciate it Howie. You like those letters you got? *[referring to the letters from his 3rd grade class]* Now, I'm filling up at least 8 minutes of your tape. The other 22 minutes you can hum, or whistle Dixie, or something. I got another 4 seconds hold on.

Mom: Howard, I'm really glad you're together with Arty. Give Arty our love too. Say, Arty has a great sense of humor too. It's marvelous to hear him talk. You two boys really seem to get along well together. Steve is some kind of a wise guy, he says, that's what he's worrying about. I'm not!

I'm still working Howard. The nuns keep asking about you. Howard, the sister in the library gave me a stamp to send away for you letter. I offered to pay her for it. she says, "no", she wants you to have that.

Steve: It just took 15 cents worth of the reel to tell you about the 6 cents stamp. By the way, tell Arty I'm not really what I seem like. It's just that... I can't really explain it. I guess I am what I seem like. I'm telling you don't get married. Louie's agreeing with me. He's agreeing from across the room. I guess after a couple of years you get smart. That's all there is to it. Evelyn's enjoying it now, but Louie's walking home. I don't understand that. I don't know. My parents send their regards –they don't know I'm here but when I tell them they'll send their regards. No, they ask about you a lot. My mother says when you come over you can have that lasagna dinner you once stood here up for. Frisky misses you. He says he never met anybody like you . I was talking about Frisky and all of a sudden somebody thought of you're grandma. Hold on..

Mom: You know Grandma says she has a stove. She has a small kitchen but a big stove. Boy you're going to get some good food there; besides what you're going to get here.

Steve: That doesn't compare to what you get in Vietnam Howie, The foods O.K. over there too isn't it? Daggers are flying across. About 40 a minute from Marilyn. Would you believe we suffered through your entire..I mean we listened to your entire tape. We recorded the whole thing to bring over to Janet and we got nothing. Come to think of it we don't have to rerecord it, that's what you said all together. I take it back, cause I don't want to get hit again. Arty said something, yours was just to fill in the spaces while he was thinking. Wait, you're coming home soon. You might have learned some Judo or something. I take it back Howie. You're really a conversationalist and a scholar. You're a scholar and a gentleman and a fine person and you've got one hell of a liar for a brother in law. But except for that it's O.K. Howie. I feel like this is the Apollo countdown over here. Instead we're counting feet on the reel of tape.

Did you ever buy your camera? I never did get an answer to that question. Marilyn wants to know why I don't let somebody else talk. I'll ask for volunteers again. O.K., I'm back! O.K. your mother is here. She's going to tell you about the oven that goes with the stove. No oven? We'll try for the refrigerator.

Mom: Say Howard, Marvin is still planning on the New Years Eve party. You know the surprise party that no one is supposed to know about?

Dad: A note to Arty. I hope the time will go very fast and before you know it the year will be up. Actually, you're a freshman over there with only one-month service there. Howie, as Steve mentioned before, I tried to re-tape, record your tape onto ours but I think ours has seen it's days. Not one word came out . Actually it wasn't a waste of time but it certainly was a waste of electricity.

I'm also waiting for the brochure from Zeigler. I guess they do get many requests and it takes a lot of time. My request was sent in almost 3 weeks ago. I'm still waiting.

Mom: Howard, this is mom again and I must say you boys have a lot of patience. Because we have a small inkling of what you went

385

thru taping that and not having it come out. Being so disappointed and all.

Marilyn: *[Mom in background, "Say something about Arty"]* What can I say about Arty, I'm married...*[background discussion].*

Lou: That last bit of speech you just heard was your family discussing what they were going to say. They haven't had much to say. Marilyn's just sitting here laughing. She's worried about what the other guys in the barracks are going to think of us. Your brother left in a hurry. Not because he didn't have much to say. It's just that he had a heavy date tonight. You know how that is.

Steve: By popular demand I won't tell you anything except that, his heavy date, I don't know. I saw him go into the Singer truck but the truck hasn't moved yet. I don't see anyone in it. *[In background "it's vibrating"].* Since you've left Marvin has taken over Howie, where you've left off. Uh-oh Marilyn's got that look. Here she goes...

Marilyn: Hi, talking about the Singer truck. It was so funny when we moved into the apartment. We had to put... Oh, this is Marilyn. Anyway, in case you didn't recognize me. When we moved into the apartment, it's really funny because we had to move everything into the Singer truck. Besides all the garbage that we put in the Singer truck, they put me back there too. It's a panel truck and the back is where you put all the sewing machines and everything. They put the mattresses there. They threw me in the back too. It was really funny when we opened the doors, when we got to our apartment. People were looking at us. They opened the doors and I came out. They were probably wondering what was going on back there. Especially since, after I came out, the 2 mattresses came out after me!

Steve: I was just requested to tell you about the honeymoon but when you come back I'll do better than that. It's a shame you couldn't be at the wedding. I didn't regret not having you at the honeymoon though. I have a complete set of slides of the honeymoon. Plus with the camera I bought and the close-up lens I took a slide of every one of the proofs. When you come home I'll be able to show you a complete set of slides of the wedding that you missed. It was great hearing from you there.

Marilyn: Howie, it's not that we didn't want you on the honeymoon. It's just that with all of us there it would have been too much. You know mom & dad came along. (laugh)

Steve: Lou's in the middle of us holding the tape recorder. It looks like a waiter in a pizza joint. (laughing) Every time it's somebody's turn he pivots on his right knee, which is worn thru to the skin now.

Lou: I have to really defend myself. As an outsider looking in, it looks pretty funny from my angle too.

Steve: What he not saying is that you've got one hell of a nutty family Howie. O.K. Lou shift, now the left knee. Arty must think we're beating up his brother-in-law here. Actually Evelyn's doing all the fighting. You think your year there is something? If you want to see real agony you should see 6 people recording.

Dad: Well I've just been told. This is dad now speaking. I've just been told that there's another 5 minutes to go so I'll sign off now. Lots of luck to both of you boys. Let's hear from you soon. Both of yeas.

Steve: There's still how many more minutes? About 5 minutes. There are now 4 minutes & 52 seconds.

Mom: Whatever Dad said a minute ago, goes for me too, Howard & Arty.

Marilyn: Howie, you know the tape sounded great with you and Arty. You really sounded like you're having a great time. You don't sound like you're in Vietnam. Are you in Vietnam or not?

Steve: Howard, did you ever think of the army as a career? I can't believe this is the same family. I'm not going to say who, but I've known people in here that can spend hours on the phone and they can't fill up a 30-minute cartridge between them. Your father wants this, but considering he's signed off I won't give it too him. Ouch! Ouch Ouch!

Dad: Come to think about it Howie, I wish you luck on the rat fight or the rat war. I don't know.

Steve: They're great sautéed. Marilyn take away all this Italian food and Chinese food. I can't eat it while I'm talking to Howie. I feel guilty really, come on. No, no pork & spare ribs. I feel like I'm adopting you. No one will say anything. Don't worry, if Marilyn didn't tell you, we have another bedroom for you to move into. I think your parents would shoot us if....

Lou: By the way, your father, your mother, your brother-in-law are sitting right along side me here. They all look good. Marilyn looks the best I've ever seen her in a long time. Marriage is really agreeing with her.

Marilyn: Yea. See that Hey. Everybody in my office says..

Steve: It's wrecking havoc on me though. I don't know . Lou spoke for I think it was 14 point 3 seconds. So, when the other side is on for Arty you're going to hear 14.2 seconds of my sweet tones. Marilyn made a funny, she's not sleeping over either tonight.

Lou: This is Louie again. You and Arthur must have the same thing Steve and I have in common. Girls under 21. I don't know how cheap they are there, but over here I understand they're getting pretty expensive. They're not walking the streets like they do over there.

Steve: Howard knows very well how expensive they are. They're not walking but he knows where they are anyway. He says be nice, and if you can't be nice , be gentle. There are 2 sisters here concerned about their 2 nice little brothers. Their baby brothers, and they're thinking about when they were in diapers and little pictures

388

of them. I hope you're playing this tape for everybody else in the barracks. Otherwise it'd be a waste. *[continues in baby talk]* You wanna speak to your baby brother? This is how-ie.   That should take a couple of days off your tour over there.

Lou: Art, hunting season starts soon. I hope to bring back a big one this year. At least something with antlers on it. I'm looking for 4-legged deer this year, not any 2-legged ones. I don't know what I'm going to be doing out in the woods there. I'm going bow hunting this year. Stan lent me a bow from the office and I'm going to try catching a couple of deer. If I catch anything, I'll send you a nice big picture of it.

Steve: I'm not going to be hunting but I know what I'm going to be doing in the woods this year.

Mom: Howard, let us know on the ETS, all the details about the ETS. I'm really looking forward, Dad & I are looking forward to having you home Howard. We can hardly wait.

Marilyn: Howie, I have to sign off now but I'm really looking forward to seeing you when you come home. I'm not voting this year. I'm not 21 yet. But if I could vote, I'd vote for Nixon even though I'd rather vote for Mickey Mouse. I'll be seeing you. I guess.... One thing I don't understand. Are you coming home December 22nd or December 24? Because the days will be different here. Clarify that a little if you can. O.K. Howie until I see you (kiss) bye.

Dad: And don't forget to bring your long johns here.

Steve: We just played this back. It's so good Howie, I decided to keep it. I really enjoyed listening to myself. You can have the empty tape. Everybody wants me to ask you to tell us in advance about when you're coming home so they can prepare your winter clothes. I just say carry a survival kit, a flask! One minute & ....your mother has 2 quilts to wrap you up with in the airport. Since you're worried about your language, Lou says he's got one of Ricky's pacifiers to keep you quite – pacified again. *[Eve in background – his nun-nun].* Ricky calls it his nun-nun. If you can repeat that, if it's not too hard for you..say it slowly Nun.......nun! Very good dumb-dumb.

Mom: Howard, how do you like our Don Rickels son in law?

Steve: I like my Phyllis Diller mother in law. *[smack]* I said that in jest. The biggest one is in the room with me. I'm not going to say who because she might not feed me next week. That still doesn't say who does it Marilyn.

Dad: He got out Howie, in his own defense because Marilyn just had the rolling pin for him.

Steve: That's the only thing she can do with it. she can't bake pies. Baking me pies.. she's baked 8 pies so far, 4 more and we have service for 12.   We use the crust as plates. Want to defend yourself Marilyn? Come-on Duh-duh-goo-goo. Just got pie in my face!

Dad: Howie, dad again. (Laughing) It was very nice of Lou & Evelyn to come here with the tape . It's now 11:50. We're really holding them back.

Steve: Would you believe we spent 2 hours and 27 minutes on a 30-minute tape? I believe 2 hours & 15 minutes. We did spend a very long time. It's all your mother's fault.

Mom: I second that, what Daddy said. I'm always seconding dad, that's right. I agree that Evelyn & Lou are very nice people. That's a very nice thing that they did. Howard, don't worry about your Bronze Star Certificate. It's in a frame. It's a very, very nice award that you got.

Steve: Your father used up the tape. It's about time they give me a chance to speak. I just wanted to say, Hello Howie, nice hearing from you. Fifteen seconds, don't resend them Marilyn. I mean it's the first time I had a chance. O.K. I'll have to sign off now, Howie. Don't worry if I'm like your father, when I sign off I'll be back about 4 more times. Poor Evelyn & Lou they're ready to go. Wait till we tell them they have to play it back, then you'll find out. Would you believe we recorded this 4 times just to get it right once? It's all for you Howie. Actually it's for Art. I figured I'd make you feel alright too. He must be nice and pensive by now. Do I hear him snoring in the background? Or is that one of the mosquitoes? I've been rehearsing this all day in my class. My class wants to meet you when you come back. I told them you're a Viet Cong. We had your post card hanging up. This is a different class then the other one. This one I don't think you've written to. The other class graduated. They're all concerned I read them your letters and they wrote you some letters. They want to know did you ever use Myrtle's recipe for German Gingerbread cookies that she mailed you? Back again....

Dad: By the way Art, let me know what kind of food you like. I'll be glad to send you some Howie tells me that the food is not so hot out there. What little food you do get. Though, from the looks of the picture he sent me, with that potbelly, I don't know whether I should believe him or not. Marilyn says you might be pregnant. I don't know. Not my boy. Keep out of the way at a distance [probably to Steve]

Steve: Maybe we can get Arty out a little early too.

Lou: By the way Arthur this tape does not destruct in 10 seconds, so behave yourself with it. You'll be playing with it for the rest of your life. Don't erase it either. It will exemplify how 6 idiots can sit around one little box, speaking into a microphone and make fools of themselves.

Steve: Howie, there's one minute to go so, Four Score and seven years ago..... Triggers in the background singing. I've got a feeling this tape was over 15 minutes ago and somebody's playing a big joke on all of us. You have their the new secret weapon. Turn this lose in the jungle and the will be over.

All together singing: Happy trials to you, until we meet again. Happy trails to you.....[tape ends]

DICTIONARY OF VIETNAM ARMY SLANG

* beaucoup: (French). many, big, huge, very, etc.

* bought the farm: to be killed.

* chop-chop: food, or eat.

* C's: "C" rations

* di di (mau) ("dee-dee (maow)"):"go away (fast)."

* dien cai dao ("dee-in-kee-daow"): crazy

* dustoff: medevac

* freedom bird: jet that flies soldiers back to the U.S.

* grunt: infantryman

* gunship: armed helicopter

* Hanoi Hannah: VietnameseTokyo Rose.

* Ho Chi Minh sandals: sandals made from tires.

* Ho Chi Minh trail: VC & NVA jungle paths and supply route.

* Incoming!: Inbound artillery/rockets

* in country: in Vietnam.

* lai day (pronounced "lye di"): "come here."

* lima charlie: "LC," short for "loud and clear"

* LZ: landing zone.

* medevac: short for medical evacuation.

* numbah-one: the best

* numbah-ten : Not good.

*nam or the 'Nam: Vietnam.

* plastic: type of explosives

* P's: piastres; Vietnamese monetary unit

* Puff or "Puff the Magic Dragon"; a C-47 Gunship

* Real Life: civilian life.

* Rog (pronounced "rahj"): "Roger," which is the
radio term for "I understand." Also,"That's right".

* roundeye: Caucasian woman.

* sapper: an enemy soldier swith strapped on
explosives. Like WWII Kamikaze.

* straight arrow: remained faithful to wife or
Stateside girl friend while Vietnam.

* The Pill: malaria tablets taken weekly.

* The World: the U.S.A

* ti ti ("tee-tee"): "small."

* xin loi ("sin loyee"): "Sorry 'bout that."

* zap: to kill or seriously wound.